Bryony Hill is married to Jimmy, the ex-professional footballer and TV presenter. She lived in France in the early 1970s, where she developed a love for French food, then moved to London, where she met Jimmy. Now living in Sussex, Bryony has published two previous books: the novel *Penalty Chick* and her spirited gardening book *A Compost Kind of Girl* (both Book Guild Publishing).

www.bryonyhill .com

To dear Annie —

ANGEL IN
AN APRON

BRYONY HILL

With best wishes, & love!
Bry (Hill.)
x x x

Book Guild Publishing
Sussex, England

First published in Great Britain in 2010 by
The Book Guild Ltd
Pavilion View
19 New Road
Brighton, BN1 1UF

Printed in Great Britain by
CPI Antony Rowe

A catalogue record for this book is available from
The British Library.

ISBN 978 1 84624 462 9

CONTENTS

ACKNOWLEDGEMENTS

This is my third book to be published, and possibly the most fun to write, and I want to thank Book Guild Publishing from the bottom of my heart for their continued support and faith in me. A wonderful relationship has developed and the team (who, with endless patience and encouragement, have corrected and cajoled me through countless hurdles over the years) have become part of the family. Laura Longrigg, my agent and dear friend, stands on an equal footing, for after all, it was she who gave me my opening gambit. My thanks also go to Catherine Gallop who has been an extraordinary and invaluable extra pair of eyes – and ears! Jimmy has stood by me now for over 34 years - man and boy - never once complaining at what was put on a plate in front of him, eating every last mouthful. His justification (however dubious the dish may have been) was that, being brought up as a child in the Second World War, he learned never to leave a scrap as you were never sure where your next meal came from. Last but not least, thanks go to my mother, who passed away recently and who taught me to cook in the first place. These recipes are dedicated to her, with love.

Introduction

She is not an angel, she is not a goddess
She is not a diamond, a ruby or a pearl.
She is what is sweetest, completest and neatest
A dear little, queer little, sweet little girl.

It was my thirteenth birthday and my godmother had given me a beautiful leather-bound autograph book. My older brother, who was on an exeat from school that weekend had invited one of his friends, Dave, for the day. Ah, Dave. What can I say? At six feet tall he towered over me and, with a shock of shaggy blond hair, he was a total sex god. I worshipped the ground he walked on, but at two and a half years my senior, in his eyes I was completely invisible. In a flurry of hope and desperation to be noticed, I baked a chocolate sponge cake, sandwiching it with butter cream. Then I cut a heart shape out of a folded piece of paper, placed it over the cake, and dusted icing sugar leaving a perfect but not very subtle impression of my intentions. He ate three slices.

Minutes before he was due to leave, having dwelt upon it all afternoon, I plucked up courage and asked him to be the first person to christen my album. He condescended with this ditty, incidentally writing 'angle' as against 'angel', but it didn't matter, I was too in love to care. In the ensuing years, he went his way, I went mine but I never forgot that special moment. In spite of unrequited first love, chocolate cake has remained my number one seduction technique ever since.

More than four decades later I like to think that I have risen from the depths of a non-being to an angel, at least in the kitchen, albeit with a slightly wonky halo. Cooking is my only saving domestic grace – I am a total nightmare in every other department. My husband, Jimmy, says that, if there was an Olympic category for untidiness, I would knock Sir Steve Redgrave's five gold medals into a cocked hat. However, in my defence, I would say that he can invite anyone to our house at any time of the day or night and I would always be able to produce a meal any angel would be proud of.

Why the apron, you may ask? Those who know me intimately may have calculated that I own more of this garment than most women own knickers – I have dozens of the things: for example, there is one cut deftly from American cloth (waterproofed cotton), several frilly vintage overalls found in charity shops and a couple converted from outgrown skirts, cut down for gardening. In an emergency I am a dab hand at improvising (no sewing needed thankfully) with a man's shirt, using the sleeves as ties. Last but not least, tucked away in my drawers is an authentic nineteenth-century French maid's apron to be donned for special occasions only.

I cannot resist dipping into boxes of remnants and samples found in fabric shops. I scramble voraciously for workable lengths of linen union, as not only is it tough but also washable, but in order to find a place in my shopping basket, it has to sport a flamboyant, floral design, the gardening theme strongly in evidence. Then once back home and scissors at the ready, I take an Ikea apron (a firm favourite) as a template, and cut around it. With a bit of stitching here and there I end up with my perfect pinafore. I am content only if I have an apron knotted around my middle – like a child with a dummy, it is my security blanket.

On the day we were married, I cooked a three-course, roast beef lunch for twenty clad in my new posh frock which was, naturally, protected by an apron. It was one that I had given Jimmy to wear when busy at the barbecue and sported a torso of a grotesquely muscular man lugging an impressive six-pack, tucked into an eye-wateringly tight pair of bathing trunks.

Nowadays, as soon as I am up and running in the morning, on goes the chosen apron for the day and, if I can squirrel a paper hankie or two, a pair of secateurs and a handful of dog treats in the pocket, I am a happy bunny. To sum it up, it is virtually impossible to find a single photograph taken of me over the last twenty-odd years, whatever the occasion, without me wearing one.

On holidays in France, rarely do I bring back designer clothes in my suitcase. What do I buy instead? You guessed. Aprons, or *tabliers* as they are called on the other side of the Channel. The French take these garments very seriously: usually made from dark, inky blue material splattered with sprigs of flowers, they are styled into a wrap-around shape with sensible holes for the arms trimmed with a colour-coordinated bias binding. As a bonus, the ample fabric covers both the back and the bottom – a bit like a sleeveless overall. The indigenous wearer can often be spotted on the vegetable plot leaning on a rake, sporting an ancient, squashed straw hat. As it happens, I have that as well. In triplicate. And the rake.

However in recent months, I find myself wide awake in the middle of the night, in a cold sweat, fearful that possibly I am letting myself go on the sartorial front. The angel getting a little too big for her cloud, as it were, finding it harder to keep the wings fluffy and the halo polished. When my second book *A Compost Kind of Girl* was about to be published, I wrote in desperation to Hilary Alexander of the *Daily Telegraph* to see if she could come to my aid. She told me to bring my favourite clothes to the makeover. What were they? My gardening apron and gumboots. She had her work cut out that day, I can tell you, but expertly she pulled out all the stops and kitted me out in a smart tailored blouse, slender trousers and killer Jimmy Choo heels. After the 'shoot' I was able to purchase some of the outfits, but since that euphoric day they have spent most of their life ignored in the back of the wardrobe and now appear on eBay!

When it comes to cooking, I wing it (as angels do) since I am far too impatient to bother with scales. Also, as we have an Aga, it tends to rule out precise oven temperatures and specific timings: you open the oven door, bung in the food, wait a while and remove it. If it isn't cooked enough, sling it back in and wait a further five minutes. After which, bingo! But I know this won't suit most of you, so I have been careful to give appropriate temperatures and timings for electric and gas cookers.

I can't remember when I first became involved in preparing food, but it certainly was before I was five. Ma was a hands-on, stay-at-home mum who taught us to read and write before we reached school age. She also showed us how to weave baskets out of cane, to make finger puppets from flour and water paste and most importantly, how to cook. Tasteless soups, watery, over-cooked vegetables and tough, unidentifiable meat were often on the tables of other families we knew. Austerity and rationing lingered after the war into the Fifties when I was a child but our mother was a heavenly cook, and her patient instruction taught me to savour the thrill that accompanies full tummies and a stack of empty plates.

In 1970, having completed a foundation year at art school in Brighton and failing to get on a degree course, I sailed away to France to be a companion/cook to a hormonal fourteen-year-old girl, her thirty-five-year-old brother (blind in one eye and prone to wearing army camouflage), two dogs and a North African housekeeper, while the parents were on a cruise in the Caribbean. In my innocence, in under a fortnight I had fallen hook, line and sinker in love with a dashing Frenchman who took me under his wing, introducing me to things of which I had only dreamed. An added bonus was that he received a hefty allowance from his father, which permitted us to dine in the best establishments where he took every opportunity to show me on a plate all that France has to offer.

Up until then I was definitely more Gordon Bennett than Gordon Ramsay and had only ever experienced simple, wholesome food shared with my family around the kitchen table, prepared from our own fruit and vegetables. Suddenly here I was in a foreign country being offered exotic and enigmatic dishes. At these Pantagruelian feasts I ate venison for the first time (simmered with wine and cherries), fried sweetbreads, creamy scrambled eggs studded

4

with truffles and occasionally dishes I would rather not have been told what they were after having consumed them.

At the start of our relationship the Frenchman took me to Honfleur, a picturesque port on the Normandy coast beloved of artists, the Impressionists in particular. For our first lunch he ordered *tourteaux à la mayonnaise*. Straddling huge platters were two equally gargantuan crabs, caught locally that morning. Up until then, the only crabs I had caught were in Walberswick, a sleepy village on the Suffolk coast, using bacon or chicken legs as bait, dropping the line off the Bailey bridge in the hope of bringing home supper. These Gallic monsters were accompanied by a bowl of unctuous mayonnaise, a lemon cut in half wrapped in muslin, a basketful of crispy *baguette* and a pair of heavy duty nutcrackers. Alcohol was also alien to me as I had not sipped anything more inebriating than a Dubonnet and lemonade on high days and holidays with my parents and for the first time in my life I tasted chilled *Muscadet sur Lie*. I thought I had died and gone to heaven.

During the following spring holidays, his father generously paid for us to travel south to Cannes on the Côte d'Azur. We journeyed overnight, first class, on the elegant sleeper *Le Train Bleu*, accompanied by rumbling indigestion and our six-month old cocker spaniel puppy, Ulla. The next day, we drove a short distance along the coast to St Raphaël and it was there that I tasted my first *bouillabaisse*, the legendary Mediterranean fish stew. It was so copious, as was the bottomless carafe of *rosé*, which kept on being replenished, that after the bill was settled we managed, with certain difficulty I hasten to add, to stagger across the square to the church where the three of us sank gratefully onto a pew, falling asleep within minutes, encouraged by the lingering aroma of incense and the soothingly cool darkness.

It is impossible to recreate this pungent combination of saffron, olive oil and rock fish effectively in England, but I have learned since to make an equivalent that sits more comfortably in northern climes, called a *bourride*.

The Frenchman was busy studying for his degree at the university of Orléans, visiting his parents in Paris once a month. When he returned to the capital his father invariably booked a table at one of the best restaurants, with me tagging along in hungry pursuit. Entering wholeheartedly into the spirit of our affair, he encouraged me to sample firstly a monumental *choucroûte* at the Brasserie Lipp – a steaming marathon of pickled cabbage and smoked sausage refreshed with tankards of chilled Alsatian beer. On another occasion he persuaded me to plough my way through a belt-releasing, zip-undoing *cassoulet* at l'Auberge de la Truite in the Faubourg St Honoré, a mere garlic breath away from the British Embassy. Between mouthfuls, I learned that a true *cassoulet* takes days to build and comprises white beans, tomatoes, various types of sausage and *confit d'oie* (preserved goose), covered with a luscious cheesy crust, eating at its most serious and decadent.

Endearingly, *père et fils* took as much pleasure in getting me to try different things as I had in savouring them and through their tutelage I learned a great deal about presentation, food combinations, sauces and which wines (and bottled waters) should accompany each dish. For example, it is virtually impossible to find a wine which complements both egg and chocolate; plain water is preferable, as wine is distorted by their complex flavours.

The irony was that during my entire four and a half year sojourn in France I never owned more than a single electric hot plate and one very large saucepan with which to experiment!

Cooking is an art, a fascinating alchemic blending of ingredients, amalgamating families and friends. Ask anyone who has experienced extreme happiness (or sadness for that matter) in their lives and I bet you a pound to a penny that they will remember exactly what they were eating either before or after the event. It's also a well-established fact that most men would rather share a meal with someone who happily slurps down every last morsel than a person who pushes and prods indifferently at a lettuce leaf. Food is sexy. It is the very staff of life. One of those memorable occasions for me was the first dinner *à deux* I shared with Jimmy. He took me to an Italian restaurant where he was a regular customer, near my old flat in Notting Hill Gate and as he was familiar with the menu, I let him choose. Our starter was a rustic dry, cured meat called *'speck'*, served with mayonnaise mixed with fresh herbs, followed by crunchy, deep-fried chicken Kiev and an orange and onion salad. Having consumed a bottle of Frascati followed by several flaming sambucas, he found the way to my heart.

A few years later, in 1985 we moved to Sussex, where we have remained happily ever since. This is where I learned to garden in earnest and now, after years of hard work and landscaping the grounds, we are very nearly self-sufficient in vegetables and fruit. Jimmy took a bit of persuading, but two years ago I achieved a childhood dream when we acquired three brown hens. The deal was that he would name them – and so he did: Cocker, Doodle and Do. Tragically Do recently had to be put to sleep as she was suffering from the avian equivalent of sheep bloat and we have now augmented our flock with a light Sussex and a soft, dove grey girl, the first sporting Fulham's colours as Jimmy confirms. They have been named (in spite of being fiercely female) Haynsie and Robbo after his old late, lamented playing mates, Johnny Haynes and Bobby Robson. Miraculously after only twenty-four hours, Robbo produced her first, quite perfect egg. One of my favourite times of the day is to be up with the dawn, checking in the still warm nests in the coop for overnight laying. The hens are very obliging, popping out on average an egg each a day, and Jimmy often has one boiled for his breakfast.

The gardener in me cannot resist seed catalogues and I flip through the pages as soon as they drop through the letter box, ticking every other carrot, lettuce or must-have beetroot. We have plum and apple trees, black and redcurrant bushes, peach and quince trees, gooseberries and a couple of young walnut trees, which will probably not fruit until well after I reach pensionable age. I try to grow crops that will enable us to pick at least something on every day of the year: salads, tomatoes, cucumbers, courgettes and beans in the summer months and all members of the cabbage family and leeks during the winter. Anything edible leftover is fed either to the chickens or to our vertically challenged labrador, Charlie – the scraps go onto the compost heap thus completing the circle.

Next spring we are taking on some new tenants: in our village lives a family of bee keepers and we have invited them to put a dozen hives in a sheltered corner of our half-acre field. They will look after them whilst the bees look after us providing delicious honey made from our own flowers.

We entertain sporadically all year round. Jimmy's family are frequent visitors, as are friends and colleagues from the entertainment and sporting world and my family lives nearby. Our favourite time for these gatherings is around Jimmy's birthday in mid-July. After too many rotten summers, we are desperate for sunshine and a few consecutive warm days so that we can eat on the terrace or in the shade under the apple tree. Lunches are leisurely, spontaneous affairs and comprise whatever is ripe and ready to pick. The asparagus bed we created from scratch reached maturity last June and now we are able to feast on bundles of it for many happy weeks.

If we are planning a dinner or lunch with friends, I would far rather be given little or no notice because it removes the hours, days – even weeks – spent agonising over recipe books. I start with Delia, ending up with Rick, via Jamie and Gary, and in the end (unwisely) I ignore the lot of them, and usually opt for a simple roast with a pudding to follow, invariably my grandmother's all-in-one pavlova. I don't do a starter as such, but hand round freshly made nibbles with drinks beforehand so that we can all sit down together for the main course.

One of the biggest compliments I have ever been paid was the day Des Lynam and Tim Brooke-Taylor came to Sunday lunch. Carelessly we had left our shopping until very late on the Saturday afternoon, planning to cook a couple of ducklings. However, when we reached the supermarket there was only one bird left. We searched the other aisles and located a couple of quails, a partridge, a wild duck and a hen pheasant. Their cooking needs vary considerably and I had set myself a nightmare challenge.

I started off with the largest fowl in the roasting dish and after half an hour, in went the pheasant, then the other birds in size order. When they were crispy and golden and the juices ran clear, I lifted them out of the pan, cut them in half or quarters with poultry shears, laid them on a platter, and poured over the gravy, scraping the sides and bottom of the pan, and left them to rest in the warm for ten minutes. I dished them up with potatoes (dug freshly from the garden) roasted in some goose fat left over from Christmas, alongside a steaming bowl of *petits pois à la française*. Laid out on a clean white table cloth, it looked like something from a medieval feast and there wasn't a crumb left. Tim B-T said that it was one of the best meals he had eaten in his life.

The recipes in this book are the result of a mixture of old family stalwarts and ones I have conjured up or interpreted. It is the sort of food we like to eat: uncomplicated, satisfying and full of natural flavours. The ultimate in comfort food. The instructions and ingredients are not set in tablets of stone and if you feel that you want to change them in any way to suit your taste buds, then it's entirely up to you. Be flexible, have confidence in yourself and above all, enjoy! You will feel positively angelic...the apron is an optional extra, but certainly your wings and halo will be firmly in place.

Sadly, not long after *A Compost Kind of Girl* was published in 2007, my mother passed away following a short illness. My two brothers and I were confronted with clearing sixty-five years of clutter from our old family home (where I was born) as it had to be sold. In so doing I came across, amongst other things, an entire collection of women's magazines to which my mother had subscribed dating from 1949 (a year after she married my father) until he died in 1966. Covered in bat droppings, mouse dirt and years of dust, they were unexpected treasure trove. Eventually, after countless car journeys, I succeeded in bringing them back to our house, where I waded through pile after pile spending many happy hours reading through the totally non-politically correct articles about men, marriage and babies, devouring the enigmatic post-war recipes, envying the fashions and wasp-waisted models and the elaborate, extravagant flower arrangements. A seed was sown...

I set about writing *Angel in an Apron* and, when it came to the thoughts on how best it could be illustrated, my mind turned instantly to Ma's magazines. Virtually every advertisement, article and story was complemented with a picture of a woman or girl or child in an apron. Everyone knows what a chicken fillet, a leg of lamb or a pork chop look like so why not move the goal posts and illustrate my recipes with something completely different? There is a distinct possibility that you will think I am totally mad but I want to convey the spirit behind my ideas, namely the fun and the satisfaction that each dish produces, inspired by these vintage pictures.

TIPS •

In retrospect, this is where I probably obtained my first tiny halo: the best bit of advice my mother ever gave me was to wash up pots and pans as you go along as against piling everything into a heap to deal with later. If you don't do as she suggested, by the time the meal is over there will be a depressing mountain of dirty utensils. Ma's answer to the problem was that, once the spuds are cooked, the broccoli steamed, you decant them into a serving dish and keep them warm. Don't worry for a moment about your guests while you busy yourself with these jobs – they're having far too much fun – just make sure you clear the decks before joining the throng.

Don't take up valuable space in the dishwasher so start by putting the pans into a basin of very hot water, don your rubber gloves and add a squirt of washing up liquid. By not allowing anything to dry to a tough crust, a mere flip around with the brush or scourer normally will remove any cooking debris in a matter of seconds. Rinse them under the tap and place on the draining board. Finally, save energy and make the tea towels redundant, leaving everything to dry naturally.

If you have a dish covered in tough, burned bits, sprinkle it with some biological washing powder and fill the pan with a kettle of boiling water. Live dangerously and break the rules, leave it overnight to soak and by morning all the nasties will come away with ease. A cheaper, more environmentally friendly solution, is to use old-fashioned soda crystals.

Finally, however tired I may be, without fail I load the dishwasher before going to bed as there is nothing more hangover-inducing than being confronted with a sink full of dishes the following day. It's well worth the pain, believe me.

Angels do have a reputation to keep up after all...

Measurements

Measurements have been given in **metric** and **imperial** but before you get started, here are some useful spoon measurements. **Cups** are also used – measuring cups can be bought in cookery shops, but a useful guideline is that a cup equals 250 ml (9 fl oz) or a proper teacup.

IMPERIAL

1 oz butter = 1 level tablespoon

55 g (2 oz) breadcrumbs = 1 breakfast cup

1 oz uncooked rice = 1 level tablespoon

1 oz currants, sultanas, raisins = 1 level tablespoon

1 oz dripping = 1 level tablespoon

1 oz flour = 1 heaped tablespoon

1 oz jam = 1 heaped dessertspoon

1 oz lard = 1 level tablespoon

1 oz suet = 1 heaped tablespoon

1 oz caster sugar = 1 heaped tablespoon

1 oz demerara or brown sugar = 1 level tablespoon

1 oz granulated sugar = 1 heaped tablespoon

1 oz golden syrup = 1 full tablespoon

1 egg = 55 g (2 oz) approximately

General calculations for entertaining (c1943)

Cocktail party: 4–5 savouries per person, 3–4 small drinks

Fork buffet: 1 starter, 1 main dish, 1 pudding, 3–4 drinks per person

Wedding: 4–6 savouries, 1–2 sweet items, 3–4 drinks per person

Teenage party: 1 main dish, crusty bread, butter and cheese, 1 sweet dish per person

FOR 25 SERVINGS YOU WILL NEED:

4. 8 litres (8 pints) of soup

2.5–2.7 kg (5$\frac{1}{2}$–6 lb) meat without bone

3–3.6 kg (7–8 lb) meat with bone

6 x 1.2–1.3 kg (2$\frac{1}{2}$–3 lb) chickens

7.2 kg (16 lb) oven-ready turkey

850 ml (1$\frac{1}{2}$ pints) of mayonnaise

2.7 kg (6 lb) fruit salad

850 ml (1$\frac{1}{2}$ pints) double cream

450 g (1 lb) butter

25–40 g (1–1$\frac{1}{2}$ oz) rice or pasta per person (uncooked)

85–140 g (3–5 oz) of rice or pasta per person (cooked)

For a trifle: 2.25 litres (4 pints) of custard and 25 sponges

For sausage rolls: 650 g (1$\frac{1}{2}$ lb) short or flaky pastry, 900 g (2 lb) sausage meat. This makes 30 medium and 50 small rolls.

ALSO NOTE:

· When I mention the addition of milk, it is up to you as to whether you use full cream, semi-skimmed or skimmed milk. My recipes are based on using semi-skimmed – a sort of half-way house.

· The recipes are for two servings unless otherwise mentioned.

· I like to use freshly ground black pepper but for white sauce my mother always insisted on white.

Soups

There is no secret formula required to create a tasty bowl of soup: a delicate broth can be made quickly from water, a carrot, a leek and a potato. Blitz the vegetables once they are cooked, add a touch of milk or cream, season with salt and pepper and it's ready to eat in less than half an hour. I use up any leftover vegetables from the day before and add them to the stock pot but, if you delay eating a soup which includes potatoes, don't let it hang around for more than twenty-four hours for, even if kept in the fridge, it may begin to ferment. As a base to most of my soups I use chicken stock (fresh or frozen) or in the absence of both, Marigold Vegetable Bouillon powder or good old, plain, bog standard tap water. If you use the Bouillon powder, make sure you taste before adding any extra salt.

ROASTED TOMATO SOUP

It is almost impossible to give exact measurements for this recipe – it depends on the size of your oven dish and what quantity you want to make. However, I shall try and be as precise as I can.

SERVES 3–4

900 g (2 lb) juicy (even over-ripe) tomatoes, washed but with stalks left on if still attached – they will add more flavour

2 large onions

2 sticks celery, washed and chopped

2 good sized carrots, peeled and chopped

2–3 large cloves garlic

1 red chilli, chopped, or ½ tsp dried chilli flakes (optional)

1 tsp sugar

3 tbsp olive oil

Salt and freshly ground black pepper

2 tbsp crème fraîche (optional)

Fresh herbs such as marjoram, thyme or basil for garnish (rosemary is an extremely pungent herb so be more economical if you use it)

METHOD

1 Preheat the oven to gas mark 6 (200°C, 400°F).

2 Wash the tomatoes and cut any large ones in half or quarters (skin and seeds intact).

3 Peel only the outer, dusty layer of skin and roots from the onions – the brown skin left behind will give some extra colour and flavour. Cut them into quarters and then again in half.

4 Crush the garlic (skin left on) by banging down on it with a wooden spoon.

5 Place all the prepared vegetables higgledy piggledy in a large roasting dish. Scatter the chilli (dried or fresh) and sprinkle on the sugar – this is a vital ingredient if cooking with tomatoes as they can be acidic.

6 Pour over the olive oil, then add about 1 teaspoon of salt and a few good grinds of black pepper.

7 Place in a hot oven for about 30–40 minutes until the vegetables are beginning to tinge with black. At this point, remove from the oven and taking small quantities at a time, push it through a sieve in order to leave behind any skin and stalks, which you throw away. (I have one of those wooden mushroom-shaped utensils to push the cooked vegetables through the sieve, but the back of a ladle works if you don't.)

8 When you are ready to serve, if you want a creamy soup, whisk in the crème fraîche – it shouldn't curdle.

9 Finish by decorating each bowl of soup with a few torn up fresh herb leaves.

TIPS •

If you intend to freeze the soup, don't add garlic now as it can make it taste fusty when thawed.

Apart from using as a concentrated tomato soup, this purée can be used for pasta or as an accompaniment to fried or baked fish. I freeze it in blocks (plastic butter or spread containers are ideal).

For a high protein, low-fat soup, dilute the tomato purée with 1 pint of water or chicken stock and add a cupful of orange lentils. Bring to the boil and simmer, stirring now and again for about 20 minutes. When the lentils are soft, whizz the soup in the pan with a hand-held blender.

If you didn't include them in the original cooking, add some extra heat with either a finely chopped fresh chilli or a pinch of dried chilli flakes.

A teaspoon of curry powder makes a spicy soup for a cold winter's day, but fry it first in a teaspoon of oil for a minute, stirring all the while before adding the liquid.

To make a thinner soup, dilute the concentrated purée with some chicken or vegetable stock – it will then feed more mouths.

ROASTED RED PEPPER SOUP

This soup is packed full of vitamin C.

FOR 4 PEOPLE
4 large red (bell) peppers
2 cloves garlic
2 large onions
Large stick celery
I large or 2 small carrots
3 tbsp olive oil
1 tsp Italian herb mixture (dried)
Salt and pepper
Chilli flakes or 1 red chilli (optional)
1 tin chopped tomatoes
$\frac{1}{2}$ tsp sugar
1 pint stock (chicken, vegetable or water)
Basil or parsley for garnish

METHOD

1 Preheat the oven to gas mark 6 (200°C, 400°F).

2 Prepare the peppers. push your thumb into the pepper and prise it apart. Carefully remove the stalk and as much of the core and pale ribs running along the inside. Rinse away the seeds and tear the pepper halves into generous sized pieces.

3 Crush the garlic (skin left on) by banging down on it with a wooden spoon.

4 Remove the outer skin and roots from the onions, leaving the remaining clean, brown skin, and cut into wedges.

5 Wash and slice the celery and peel the carrot(s).

6 Put all these prepared vegetables into a roasting dish and drizzle with the olive oil. Sprinkle the herbs over the top, together with the salt and several good grinds of pepper.

7 If you are using chillies, slice a fresh red or green one down the middle and remove the seeds and the rib-like bits, and cut up roughly. If you are using dried chillies, scatter enough over the vegetable mix to give a gentle kick but not enough to burn the roof of your mouth – 1 tiny salt spoon's worth is all you need.

8 Put the roasting dish into a hot oven and cook for at least half an hour – until the peppers start to singe. Sieve to remove skin and any fibrous stuff.

9 Put into a pan and add the tin of chopped tomatoes – I always buy chopped ones in juice, rarely the whole plum tomatoes because there are many more packed into a tin. Add the sugar, stock or water and heat on the stove.

10 Finally, blitz with the hand-held blender, have a sip and check the seasoning. When you are ready to serve, scatter over a few torn basil leaves or chopped parsley.

TIP •

It's worth wearing disposable latex gloves or your Marigolds when preparing fresh chillies because, if you touch your face or any other sensitive place, you will be most uncomfortable for a while.

COMFORTING LEEK AND POTATO SOUP

FOR 4 PEOPLE
4 large leeks
2 large potatoes
1 large carrot
1 stick celery
25 g (1 oz) butter
850 ml (1 ½ pints) water/vegetable or chicken stock
Salt and pepper
225 ml (½ pint) milk
Chives for garnish

METHOD

1 Prepare the leeks by trimming some of the dark green tips and cut off the roots. Run a pointed knife down the whole leek to the depth of about two layers. Peel off these outer leaves and then if you are happy with the appearance of the leek, cut it in two lengthwise. Pull the leaves apart and wash well in two or three lots of clean water. The mud tends to lurk on the inside of the upper parts of the leaves. Drain and slice but not too meticulously.

2 Peel and chop the potatoes and carrot into small pieces. Slice the stick of celery.

3 Put the butter into a saucepan and melt. I use butter for this soup instead of oil because it gives a nice flavour and it's worth the extra calories. Add all the vegetables and stir for a minute or so. Let them sweat for about 5 minutes and then add the stock or water. Bring to the boil, cover and simmer for about 20 minutes until the potatoes are cooked – test this by squashing a piece against the side of the saucepan – if there is any resistance, continue cooking for a further five minutes.

4 Remove from the heat and blitz until nearly smooth, leaving a few bits and pieces for texture. Taste and then season to taste. Add the milk and give a second quick blitz.

5 Serve with some chopped chives sprinkled on top.

TIP •••

In the winter months when your chives have disappeared underground, rather than buy pots of the herb in the supermarket, get half a dozen shallots, fill a flower pot with soil or compost and bury the bulbs close to each other, up to their necks. Place on a windowsill in the kitchen, water and wait for lovely green shoots to appear. Snip them off with scissors – they will taste like fresh chives. You will manage to obtain several 'pickings' and when the bulbs are exhausted, chuck them into your compost bucket. I always have one pot of shallots on the go and a replacement waiting in the wings.

ANOTHER JOLLY NICE LEEK SOUP

This soup really tastes of the vegetables, but if you want to blitz it you end up with a thick, creamy soup which tastes different, but equally enjoyable.

2 large leeks
2 potatoes
1 tbsp butter
600 ml (1 pint) strong chicken stock
Little single cream (optional)
Little chopped parsley or chopped chives
(see Tip on p. 18)

METHOD

1 Wash and slice the leeks finely.

2 Peel and chop the potatoes into tiny cubes.

3 Melt the butter (about a tablespoon) in a pan and add the vegetables. Stir and let them sweat for 2 minutes. Add the stock, stir and bring to the boil. Simmer gently with the lid on until the potatoes are cooked – about 15–20 minutes. When you are ready to serve, add the cream if desired and sprinkle each bowl with some parsley or chives.

GREEN PEPPER SOUP

This lovely green soup can be served hot or chilled. To make it even prettier, swirl in a little cream and decorate with chopped chives.

8 oz green (bell) pepper
1 large onion, peeled
1 dessertspoon oil
20 g ($^3/_4$ oz) butter
$^1/_2$ tbsp flour
2 beef or chicken stock cubes
300–425 ml ($^1/_2$ – $^3/_4$ pint) boiling water
225 ml ($^3/_4$ pint) milk

METHOD

1 Carefully remove pepper stalk and as much of the core and pale ribs running along the inside. Rinse away the seeds and slice.

2 Slice the onions and sweat the pepper and onion in the oil and butter.

3 Sprinkle on the flour and stir in. Remove from the heat.

4 Dissolve the stock cube in the water and add this to the vegetables. Mix well and bring to the boil; simmer for about 15 minutes.

5 Put into a blender (or use the electric hand blender directly in the saucepan) and whizz. Pour back into the saucepan (if you used a blender) and add the milk, stirring well. Season with salt and pepper as necessary. Sieve into a bowl.

VERY SIMPLE CHICKEN NOODLE SOUP

This is a 'cuddle in a cup', especially if you have the sniffles. If you are spending time working at your desk at the computer or digging in the garden, the chances are you have little time on your hands to rustle up something nourishing and tasty. If you have some good, strong chicken stock available, then you can make this quick and easy soup. When there isn't any in the house, I use a good quality chicken stock cube diluted with 500 ml (18 fl oz) boiling water.

600 ml (1 pint) concentrated chicken stock (or good quality chicken stock cube as mentioned, diluted)

Salt and pepper to taste (if you are using a stock cube, taste first before adding salt or pepper)

½ bundle rice noodles or 25 g (1 oz) dry, fine egg noodles

2 finely sliced spring onions

METHOD

1 Heat the chicken stock and test for salt, then season accordingly.

2 When this is boiling, add the noodles. Check to see whether they are cooked before adding the spring onions.

3 Serve in a chunky mug.

TIPS ••

I break the noodles up before cooking, otherwise it is impossible to eat tidily and everything runs down your chin! Check with the instructions on the packet to see if you need to boil them or merely let them sit in the stock before eating. Usually they are added to the boiling liquid and left for a few minutes to swell.

You can make this soup a bit more oriental by substituting some of the salt with a splash of soy sauce.

EVERY DAY SOUP

450 g (1 lb) leeks
2 carrots
1-2 sticks celery
1 tbsp butter or olive oil
Chilli flakes (optional)
600 ml (1 pint) (approx.) water or stock
Salt and pepper
Baguette to serve

METHOD

1 Wash the leeks well and chop roughly.

2 Peel and chop carrots and slice the celery.

3 Melt the butter or olive oil in a saucepan and, when hot, add all the vegetables. Stir and leave to sweat on a medium heat for 2-3 minutes and then stir again. (It is not vital to do this step, but if you have the time it does help release the flavour in the vegetables.)

4 Add the chilli flakes depending on how hot you like it. (I'm a scaredy cat and would add only about enough to cover the end of a knife point – remember that dried flakes are hotter than a fresh chilli as the seeds are included.)

5 Add the water or stock (chicken, vegetable or made up with Bouillon powder); stir, cover and simmer for about a 15 minutes until the vegetables are soft. I like a few lumps

in my soups and find that, if I purée in a blender, the character – and flavour – of the soup alters considerably. Therefore I find a potato masher an ideal tool, leaving just the right amount of 'bite'.

6 Check the seasoning and add salt and pepper as necessary.

TIPS •
You can smarten up this hearty soup with a spoonful of crème fraîche or double cream and a sprinkling of chopped parsley.

If you don't manage to finish a baguette, put the remainder into a plastic bag. The next day, remove from the bag and place in a hot oven for a couple of minutes and it will come back to life. If you forget to put it into a plastic bag and it seems too dry to bother about, flash it under the tap to moisten the crust and then place it in a hot oven but for a minute or two longer. It will be just like a fresh loaf.

WINTER WARMER SOUP

This is a meal in itself and will warm you from tip to toe.

1 tin beans (whatever you have handy, e.g. mixed salad beans, white beans, chick peas)

1/2 small green cabbage (about 225 g [8 oz]) – your choice of variety

1 medium onion

2 carrots

1 stick celery

1 clove garlic

1 fresh red chilli or 1/4 tsp dried chilli flakes

1 tbsp olive oil

1 tin chopped tomatoes in juice

1/2 tsp sugar

600 ml (1 pint) stock (Bouillon powder, chicken or vegetable)

Salt and pepper

1 tbsp chopped parsley

2 tbsp grated Emmental cheese

METHOD

1 Pour the can of beans into a sieve and rinse well.

2 Wash and shred the cabbage thinly.

3 Peel and chop the onion, carrots, celery and garlic into little pieces.

4 Heat the oil in a saucepan and add the carrots, onion, celery and garlic. Add the chilli flakes or fresh chilli. Stir and sweat for a couple of minutes. Tip in the cabbage and stir over a high heat for a further minute – it will become bright green.

5 Add the beans, tinned tomatoes, sugar and stock, stir and bring to the boil. Simmer until the vegetables are cooked.

6 Season with salt and pepper to taste.

7 Sprinkle the parsley over and finish each bowl with a spoonful of cheese (this will melt) and serve.

TIP •

If you have any fresh pesto left in the fridge (see recipe on page 168), add a teaspoon to each bowl of soup instead of the chopped parsley.

LUSCIOUS WATERCRESS SOUP

This soup is peppery, tangy and a brilliant green and very healthy.

1 large onion
1 large or 2 smaller potatoes
1 stick celery
1 carrot
**1 large or 2 small bunches fresh watercress or
a bag of organic watercress**
20 g (³/₄ oz) butter or 1 scant tbsp oil
425 ml (³/₄ pint) stock (or plain water)
150 ml (¹/₂ pint) milk and/or cream
Salt and pepper
1 tbsp cream or crème fraîche

METHOD

1 Peel and chop the onion into fine slices so that they cook quickly.

2 Peel and chop potatoes into small chunks.

3 Chop celery.

4 Peel and chop carrot.

5 Trim the hairy stalks from the watercress and wash thoroughly to remove any grit or yellowing leaves and chop roughly.

6 Put the butter or any sort of oil in a pan and heat. Add all the vegetables except the watercress and stir for a couple of minutes to bring out the flavours.

7 Add the stock (or plain water), stir and cover. Bring to the boil, reduce the heat and simmer until the potatoes are soft.

8 Throw in the watercress, stir and heat through for a couple of minutes until it wilts.

9 Stir in the milk. Remove from heat and whizz with hand-held blender. (I use this more than a full blown food processor because it is instantly ready to function and is easy to clean.)

10 Taste and season with salt and pepper. Add a swirl of cream and serve at once. If you are using crème fraîche you may want to use the blender again to mix it in thoroughly.

TIP •

Try and find a greengrocer who sells glossy bunches of fresh watercress. Place it in a glass with a little water as soon as you get home to keep it in tip top condition.

CAULIFLOWER SOUP

Or (as it's known in this house), Windy Pop Soup

1 medium-sized cauliflower
1 large onion
1 stick celery
1 large carrot
2 cloves garlic
25 g (1 oz) butter or 1 tbsp oil
600 ml (1 pint) chicken stock, Bouillon or water
1 cup milk
Salt and pepper
1 tbsp cream (optional)
Parsley or chives for garnish

METHOD

1 Remove outer tough leaves from the cauliflower but keep any of the more tender inner leaves and slice these finely. Wash well. Cut the florets away from the central 'trunk' of the cauliflower and either slice or chop into chunks. Discard the 'trunk'.

2 Peel and chop onion. Slice the celery and peel and chop the carrot.

3 Crush the garlic (skin left on) by pushing down on it with a knife blade or wooden spoon. The skin can then be easily removed.

4 Put either the butter or oil into a saucepan and heat. Add the onions and stir for a minute then tip in the celery, carrots, cauliflower florets and leaves, and garlic. Allow these to sweat for 5 minutes.

5 Add the water or stock and stir. Bring to the boil, reduce the heat and simmer until the vegetables are soft – about 20 minutes.

6 Remove from the heat and whizz in a blender or squash with the potato masher. Add the milk and whizz again. Taste and season with salt and pepper, adding more if necessary.

7 This soup is elevated to a different level with the addition of a little cream, swirling it with the spoon to make it pretty. Sprinkle with some chopped parsley or chives and serve.

TIP •
Never overcook vegetables for soup as it ruins the fresh flavour.

BUTTERNUT AND GINGER SOUP

This is a lovely, warming soup and the hint of ginger and chilli gives it extra oomph. It will serve two people generously but also four as a starter.

½ butternut squash (about 450 g [1 lb])
1 cm (½ inch) fresh root ginger
1 clove garlic (optional)
1 onion
1 stick celery, chopped
Pinch of dried chilli flakes
25 g (1 oz) butter
600–850 ml (1–1 ½ pints) vegetable, chicken stock or made-up Bouillon
Salt and pepper
1 cup milk

METHOD

1 Peel the butternut with great care – it is quite tough and an ordinary knife might jump and cut you. Instead, I slice the butternut first into large rounds and then, using a vegetable peeler, work my way around the skin. Scoop out any pips and stringy bits from the centre with a spoon. Cut into 2.5 cm (1 inch) sized chunks.

2 Peel and grate the ginger.

3 Peel and chop the garlic and onion.

4 Slice the celery.

5 Melt the butter in a saucepan and add the onion, celery, garlic and ginger and chilli flakes. Stir for a minute or two and add the butternut. Stir again, add the stock and bring to the boil. Allow to simmer for about 15 minutes until the vegetables are soft.

6 Season with salt and pepper.

7 Using an electric hand blender, blitz the soup in the saucepan and add the milk. Blitz again and taste, adjusting seasoning if necessary.

TIP •••

If you are having to cook a lot of onions at one time and have other jobs to do, put the sliced onions in a frying pan with a tablespoon of oil and add enough water barely to cover them. Bring to the boil whilst stirring and then reduce the heat and let them get on with it whilst you carry on with other things. The liquid will evaporate as the onions cook. You can either continue to fry them stirring every now and then until they are golden brown, or use them as they are if no further colour is desired.

ALTERNATIVE BUTTERNUT SOUP

3 thick rounds butternut squash cut from the 'neck' end
2 carrots
1 large clove garlic
2 leeks
2 sticks celery (save some leaves for garnish)
Knob of butter
850 ml (1½ pints) chicken stock or Bouillon
1 cup milk
Salt and pepper

METHOD

1 Remove the rind from the butternut, taking care not to cut yourself (see page 26). Cut into small chunks.

2 Peel and chop the carrots and garlic.

3 Wash the leeks and celery and slice finely.

4 Melt the butter in a pan and add the vegetables, stirring for 2 minutes. Add the stock and bring to the boil. Simmer for 15 minutes or so until the butternut is soft.

5 Using a potato masher, crush the vegetables in the saucepan but not to a complete purée. Add the milk, stir and taste.

6 Season with salt and pepper.

7 When you are ready to serve, sprinkle the soup with some raw celery leaves torn into small pieces.

HAM AND LENTIL SOUP

This is a double recipe – buy one, get one free. For a change, every now and again I like to cook a small piece of smoked gammon partly because there is no waste and also because it leaves me with a wonderful quantity of delicious stock. I soak the ham for a few hours in cold water before cooking it in case it is very salty, which it can be and this would make the stock tricky to use afterwards. I prefer smoked gammon to what is called 'green' gammon as it makes a tastier soup.

COOKING THE GAMMON

1 Place the gammon into a large saucepan and surround it with any vegetables you have to hand, for example:

2–3 peeled onions but kept whole

2–3 sticks celery cut into finger length pieces

3–4 carrots cut into chunks if large, or kept whole if small

Bouquet garni (see Tip below)

Potatoes, kept whole if small, or cut in half if large (if I am serving the gammon hot I will add enough potatoes for the amount of mouths to feed along with the other raw vegetables)

2 Add enough cold water to cover the surface of the ham and vegetables and add approximately 12 peppercorns. Cover, bring to the boil and simmer on a gentle bubble until the ham is cooked. This isn't an exact science because it depends on the size of your piece of ham but a good way to tell is as follows: if you can pull the dark brown rind away easily from the meat (using tongs) then it is done. If there is any resistance, leave it to cook a few minutes longer.

TIPS •

I serve the hot ham sliced thinly, surrounded by the vegetables and pour a ladle full of ham stock on top. Sprinkle some chopped parsley and serve with some freshly made English (Coleman's) mustard – an absolute must! If I have time I will make a parsley sauce using some of the stock and adding a little milk.

Bouquet garni: Gather together several stalks of parsley, a couple of bay leaves, a couple of sprigs of fresh thyme and tie them with some thread or string so that they can be removed easily after cooking.

Don't throw the rind of the gammon in the bin. Using a large clothes peg, attach it to a branch on a tree or bush – woodpeckers love it.

NOW FOR THE SOUP

The amount gleaned from this recipe depends of the size of the original gammon and the liquid needed. I judge 600 ml (1 pint) of soup to equal two servings.

1½ cups red lentils (per 850 ml [1½ pints] ham stock)
Mint leaves for garnish
Milk (optional)

METHOD

1 The most important thing (as I mentioned before) is to taste it the ham stock before you start. If it is too salty then don't use it neat – take 600 ml (1 pint) of the ham stock and dilute it with water until you are happy that the balance is right. Repeat the process with the remaining stock and freeze once cold in suitable quantities to use later.

2 There will probably be some vegetables left over including potatoes and maybe even some parsley sauce, which you can add at this point. Rinse the lentils in a sieve to remove dust and to check for tiny stones.

3 Bring the stock and vegetables to the boil and then add the lentils. Stir every now and again. This will take about 20 minutes of simmering before the lentils are cooked. At this point, use the potato masher and crush the lentils and vegetables to make a hearty, lumpy soup.

4 Check for seasoning and adjust accordingly. If you want to, you can add a little milk (about a cupful) to make it look creamy and then, when you are ready to serve, add a few chopped fresh mint leaves – they go really well with the ham stock.

TIP •
Instead of lentils you can ring the changes by using frozen peas – approximately 450 g (1 lb) peas to 600 ml (1 pint) stock.

CREAM OF CARROT SOUP

450 g (1 lb) carrots
1 medium potato
1 medium onion
1–2 cloves garlic
1 stick celery
25 g (1 oz) butter
600 ml (1 pint) chicken stock
1 tbsp crème fraîche
Salt and pepper
**Few fresh coriander leaves (if you have them handy)
or chives or parsley**

METHOD

1 Peel and chop the carrots, potato, onion and garlic.

2 Wash and slice the celery. Melt the butter in a saucepan and add the vegetables. Stir and cook for about 3 minutes to bring out the flavour. Add the stock, bring to the boil and simmer until the vegetables are cooked (about 15 minutes).

3 Cool slightly before blending. I prefer this soup to be lump free and therefore I blend it in the food processor until it is smooth. Pour the soup back into the pan to heat up again and whisk in the crème fraîche.

4 Season with salt and pepper to taste.

5 Sprinkle each bowl with the coriander or other herbs to garnish.

TIP •

To add a tangy taste to this soup, add the juice of 2 small/medium oranges when you blend the vegetables.

POTAGE MONGOLE

This soup and the Mushroom and Pea Soup that follows are rustled up in less time than the time it takes to open the cans.

1 tin green pea soup
1 tin tomato soup
1 soup tin milk
1 soup tin single cream
¼ tsp curry powder
Chopped parsley and croutons to garnish

METHOD

1 Combine all the ingredients except for the garnishes together in a pan and heat through, stirring constantly.

2 When boiling point is reached, remove from the heat, decorate with some chopped parsley and serve with croutons (see Tip below).

TIP •
Croutons are quick and easy to make and not only use up stale bread, but also bulk out a portion of soup. Cut thick slices of bread (about 1 cm/¹/₂") and remove crusts. Cut into squares and place on a non-stick baking sheet. Drizzle over some ordinary olive oil and bake in a moderately hot oven until golden and crisp.

MUSHROOM AND PEA SOUP

1 tin mushroom soup
1 tin pea soup
1 soup tin milk
1 soup tin water
1 onion, thinly sliced

METHOD

1 Combine all the ingredients together in a pan and heat through, stirring constantly.

2 Heat gently to boiling point, stirring constantly, and simmer for approximately 5 minutes or until the onion is soft and cooked through.

COLD SHANNON SOUP

If you like the classic, cold Spanish tomato soup, *gazpacho*, you will like this.

FOR CONCENTRATED STOCK
450 g (1 lb) tomatoes, cut in half
1 fennel bulb, sliced
2 onions, chopped
1-2 cloves garlic, skins on, chopped
Basil
1 tsp sugar
2 tbsp olive oil
Salt and pepper
Chicken stock
Juice 1/2 lemon
Dash Tabasco sauce or 1 dessertspoon hot chilli sauce
2 tbsp cream or crème fraîche (optional)

METHOD

1 Roast all the ingredients (except the chicken stock) in a hot oven for about an hour to make a concentrated stock.

2 When all the vegetables are well and truly cooked, pass the mixture through a sieve. Measure the purée and add an equal amount of chicken stock.

3 Add the lemon juice, Tabasco sauce or chilli sauce and mix together. When the soup is cold, add a couple of tablespoons of cream or crème fraîche if desired and stir. Chill thoroughly.

4 Serve in individual bowls with a sprinkle of chopped chives or basil.

LETTUCE AND MINT SOUP

1 cup chopped raw potato
1 cup chopped onion
25 g (1 oz) butter
600 ml (1 pint) chicken stock
3 cups sliced lettuce – the outer leaves are fine (keep the hearts for a salad)
½ cup fresh mint
Salt and pepper to taste
Cream to decorate
Freshly chopped herbs to decorate

METHOD

1 Sweat the potato and onion in the butter for 5 minutes, then add the stock. Stir and bring to the boil. Simmer with the lid on until soft.

2 Add the lettuce and a small handful of mint leaves (about half a cup) and bring back to the boil, but do not replace the lid – this will keep the vegetables nice and green. Stir and cook for 2–3 minutes.

3 Remove from heat and put into a blender. Whizz until smooth. Season with salt and pepper and decorate with a swirl of cream and some chopped, fresh herbs. Serve either hot or chilled.

TIP •

If you grow your own vegetables and are anything like me, you either have a glut of lettuces or none at all because they have all been eaten or if not, they have bolted. This soup is a good way of using up some of the lettuces, even if they are a little past their grow-by-date and are on the verge of running to seed. However, taste a leaf first before making the soup in order to check that it isn't too bitter.

WHITE ONION SOUP

2 large white onions, peeled and sliced
25 g (1 oz) butter
1 large potato, peeled and chopped into medium-sized pieces
600 ml (1 pint) milk
Salt and pepper to taste

METHOD

1 Sweat the onions in a pan with the butter. Put on the lid and simmer gently over a very, very low heat for at least an hour. They should never brown but remain cream-coloured and transparent.

2 Boil the potatoes in unsalted water until mushy.

3 When the onions are done, add 1 cup of potato water and the potato. Heat almost to boiling point then pass through a sieve.

4 Add the milk to the puree and re-heat, seasoning with salt and pepper.

SWEETCORN AND COURGETTE SOUP

This is wonderful with your own home-grown sweetcorn. If you don't have any in your veggie plot, try to buy a 'super sweet' variety, as this retains more flavour than the others. If neither is available, open a can.

1 large fresh corn on the cob
15 g (¹/₂ oz) butter
1 medium courgette, chopped
1 medium onion, peeled and sliced
1 stick celery, sliced
2 cloves garlic, peeled and chopped
600 ml (1 pint) chicken stock
Salt and pepper to taste
225 ml (8 fl oz) milk
Dash of cream (optional)
Freshly chopped parsley for decoration

METHOD

1 If using fresh sweetcorn, up-end the cob and run a sharp knife firmly from top to bottom, removing the kernels. If using a can, open, drain and rinse.

2 Melt the butter in a saucepan and add the vegetables, stirring every now and then for 5 minutes.

3 Add the stock, stir and bring to the boil. Simmer with the lid half on (propped open with the wooden spoon) for about 15 minutes, or until the vegetables are cooked and soft.

4 Whizz in the saucepan using a hand-held blender, but not totally to a smooth cream – leave a few bits and pieces of vegetables for a little crunch. Season with salt and pepper and taste and adjust accordingly.

5 Add enough of the milk and/or cream to make the soup fairly runny, then stir. Put to one side to eat later or re-heat immediately (but do not boil).

6 Serve with the parsley on top.

TRICK PRAWN BISQUE

I was given this wonderful recipe by an old girlfriend, Carole, who was witness at our wedding. It was her mother's and when she gave it to me I had to promise not to pass it on – if I did, she said, 'it would be served at every dinner party in Notting Hill!' I have kept my word to this day, but since Carole has recently moved to the West Country and we live in Sussex, the embargo has been lifted.

First of all, in advance (a week or so) make some chilli sherry. For this recipe you will need only a small amount, but it will be a useful addition to salads, marinades and other soups. Find a small bottle or jam jar and fill it with medium dry Amontillado. Drop in either a couple of fresh red chillies, or a teaspoonful of dried, crushed chillies. Leave on a sunny window sill for a few days, shaking it now and again.

115 g (4 oz) fresh prawns
1 tin tomato soup
1 tin lentil soup
Cream for decoration
Chilli sherry

METHOD

1 Put a few whole prawns to one side for later.

2 Blitz the rest of the prawns in a blender, add them to the two tins of soup and heat gently up to boiling point.

3 When hot, add a drizzle of the chilli sherry and pour into bowls. Put a few whole prawns into each dish and decorate with a swirl of cream. Serve immediately.

Eggs

Rule 1: *Un oeuf* is enough.
Rule 2: There's no 'f' in *oeufs*!

When I was four years old, out of the blue my father presented my mother with 40 chickens, the idea being that we would sell our eggs to the village baker to make some extra cash. To begin with things went more or less according to plan, in spite of the meddlesome intervention of a fox. Then, all of a sudden the supply completely dried up. My parents were mystified and anxiously researched in their hen-keeping books for an explanation, but to no avail.

It wasn't until a few days later that my mother's radar sensed that the house had become unnaturally quiet and I was nowhere to be seen – or heard. She eventually found me at the bottom of the garden, hidden away behind the tool shed, stirring a sloppy mud pie in a large, galvanised bucket. Caught in the act, I waited in trepidation for her wrath to explode as she looked over the low flint wall into our neighbour's field. On the other side, nestling in the long grass and ox-eye daisies were a week's worth of egg shells. Unbeknown to my parents, I had been stealing them each day in order to create my first culinary dish. Remarkably, instead of admonishing me, they decided the best policy was to encourage this initial foray into the world of cooking and, thanks to their wise parenting, I have never looked back. A prime case of egg poacher turned game keeper if ever there was one...

My father, who was an estate agent, every so often turned up at home at lunchtime, without prior warning, accompanied by a client or two in the hope of grabbing a bite to eat. The scenario was always the same. 'My wife will feed us!' he said with alacrity. 'Absolutely no problem! She's great in emergencies and I would take her into the jungle any day,' he added for good measure.

One Saturday, Ma heard a car enter through the gate at a quarter to one and was enthralled to see a gleaming, coffee-coloured Rolls Royce slither down the drive and park under the oak tree. The heavy doors opened and out of its leather upholstered depths stepped the world famous actor, Michael Wilding, and his current wife Susan. Fabulously blonde, über glamorous and, sticking to the script, swathed in floor-to-ceiling pastel mink. For those of you too young to remember, Michael had previously been married to Elizabeth Taylor and was definitely 'A' list material with a string of successful films to his credit. Realising that she now had three extra mouths to feed, Ma went out to greet them, first wiping her damp hands on her apron.

'Please come in and join us for a bite to eat,' she said, lacking some of Dad's confidence. 'You'll have to take pot luck!' Armed with a bottle of sherry and a packet of Twiglets, she ferried our guests into the sitting room along with my father before disappearing into the kitchen to rustle up a platter of egg and mayonnaise sandwiches. I was despatched to the vegetable plot with a colander and knife to pick a lettuce and gather some tomatoes. The Wildings were a delightful couple, charming to the extreme with no airs nor graces and they entered totally into the ad hoc spirit of the occasion, even taking Ma and me along with them in the Rolls when it was time to view the property after lunch.

As I have already mentioned, we are lucky to have our own hens and therefore a constant supply of eggs. If you have nothing else in your larder apart from these miracles of nature, you will always be able to produce a meal in minutes. Savoury or sweet, the possibilities are endless. I never store eggs in the fridge, but in a cool part of the kitchen out of direct sunshine.

JIMMY'S WAY OF BOILING AN EGG

Remember when you are boiling an egg that the fresher it is, the longer it needs to cook so, if you intend to eat the one which is still warm from the coop, add an extra minute or two. (Someone told me that he keeps his 'coop' eggs for a day or two in order to let them 'set' a bit.) This is how Jimmy cooks his. I cook them this way but am not always as successful as Jimmy – give it a go and see if it works for you! Three minutes for cooking seems fairly foolproof for shop-bought eggs.

METHOD

1 Take one egg (at room temperature), place it in a saucepan and cover with cold water. Put on the stove and bring to the boil. Wait a couple of minutes then carefully lift out the egg with a spoon.

2 If the water evaporates quickly off the shell this means that the centre of the egg is hot, indicating a firm white and soft yolk. If not, put the egg back into the hot water and boil a minute longer.

3 Eat – if the weather permits – in the garden or on a sunny balcony armed with a battalion of soldiers to dip into the egg.

DELECTABLE BAKED EGGS

If you are of the same vintage as me, dig out the box of china ramekins you were given as a present in the seventies from the back of a cupboard and give them a good wash. Alternatively, rescue a few from the collection of glass dishes, saved from endless naughty chocolate puddings. These delicate eggs make a lovely starter served with toast or French bread.

As many eggs as people
Pot crème fraîche
Salt and pepper
Freshly grated nutmeg

METHOD

1 Preheat the oven to gas mark 5 (190°C, 375°F).

2 Butter the insides of the ramekins and break an egg into each ramekin.

3 Add 1 tablespoon crème fraîche, a little salt and a couple of twists of pepper plus one or two gratings of nutmeg to each pot – just enough to give a hint of the exotic.

4 Place the pots in a dish half filled with water. Bake in a hot oven for about 10 minutes. Very fresh eggs may take a minute more. You want the white to be firm and the yolk soft, so you may need to check during the cooking time. Give them a shake and if the white wobbles they need a touch longer.

THE ABSOLUTE OMELETTE

Once again, home-produced eggs have no equal but free-range eggs from a supermarket are a good substitute. If there are two or three of us I make one giant omelette to divide when cooked.

For each person you will need:
2–3 eggs depending on appetites and the size of the eggs
Knob of soft butter
Extra 1 tsp butter for cooking
Salt and pepper

METHOD

1 Beat the eggs with a fork, but don't overdo things. (A Parisian taxi driver told me that when he made an omelette, he added a sizeable knob of very soft butter to the raw egg along with salt and pepper before giving it a good whisk. Butter is cream after all but in a different form.)

2 Put an empty omelette pan onto a hot stove and allow to heat thoroughly. Put another good sized blob of butter into the pan and let it melt by tilting the pan so that it covers the bottom. Replace onto the heat and wait until the fat stops sizzling and goes quiet. This stage is crucial. Watch the butter very carefully until you can see it just beginning to take on a light brown colour. Now is the time to tip in the egg mixture.

3 Give it a quick swizzle with the fork you used to beat the eggs, leave for a moment, then a second and possibly third swizzle. The idea is to move the eggs around the pan but not into a scramble, allowing them the opportunity to set and develop a nice brown bottom. Above all, don't overcook and remove from the stove when the surface is still a fraction 'yaggy' – the residual heat will ensure that it continues to cook.

4 Gently flip the omelette onto a warm plate, folding as you do so.

TIP •
I always crack my eggs individually into a saucer first before adding them to the others for the following reasons: the law of averages dictates that the last egg you break will either have bits of shell in it, or some odd-looking floaty bits – it might even be bad. If this is the case you have no option but to throw the lot away and start afresh. Should a piece of shell fall into the raw egg, remove it by using a piece of shell as a scoop and it will attract the particle like a magnet.

To vary, before cooking the omelette turn on the grill to heat up and grate some cheese into a bowl: Gruyère, Emmental or Cheddar – or a combination of any of them.

When you reach the stage where the base of the omelette is browning nicely and firm, but the egg is runny on top, remove from the heat and scatter over the grated cheese. Place under the hot grill and watch it like a hawk. The cheese will melt and the remaining uncooked egg will puff up. This takes less than a minute.

Serve immediately with a salad of butterhead lettuce and a vinaigrette made from any oil other than olive, e.g. sunflower or rapeseed oil – the lightness of the dressing will complement the cheese in the omelette.

THE PERFECT FRIED EGG

Please don't ever fry an egg in a puddle of oil.

1 egg per person
Knobs of butter
Salt and pepper to season
Baguettes

METHOD

1 First crack your egg into a saucer and check for bits of shell. Then take your small omelette frying pan, put it on a high heat and drop in a good knob of butter (about 1 teaspoon). While it is melting swill it around the pan to cover the bottom.

2 When it is really hot and the butter is beginning to turn brown, drop in the raw egg. It will spit and curse at you, but this is exactly what you want – the very hot fat will make the edges of the white go lacy and crisp.

3 Flip some of the hot butter onto the middle of the egg with a spatula – this will cook the raw film of white over the yolk.

4 Season with a little salt and pepper and *voilà*! Slide it carefully onto a warm plate and eat with some crusty baguette which you can use to mop up the runny yolk.

TIP •

If you happen to be in a hypermarket in France, go to the kitchen section and look for small, round metal dishes with two handles – a bit like flat-bottomed balti dishes – this is what the French use to cook their *'oeufs sur le plat'*. Le Creuset also make small cast iron, enamelled dishes, which are perfect for the purpose. These can accommodate a couple of eggs at a time (one helping across the Channel) and they serve them at the table in the dish in which they were cooked.

PROPER SCRAMBLED EGGS
2 large eggs per person plus 1 extra
2 tbsp double cream (about ¹/₂ small carton)
Salt and pepper
20 g (³/₄ oz) butter

METHOD

1 Crack the eggs one by one in a separate dish to check that they are fresh and there are no fragments of shell left behind. Transfer to a mixing bowl and beat them lightly but not too much.

2 Add the cream and a good pinch of salt and pepper and mix well.

3 Heat some of the butter in a non-stick pan and, when it goes silent but not brown after having bubbled, pour in the raw egg. (Some of the gods of the cooking world say that scrambled eggs should be cooked on a very low heat for a very long time – the reverse of an omelette. Not having the patience to dilly dally, I turn the heat down a touch and stir the eggs continuously until they begin to thicken and turn into soft, billowing lumps.)

4 At this point, drop in another small knob of butter and stir gently, folding it in until it melts.

5 Serve immediately, scooping the lovely creamy egg onto warm plates.

TIP •••
The secret is not to cook the eggs too much, so remove from the heat when you think they are slightly underdone – they will continue to cook off the heat.

MEXICAN BREAKFAST EGGS

This kick starts the day like no other. I eat it with plain crispbread, drinking fizzy water as against tea or coffee and get up from the table with my halo shining – and, thanks to the chilli, my nasal passages are squeakily clear.

1 tbsp oil – any type except olive oil
**1 small red onion, very finely chopped, per person,
or 1 large enough one for two people**
2 tomatoes per person, very finely chopped
1 red chilli
1 or 2 eggs per person
Salt and pepper
Fresh coriander for garnish
**1 ripe avocado, peeled and cut into thin slices
(at the last moment)**

METHOD

1 Put the oil into a non-stick frying pan. Add the onions and fry for a minute or two, then add the tomatoes and very finely chopped chilli – as much as you want – I use half for one serving. Cook for a further 3 minutes until the onions are soft.

2 Crack the egg(s) in a separate dish and, if clear of bits of shell, drop into the hot mixture and swizzle immediately with the spatula. You are not aiming at either an omelette nor scrambled eggs – something in between. Do not overcook.

3 Remove from heat and season with a little salt and freshly ground pepper.

4 Pile onto a warm plate and sprinkle with a spoonful of chopped, fresh coriander, with the sliced avocado on the side.

FARMHOUSE EGGS

4 free-range hard-boiled eggs, chopped
900 g (2 lb) potatoes, peeled
300 ml (8 fl oz) white sauce (see page 177)
4 tbsp grated cheese
55 g (2 oz) butter
Salt and pepper

METHOD

1 Preheat the oven to gas mark 7 (220°C, 425°F).

2 Boil the potatoes and mash with the half the butter.

3 Put into a shallow gratin dish and make a wall around the edge. Chop the eggs and fold into the white sauce and pour into the hollow.

4 Sprinkle with grated cheese and dot with the remaining butter. Put into the oven and cook until golden brown.

SURPRISE CHEESE SOUFFLE

The word 'soufflé' often produces more panic in men than the word 'marriage' or 'diet' in women, but trust me, I'm a cook. Even if it sinks in the middle – which it won't (and if it does, blame the oven) – it will be edible whatever the result. This recipe is for two and ideal for a light lunch, served with a crisp, green salad.

WHITE SAUCE:
55 g (2 oz) butter
2 tbsp flour (approximately 55 g [2 oz])
300 ml (½ pint) milk

115 g (4 oz) any hard cheese or cheeses you have in the fridge
1 generous tsp Dijon mustard
Salt and pepper

**Pinch of cayenne pepper (to cover the tip of a knife)
2 eggs, the yolks separated from the whites
2 extra eggs, whole**

METHOD

1 Preheat the oven to gas mark 5 (190°C, 375°F).

2 First make a white sauce: put the butter and flour into a non-stick pan and melt on a gentle heat, stirring all the time. When this begins to boil, stir for a minute or so – this helps the flour particles 'burst' and will thicken the sauce quickly when the milk is added. Put the wooden spoon to one side and grab an egg whisk. Pour half the milk onto the hot melted butter and flour and whisk to prevent lumps from forming. Add most of the remaining milk – you want a fairly stiff white sauce, stiffer than for pouring. As the milk heats, stir continuously once again with the wooden spoon and, when it begins to bubble, it will be at its optimum thickness. Add more milk if required. Withdraw from the heat.

3 Grate the cheese and keep about 1 tablespoon to one side; add the rest to the hot sauce, stirring until it melts. Add the mustard, about a ¼ teaspoon salt, several good grinds of pepper and the cayenne. Stir well. Leave on one side to cool slightly.

4 Get a nice clean bowl and whisk the egg whites until stiff but not rigid – a consistency a bit like hair mousse or shaving foam, depending on which is the more familiar.

5 Add the egg yolks to the cheese sauce and stir in well. Next, with a metal spoon (this cuts the whisked white into the sauce more easily than a clumsy wooden spoon), add the egg white and fold in. It doesn't need to be completely mixed in.

6 Butter a soufflé dish which will take a pint of liquid and pour in half the soufflé mix. Take one of the extra eggs,

crack it into a saucer to check that it's fresh and clear of any shell. Make a small depression with the back of a spoon in one side of the soufflé mix and drop in the raw egg. Do the same on the other side of the dish with the other egg.

7 Pour over the remaining cheese mix, remembering where the eggs are. Take the grated cheese you kept in reserve and sprinkle this where the eggs are hidden underneath.

8 Bake for about 25 minutes. It should have risen nicely and have a lovely golden brown crust on top. If it wobbles alarmingly and you think it could do with a bit more cooking, shut the door and wait a further 3–5 minutes. (Don't go off and do anything else or answer the phone – they'll ring back later if it's important.)

9 Once you are happy with the way it looks – puffed up and golden brown – take it out of the oven and serve immediately with justifiable pride.

TIP ••
I always open the oven to see how it's getting on because the Aga doesn't have a glass door –if you open it carefully so that a blast of cold air doesn't rush in, you should be fine and the soufflé won't sink.

GRATIN OF SWISS CHARD WITH DROP-IN EGGS

Enough Swiss chard for 2–4 people (see Tip below)
25 g (1 oz) butter
25 g (1 oz) flour
300 ml (½ pint) milk
85 g (3 oz) grated hard cheese (any sort you like)
I tsp Dijon mustard
Salt and pepper
¼ tsp freshly grated nutmeg
2 eggs (or 4 if you are hungry)

METHOD

1 Preheat the oven to gas mark 5 (190°C, 375°F) or turn on the grill.

2 Trim the ends of the chard and wash well. This can be done in advance *but don't slice it until you are about to cook it as the white stalks will oxidise and turn black*. Slice the leaves roughly (don't shred) and place in a saucepan with a little boiling water. Cook for about 5 minutes, pushing down on the chopped leaves and stirring every so often. Drain in a colander and squeeze out as much water as you can with the back of a wooden spoon.

3 Arrange the almost-cooked chard in a buttered gratin dish and make two (or four) little hollow nests.

4 To make your cheese topping sauce: put the butter and flour in a non-stick pan and stir as it melts. Let it bubble for a minute and continue to stir. Pour in the milk stirring vigorously or use an egg whisk at this stage to prevent lumps from forming. Stir until it boils and thickens.

5 Remove from heat and stir in the grated cheese, mustard, pinch of salt and couple of grinds of pepper. Add about a quarter of a teaspoon grated nutmeg. (I always have a few whole nutmegs in the larder and one of those tiny graters, but an ordinary [fine] grater will do just as well.)

6 Next, crack an egg at a time into a separate saucer to check for bits of shell and freshness and drop each into the preformed nest in the chard before adding the others.

7 Pour over the cheese sauce and bake in the oven for about 10 minutes or under a preheated grill for 5 minutes. The cheese topping should be a light golden brown and bubbling, and the eggs (hopefully) will be softly cooked. Serve immediately.

TIP ••

Chard reduces far less than spinach when cooked, so what you pick is more or less what you'll end up with, unlike spinach, which shrinks to nothing. I cook the green part and white stalk together. I calculate that for a main dish for two people you would need about 450 g (1 lb) of chard.

I love a crunchy topping on almost any savoury dish and always do one for cauliflower cheese, fish pie and the chard recipe above. All you need are one or two slices of bread (brown or white – or a mixture of both); whizz them in a blender to turn into crumbs. Grate a little cheese (25 g [1 oz]) and mix this roughly with the breadcrumbs. Scatter over your dish and dot with a little butter. Either heat in the oven or brown under the grill.

ANOTHER CHARD DISH

Approximately 450 g (1 lb) chard leaves
1 medium sized red onion, peeled and sliced thinly
1 clove garlic, peeled and chopped
1 packet sliced or cubed pancetta
1-2 small courgettes, sliced
Salt and pepper
**2-3 tbsp grated Gruyère/Emmental
and/or Cheddar cheese**
Olive oil for drizzling

METHOD

1 Prepare the chard by washing thoroughly. Slice finely, stalks and all. Put into a pan with a splash of boiling water, bring to the boil and stir so that the sliced stalks hit the boiling water quickly – if not, they could turn black. Cook for about 5 minutes, stirring every now and again. Drain and put to one side.

2 Cook the onion and garlic in a small pan until soft – about 6 minutes. Put to one side.

3 Chop and fry the pancetta in the pan until crisp. Drain off the fat.

4 Mix the bacon into the cooked chard, onion and courgettes, season with salt and pepper and pour into a buttered gratin dish. Sprinkle with the grated cheese, drizzle with a little olive oil and bake in a hot oven for about 20 minutes, or until the top is golden brown.

QUAIL EGG NIBBLES

These make an unusual nibble with a drink or as part of my Picky Picky Lunch (see page 160).

**As many boxes of fresh quails' eggs as you need
(I can easily eat six eggs in one sitting)
Celery salt**

METHOD

1 Cook the eggs as per the instructions on the box, then plunge into cold water. Take an egg, tap the outside on the work surface and then roll it gently between the palms of your hands. This should loosen the shell and make it easier to peel off. (I do this with ordinary hens' eggs and it works very well.) Rinse the eggs under a running tap to remove any remaining shell as there is nothing more unpleasant to crunch on.

2 Arrange the hard-boiled eggs on a pretty dish. Decant some celery salt into a small pot/container (e.g. a decorative eggcup) and snuggle in the middle of the eggs. Each person then dips the tip of an egg into the celery salt.

TIP •

If you use solid silver or silver-plated cutlery to eat an egg dish it will tarnish. This is how to remove the stains in a matter of seconds if you don't have time to get out the polish. Put a small piece of aluminium foil (or a couple of milk bottle tops if you have any) into a saucepan. Add a teaspoon salt and a little boiling water. Put the stained parts of the forks or spoons into the pan making sure they are in contact with the aluminium foil. The stains will disappear in seconds as if by magic – it will smell of bad eggs but that's the sulphur. Rinse and dry and your job is done.

EGG AND LENTIL CURRY

2 tsp grated fresh root ginger
2 cloves garlic, chopped
2 tsp green chillies, chopped
1 tbsp curry paste (up to you how hot you like it!)
4 cardamom pods, crushed
225 g (8 oz) green lentils
225 g (8 oz) tin coconut milk
1 tbsp tomato purée
Just under 300 ml ($^1/_2$ pint) water
1 bag washed baby spinach
6 tbsp fresh coriander, chopped
6 hard-boiled eggs, peeled and left whole
Salt and pepper

METHOD

1 Fry the ginger, garlic, chillies, curry paste and cardamoms for about 1–2 minutes.

2 Stir in the lentils, coconut milk, tomato purée and water. Bring to the boil and simmer for 30–40 minutes.

3 Add the spinach, coriander and hard-boiled eggs. Stir and cook a further 5 minutes.

4 Serve at once with plain boiled rice, mango chutney and a tomato and onion salad. (See page 161 for other side dishes.)

TIP •

If you have forgotten how long you have had your hens' eggs (ones purchased at the side of the road don't always indicate the date of lay) before cooking, place them in a basin of cold water. If they are fresh they will remain at the bottom but the older they are they will up-end themselves and eventually float. This is because there is a pocket of air in the egg and as the shell is porous they take on more air as they mature. You can slow this process down by storing your eggs pointed end down.

Some chefs say that egg whites from older eggs make better meringues so use these if you have any of that vintage rather than for a boiled egg – keep the ultra fresh ones for that treat.

Meat

When Jimmy and I first started 'stepping out', he took me to all sorts of exciting events. One of them was the Horse of the Year Show at Christmas time, at Olympia. He knew a lot of the people taking part and it made the evening more fun. We had been invited to a private box and the dress code was formal. Having little spare cash and also no warning, buying a new dress was out of the question so I decided to make something from a length of gold, sequined silk I had bought at the Dior factory in Orléans when I lived there in the seventies. It took me two days to create a simple sheath, which I secured at the waist with a gold belt. I felt a million dollars when Jimmy's face burst into a wide smile when I put it on for the first time. However, pride comes before a fall. During the evening, I felt my dress grow and grow...and grow... Half way through the second course, I kid you not but it was ten inches longer than when we left home. Little did I know that, with weighty fabric, you need to let it hang for at least a fortnight.

Things did get marginally better when we bumped into Ted Edgar, the show jumper who is married to David Broome's sister, Liz, and who was taking part in several of the events. He looked at me approvingly and said, 'I wish James could choose 'is 'orses the way 'e can choose 'is women!' For this reason alone, I have never knowingly eaten horse flesh in spite of spending five years of my life in France.

Roasting Meat – some helpful advice

A roast joint seems a simple enough thing to cook but like soufflés, often frightens the life out of the most competent cook. Some like their meat well done, even to the point of being carbonised, some pink and some as the French say, *bleu* – very rare indeed. If you are a mixed bunch give the outer slices from each end first to those with that preference and so on. It is far better to discover as you carve that perhaps the middle is a little under-done. If this is the case, you can always put it back into the oven to cook a few minutes extra but you can't reverse the process. I never weigh my meat – I judge the cooking time by the thickness, and rarely cook a piece (however large) for more than 90 minutes. A long piece of fillet takes no more than 30–40 minutes and a rib (with the bone in, which conducts heat) depends on how many ribs deep it is.

My advice would be to buy a meat thermometer, which removes both guess work and anxiety. I don't use one myself, and lead a dangerous life playing Russian roulette whenever we allow ourselves the luxury of having roast beef. Also, for this reason, we never have anything other than rib which has to have a nice amount of fat (which makes it even more tender). I don't buy topside because it is too lean and fillet is exorbitantly expensive. If you have a tame, friendly butcher ask him nicely if he could possibly cut the rib next to the sirloin.

I apply the same rules for pork as for lamb in that I don't normally opt for a leg – after all, it's done all the walking, has little fat and I don't think has the sweetness of shoulder. A shoulder (both lamb and pork) can be boned, stuffed and rolled or even roasted flat on a barbecue.

Making the gravy

I always add a sliced onion and a sliced stick of celery to the roasting dish. As these cook with the meat they will caramelise and provide a dark brown, savoury base for gravy. While the meat is resting somewhere warm I drain off any excess fat (not down the sink!), add 1 tablespoon flour and stir it into the juices. I then add any vegetable or potato water I have kept in reserve or some boiling water from the kettle, stir and then put back in the oven to thicken. If the onion or celery have burned during the roasting of the meat, I will strain the gravy, but, if not, I leave it as is.

Beef

At the supermarket one of the first areas I visit is what I call the 'sin bin' – the shelves where items are reduced. Some days I am lucky, some not. Once I was fortunate enough to buy a whopping piece of rib eye beef for half its original price. This was a terrific find, because like gammon there is no waste. I thought I would freeze it and keep it for a large Hill family get-together, but as Jimmy and I rarely have beef I cut it into four substantial slices about 4 cm (1½") thick, three of which I froze and kept the fourth for us to share that evening. This piece of rib eye eventually fed Jimmy and me three times, once hot, then cold with chips and a third time minced and used as a stuffing for an aubergine. The six helpings worked out at only pennies per head.

The first piece was too thick to fry (the outside would have burned before the middle was cooked), so I worked out a combination of frying and finishing off in the oven. It tasted exactly like traditionally roasted beef. The following recipe is how I achieved this.

ROASTING A THICK SLICE OF STEAK

I use a cast iron frying pan for this. If you don't possess such a pan, use an ordinary frying pan and, after you have browned the meat on both sides, transfer it to a preheated oven dish.

1 clove garlic
Salt and pepper
1 good piece of rib eye beef about 2.5–5 cm (1–2 inches) thick
1 dessertspoon oil

METHOD

1 Set the oven to gas mark 9 (245°C, 475°F).

2 Crush the garlic clove and rub this with your hands all over the piece of meat. Turn it on its edge and sprinkle salt on the fat only, not the meat.

3 Heat your frying pan and add the oil. When this is hot but not smoking carefully lay the beef in flat. Let it cook for 2 minutes in order for it to seal and get a bit of colour. Remove with tongs and

wait a few moments for the pan to heat up again and brown the other side. When this is done, up end the meat fat-side on the pan and hold it with your tongs for a minute or two to seal the fat.

4   Reposition the meat flat in the pan. Aga owners can now put this into the top oven for about 15 minutes (depending on how rare you want your meat and how thick it is). If you cook on gas or electricity, now is the time to transfer the meat onto a roasting dish to complete the cooking in the preheated oven.

5   When the beef is done to your liking, remove from it the pan and let it rest somewhere warm while you make a little gravy. Pour a small quantity of vegetable water (leek water, for example) into the pan and bring to the boil on the stove, scraping any nice bits from the sides of the pan.

TIPS •

As I mentioned earlier, I never, ever cook meat by weight. It's all a bit 'suck it and see', but it is better to remove the meat from the oven too early (it can always be put back for a few more minutes) than too late.

When a roast is cooked and you leave it to 'rest', cover the cooked joint in cling film – it keeps in the heat, the juices and the flavour.

When it comes to carving, I try to slice it horizontally into thin slices as though it were a large piece of rib. You need a sharp knife and a proper carving fork to do this (to protect your hand), but it can also be cut vertically into narrow slices.

NO-NONSENSE CORNISH PASTIES

You need beef – the best you can afford. Since the cooking time is short you want a tender cut, not braising steak – you only eat pasties once in a while. It is tricky to give you exact measurements: you want to fill the pasties but not to bursting point and it all depends on the size you cut the pasty rounds. You will notice that I don't include carrot (too sweet) or turnip (too strong).

MAKES 6 PASTIES

Ready-made short crust all-butter pastry – or flaky if you prefer
Approx. 175–225 g (6–8 oz) either rib eye, rump or fillet steaks
115 g (4 oz) potatoes
50 g (2 oz) onions
Salt and pepper
1 egg, lightly beaten with a little water

METHOD

1 Preheat the oven to gas mark 6 (200°C, 400°F).

2 First of all, make sure the pastry is at room temperature so that you can roll it out fairly thinly. Even though it comes ready rolled, I find this too thick – anyway, by making it thinner it goes further.

3 Remove any stringy bits from the meat and cut up into very little pieces, but do not mince.

4 Peel the potatoes and chop these into tiny cubes.

5 Peel and slice the onions thinly.

6 Roll out the pastry to less than 5mm (¼ inch) in thickness. Select a saucer about 10 cm (4 inches) in diameter and cut out rounds from the pastry.

7 In the centre of the pastry put a little pile of steak, potato and onion and give a really good sprinkle of salt and pepper. Moisten the edges with the beaten egg and fold up in half, sealing these edges. I crimp them using the prongs of a fork to make it decorative. Pick hold of this edge and make the pasty sit vertically so that the crimped edge is upright like the spine of a dinosaur. Brush the pastry with the beaten egg mix, repeat the process until all the ingredients are gone.

8 Place on a metal baking tray and cook on the middle shelf for about 20–30 minutes until the pastry is golden brown but not burned.

SIMPLE BEEF AND MUSHROOM STEW

Please don't buy a packet of prepared stewing or braising steak – buy it in nice large, steak sized bits and take a little time to prepare it yourself.

450 g (1 lb) stewing steak, nicely marbled with fat
2 tbsp flour
Salt and pepper
1 tbsp dripping or oil
1 large onion or 2 smaller ones
1 packet mushrooms of your choice: it doesn't matter if they are button, small open, large field mushrooms, chestnut or shiitake
½ bottle decent red wine (drink the rest with the meal)
Parsley, finely chopped, for garnish

METHOD

1 Preheat the oven to gas mark 2 (150°C, 300°F).

2 Begin by preparing the meat by removing any large bits of fat and suspicious-looking gristle. Whatever remains will melt during cooking and help make the meat tender. Cut into 2. 5 cm (1 inch) cubes. Put about 2 tablespoon of flour into a small food bag and add a teaspoon of salt and several good twists of pepper. Shake for a few moments for the salt and pepper to mingle with the flour. Next, add the meat to the bag and squidge and shake it around so that it is coated with flour. This will encourage the meat to brown quickly in the fat and there will be no need to thicken the gravy at the end of cooking.

3 Heat the dripping or oil in a casserole and drop in the meat, first shaking off any excess flour. If you are cooking a large quantity do not tip it all in at once or the heat will disappear quickly and you will end up with a grey, sludgy lump instead of individual, nicely browned chunks. Turn the meat several times in the fat, remove with a slotted spoon and put to one side in a bowl while you continue browning the remaining meat.

4 Peel and slice the onion(s) finely and, once the meat is browned, re-heat the pan and tip in the onions. Stir every now and again and cook until they are soft and beginning to take on a little colour.

5 Rinse the mushrooms under a tap, removing any speckles of compost, shake dry and slice or chop roughly. Button mushrooms can remain whole. Add these to the onions and then add the browned meat and any juices. Pour in the wine, add the bayleaf but no further seasoning. Stir well, bring gently to the boil, cover and place in the oven to cook slowly for about 2 hours. By this time the meat should be lovely and tender. Check the seasoning and adjust accordingly.

6 Sprinkle with a little chopped parsley and serve with baked or mashed potatoes and buttered cabbage.

TIP •

This stew can be pepped up with the addition of a teaspoon or two of smoked or hot paprika added at the same time as the mushrooms and meat, and perhaps a spoonful or two of sour cream, Hungarian style, just before serving up.

DRIP MINCE

This is great one-pot cooking and will provide an economical and nourishing meal for a student or person on their own. Try and find the time to mince the meat because bought mince can be quite fatty and dearer. You will end up with a comforting, savoury dish with the texture of steak and kidney pudding. The ingredients listed below are for the basic recipe. Add any of the following if you wish to add extra flavour: dried or fresh herbs, garlic, Worcestershire sauce, chilli, paprika, a teaspoon or two of Marigold bouillon, even a glass of red wine. There will be enough for two to three hearty servings.

225 g (¹/₂ lb) lean minced meat, either lamb or beef
1 tbsp flour
Salt and pepper
1 onion, peeled and sliced
1 carrot, peeled and chopped
2 potatoes, peeled and sliced

METHOD
1 Mix the mince with the flour and salt and pepper plus any of the selected flavourings and put into a greased, 600 ml (1 pint) pudding

basin. Place this in a steamer on a pan a third filled with water.

2 Place the onion on top of the mince. Put on the lid and bring to the boil. Allow to cook for at least an hour, checking every now and again to see that the pan hasn't boiled dry.

3 Place the carrot and potatoes on top of the mixture. Replace the lid and continue steaming for another hour – the steam from the lid will drip onto the meat and potatoes.

Lamb

In general and out of choice we buy the cheaper cuts of lamb – the meat is often sweeter and more tender, satisfying our taste buds more so than the costlier parts of the animal. Breast of lamb is a particular favourite, although I never dreamed that I would write this in a million years and I have Jimmy to thank for encouraging me to experiment. My memory was clouded by the repugnant 'Rag and Bone' stew we were fed every Thursday at school, the smell choking us at breakfast time as it boiled away in the kitchen. The resulting lunchtime dish comprised chewy bits of gristle, bone and unidentifiable objects floating in a slop of greasy water, at the bottom of which lurked an opalescent pulp of

pearl barley. It was truly disgusting. Now, thank heavens, I have realised that, if it is treated with respect, breast of lamb is one of the nicest parts of the beast, comfortably feeding two people, all for a snip. Great in times of a credit crunch. I have a couple of favourite ways of cooking it, and these recipes are given on pages 61–62.

Shoulder of lamb

If I am cooking for a group of six (hearty eaters) or eight (more modest appetites), I buy a large shoulder with the fillet still in situ. Since I don't want to spend my time slaving away in the kitchen, and want to enjoy our friends' company, I aim to get the maximum of preparation done in advance before they arrive. The first thing I do is to go into the garden and collect a mixed bunch of fresh herbs (whatever is available), which could include oregano, summer savory, rosemary, mint, parsley or basil. These are washed and chopped roughly and put into a bowl. Next I add two or three crushed cloves of garlic. I love the tang of lemon with meat so I add the zest and juice of an unwaxed lemon to the other ingredients, followed by a good teaspoon of sea salt, lots of freshly ground pepper and perhaps a pinch ($^1/_4$ teaspoon) of dried chillies. Last to go in are about 3 tablespoons of ordinary olive oil.

With a sharp knife, I score the skin on the shoulder, criss-cross fashion, and then rub the herb mixture into the crevices, wrap the meat in cling film and return it to the fridge. An hour before putting it into the oven, I take it out of the cold to allow it to reach room temperature. I slice a large onion and a couple of sticks of celery, put them in the bottom of the roasting dish with the lamb on top. Into the hot oven of the Aga it goes for about an hour; then it is finished off in the bottom (simmering) oven, where it sits quite happily until we are ready to eat. This could be up to an hour or more later. At the time of serving, any excess fat is drained off and the meat carved on top of the wonderfully pungent, succulent juices, during the slow cooking.

For those of you with electric or gas cookers, preheat the oven to gas mark 7 (220°C, 425°F) and cook the lamb for 40 minutes, reducing it then to gas mark 2 (150°C, 300°F) to cook for a further 1½ hours.

PERFECT RACK OF LAMB

Ask the butcher if he can 'chine' the joint – this means sawing through the bone so that you can carve easily.

**1 or more racks of lamb (depending on how many you
are feeding) counting three cutlets per head
Salt and pepper
Herbs (optional)
Garlic (optional)**

METHOD

1 Preheat the oven to gas mark 5 (190°C, 375°F).

2 Heat a frying pan (one that goes into the oven if possible – if not, use an oven-friendly metal roasting dish later). Place the fat side of the rack onto the hot pan and cook it for a few minutes, pushing down with tongs so that as much of the fat as possible is sealed and takes on a bit of colour.

3 Turn the meat over fat side up and sprinkle with salt and pepper. You can add some herbs at this stage and garlic if you wish. Put the meat into a roasting dish (or keep in your frying pan). Roast on the middle shelf for about 15–20 minutes if you like your lamb pink, 5 minutes more if you like it slightly more done. Remove from the oven and keep it warm, letting it rest for 5–10 minutes.

4 To serve, carve the meat, separating the cutlets.

RACK OF LAMB WITH A HERBY CRUST

1 or 2 slices brown or white bread

Herbs (dried or fresh) – any combination of parsley, thyme, rosemary and oregano

Garlic to taste

1 lemon

Salt and pepper

1 or more racks of lamb (depending on how many you are feeding) counting three cutlets per head

Olive oil

METHOD

1 Preheat the oven to gas mark 5 (190°C, 375°F).

2 Whizz the bread to a roughish crumb consistency and mix with your chosen herbs. If you are using fresh ones, chop them first.

3 Crush the garlic but if the cloves have a little green shoot in the centre, pick this out first as it can make the flavour too fierce.

4 Grate the zest of a lemon (half a lemon to one rack). Add a good pinch of salt and several grinds of pepper. Mix this together.

5 With a sharp knife criss-cross the fat on the rack and then push on the crust mixture. Bits will fall off – scoop them up and replace creating a thickish layer. Drizzle with a little olive oil and roast for about 20 minutes if you like your lamb pink, or 30 minutes if you like it well done.

6 Let it rest for 5 minutes then slice the meat into cutlets.

BREAST OF LAMB SPARE RIBS

Tender, sweet and extremely economical.

1 large onion
4 tbsp tomato ketchup
1 tbsp sweet chilli sauce or 1/4 tsp dried chilli flakes
2 tbsp white, red wine or cider vinegar
1 dessert spoon demerara sugar
Garlic
Juice 1 lemon
Pepper
2 tbsp soy sauce
1 breast lamb cut into pieces – ask the butcher to do this if you need help as you may need a hacksaw to cut through the bones

METHOD

1 Preheat the oven to gas mark 5 (190°C, 375°F).

2 Slice the onion and add all the other ingredients in a large dish (bar the lamb!). Mix thoroughly.

3 Add the ribs and smother them with the barbecue mixture. The meat can now wait happily in the fridge until you are ready to put it in the oven – but make sure you cover with cling film first to keep in the garlic smells.

4 When you are ready to cook, tip everything onto an oven dish and place in the hot oven, basting the ribs from time to time with the juices – about 30 to 40 minutes should do the trick – you don't want them to burn but you do want to end up with a sticky, brown, caramelised coating.

5 By the nature of the beast, there will be a lot of fat which has come off during cooking. Drain off as much as you can into a spare container.

6 Serve with new potatoes steamed on a bed of mint and a green salad.

TIPS •

This mixture is also perfect for pork spare ribs.

I use a baked bean can for the excess fat, which I subsequently turn into a fat ball for the birds when I have a spare moment by mixing in some of their seed.

BRAISED BREAST OF LAMB

This is a lovely, welcoming meal ideally prepared the day before, giving the flavours time to develop.

1 stick celery
2 onions
2 good sized carrots
1 tbsp oil
1 lamb breast cut into chunky pieces, not individual ribs
1 bay leaf
$\frac{1}{2}$ tsp salt and freshly ground pepper
Water

METHOD

1 Preheat the oven to gas mark 2 (150°C, 300°F).

2 Slice the celery. Peel and slice the onions and carrots.

3 Heat the oil in an oven-proof casserole (enamelled cast iron is ideal but not essential) and add the vegetables. Sweat these for about 2 minutes, stirring once or twice.

4 Add the pieces of lamb, bay leaf, half a teaspoon salt and several grinds of pepper. Add enough water almost to cover the meat and mix everything together.

5 Bring to the boil and then put into the oven for about 1½ hours. If you are preparing this for the following day, allow to cool and keep overnight in the fridge.

To finish off the cooking, preheat the oven to gas mark 5 (190°C, 375°F) and proceed as follows:

6 Take the meat out of the casserole, place onto a roasting dish and then into the oven to brown for about 15 minutes.

7 Drain the juices into a jug so that the fat floats to the top and spoon off or drape pieces of kitchen paper on the surface to mop it up. If this stage is done the day before the fat will become hard and easy to remove in one piece.

TIP •

I do one of two things with the vegetables which have cooked with the lamb. Either I combine them with the de-greased juices and mash them with the potato masher to serve alongside the meat or I leave them as they are and dish them up with the juices poured into a jug. Mashed potato and another vegetable such as broccoli completes the dish.

IRISH STEW

Scrag end of lamb (you want bones for flavour) is rarely available at the supermarket but check with your butcher – you are more likely to see it called stewing lamb. They resemble rather untidy chops. This isn't a posh dish, but it's a good'un: warm, comforting and easy to eat – and cheap as chips. As far as I am concerned (and the way my mother taught me), Irish stew is cooked on top of the stove, in a saucepan, and with no added fancy ingredients. If this frightens the life out of you, by all means add celery, carrots and herbs, but it will be a different dish altogether.

**1 or 2 pieces (175 g [6 oz]) scrag per person or value
cutlets – you are not looking for uniformity
Potatoes (enough for as many people you are cooking for)
2 or 3 medium onions
2 tbsp pearl barley
Water
½ tsp salt and freshly ground black pepper
1 tbsp chopped parsley**

METHOD

1 Rinse the pieces of scrag end in order to remove any nasty little chips of bone.

2 Peel the onions and slice.

3 Peel the potatoes and leave whole unless they are like big bakers – if so, cut these in half or quarters.

4 Place the lamb in a saucepan and cover with cold water. Bring to the boil and simmer for a couple of minutes. Remove from the heat; scoop off the scum then drain the lamb through a sieve.

5 Put the meat back into the saucepan, add the vegetables and pearl barley and cover with new cold water. Season with about half a teaspoon salt and lashings of black pepper. Cover with a lid, bring to the boil and simmer for about 1½ hours or until the meat falls easily falls off the bone.

6 Remove from the heat and, keeping the vegetables and meat in the saucepan, drain off the stock into a jug. Let it settle for a moment and mop up the fat using kitchen paper. Once this is de-greased, return the stock back to the saucepan with the lamb.

7 When it is ready to serve, sprinkle over the chopped parsley.

TIPS •

If you don't want to serve this on the same day, the lamb can stand idle for as long as 24 hours – during which time the flavours continue to improve. If you intend to eat it the following day, don't bother with taking off the fat now – wait until it is cold and the fat will have solidified into a hard disc, which can then easily be removed.

You may find that during the cooking the potatoes disintegrate into the stock, depending on the variety. Don't worry as they will add to the flavour and thicken the juices; but you may wish, for the potato lovers in your family, to cook a few extra and serve them separately.

PAN FRIED LAMB PATTIES

These tasty patties (rather like a burger but not served in a bun) can be prepared in advance and kept in the fridge. I dislike buying ready-minced meat and prefer to buy a piece of meat which I can dismantle, removing gristle and excess fat, and pass it raw through my old fashioned mincer. I know then what I am buying. The last time I made them I used some New Zealand chump chops which were reduced and they were delicious: I cut the meat from the bone, removed most of the fat (a little left keeps the patties tender – it can be drained off after they are cooked) and they were delicious. If it makes your life easier and you are short on time, then please do buy ready-minced lamb!

Approx. 115 g (4 oz) lamb per pattie/per person (you may feel 175 g [6 oz] each would satisfy your family/friends; I would probably buy half a shoulder of lamb or lean stewing lamb)

1 onion or 4 spring onions for two people (i.e. for 225 g [8 oz] meat) finely chopped

1 dessertspoon chopped fresh mint or 1 tbsp chopped fresh coriander

juice and zest 1/2 lemon

1 fresh red chilli, chopped or 1/4 tsp dried chilli flakes – more if you want

1/2 tsp dried, ground cumin

1 clove garlic, crushed or chopped

Salt and pepper to taste

1 tbsp oil

METHOD

1 If you are mincing your own lamb, either pass the meat through a mincer or chop in a food processor.

2 Add the onions, mint or coriander, lemon, chilli, cumin, garlic, seasoning and mix well by hand. Put the meat in an airtight container and keep in the fridge for an hour or so (more if you want) for the flavours to develop.

3 When you are ready, remove from the fridge, level off the meat mixture in the container and divide in half. Either moisten your hands under the tap or rub in a little oil; remove one half of the meat and shape into a round patty with your hands and put on a

plate. Do the same with the other half of the meat. By lubricating your hands it is easier to shape the patties.

4 Heat the oil in a frying pan and add the patties. Let them brown for about 3 minutes and carefully turn them over using a fish slice or spatula so that the other side browns. Either continue cooking on the hotplate but at a reduced heat so that they cook without burning, or place the pan (if it is ovenproof) into a medium/hot oven (gas mark 5, 190°C, 375°F) to carry on cooking for a further 10 minutes.

5 Drain off any excess fat, then add a splash of boiling water from the kettle to mix with the juices in the pan to give an instant gravy.

6 Serve with new potatoes, a green salad or vegetable of your choice and perhaps some chutney and cucumber raita (see recipe page 187).

OVEN ROASTED LAMB CHOPS
A LA LYONNAISE

¾ lb new potatoes
1 large shallot
1 or 2 lamb chops per person
1 cup chicken stock
Garlic (optional)
Salt and pepper
¾ tsp dried mixed herbs
Salt and pepper to taste

METHOD

1 Preheat the oven to gas mark 6 (200°C, 400°F).

2 Wash but don't peel the potatoes and cut lengthways into slices about the thickness of a pound coin. Place on the bottom of a small roasting dish.

3 Peel and slice the shallot and sprinkle this on top of the potatoes.

4 Rinse the chops to remove any small chips of bone and place on the vegetables. Pour over the chicken stock, add the chopped garlic if required. Season with salt and pepper and sprinkle the herbs.

5 Place in the top half of the oven and roast for about 20 minutes, making sure the potatoes are thoroughly cooked. Drain off any surplus fat and serve with broccoli florets and a sliced courgette steamed together.

OLD-FASHIONED SHEPHERD'S PIE

Some of you may not relish the thought of eating cold roast lamb – I enjoy it but it has to be accompanied by a baked potato, some sort of vegetable (carrots, leeks or broad beans) served in a white or parsley sauce and lots of chutney. Jimmy would eat any cold meat provided it is accompanied with a bowl of chips! Shepherd's pie made from leftover roast meat has a completely different flavour from bought raw mince.

**175–225 g (6–8 oz) leftover lamb from a roast
(with most of the fat cut away)
1 tbsp dripping (from the joint) or oil
1 onion, sliced
1 clove garlic
Leftover gravy if you have it
(but not more than twenty-four hours old)
Water
Salt and pepper
1 tsp Worcestershire sauce
350 g (12 oz) potatoes for topping
Milk and butter for mash**

METHOD

1 Strip the cold, cooked meat off the bone removing excess fat (mince the waste and give it to the birds).

2 Preheat the oven to gas mark 5 (190°C, 375°F).

3 Cut the meat into smallish chunks and either pass it through a mincer or whizz quickly in a food processor. It may not look as though there is enough to feed a flea but a small amount (with

the onions and gravy added) goes a long way. I don't add carrots because they can make it too sweet. Serve these as a separate vegetable.

4 Put the lamb dripping or oil into a saucepan to heat and add the onions. You want these to take on a bit of colour as they will add more flavour – particularly if you don't have any juices or gravy left from the day before.

5 Add the garlic and minced lamb, stir and fry for a couple of minutes. Add the gravy and enough water to moisten the meat – you don't want it to swim in too much liquid. Season with salt and pepper and add the Worcestershire sauce. Simmer for about 30–40 minutes, stirring every now and again.

6 In the meantime, peel and boil the potatoes until soft.

7 If you find that the mince is still a bit runny, either mix 1 tablespoon of cornflour in a little cold milk and add this to the mince, or make a *beurre manié* – see Tip below) and stir this into the mince. Both will thicken the juices.

8 Check for seasoning then pour the mince into a pie dish. (This can be done in advance and the potatoes cooked later and piled onto the cold mince before heating through.)

9 For the mash, add enough milk and butter to make it soft and fluffy but not sloppy. Season well with salt and pepper. (I use a masher to crush the potatoes and once the milk and butter have been added I give it a good whisk with a fork.) Pile the mash on top of the mince and spread it over the meat. Decorate using the prongs of the fork. Dot with a little butter and heat in the oven until golden and bubbling. We like to eat this with tomato ketchup.

TIP ••••••••••••••••••••••••••••••••••••••

To make a quick *beurre manié*, cut up 1 tablespoon butter into little cubes and roll them in 1 tablespoon flour in a dish, covering it completely. Drop as many flour-coated lumps into the dish as required to thicken the sauce.

Pork

Also known 'as the gentleman who pays the rent', because in times gone by a single pig reared in small households would feed the family for an entire year. Every last bit was used – even the bristles were made into brushes – with enough left over to sell enabling the family to pay for the year's rent, hence the sobriquet. Only the squeak couldn't be sold.

The whole point of roast pork is lots of gorgeous crackling. Our local butcher gave me a tip: first make sure the skin is well scored, then take a capful of cider vinegar and with a good sprinkling of sea salt, rub this into the skin and roast – no basting needed. It virtually never fails.

For boiled gammon see the recipe on page 28.

BARBECUED SPARE RIBS

4 tbsp tomato ketchup
3 tbsp cider vinegar
2 dessertspoons demerara sugar
3 tbsp soy sauce
2 cloves garlic, crushed
pepper
1 large onion, sliced
3–4 spare ribs per person
(from free range, happy pigs if possible)

METHOD
1 Preheat the oven to gas mark 5 (190°C, 375°F).
2 Mix all the above ingredients and pour over the spare ribs which you have placed in a roasting dish. Bake on a high shelf in the oven and baste every 20 minutes or so until most of the liquid has evaporated and the sauce has become sticky. (This could take an hour.)
3 Serve with steamed new potatoes and a green salad and lots of napkins to mop up messy mouths and fingers.

ROAST PORK

I only ever buy shoulder for roasting – the same applies to lamb. The meat, although a bit untidy to carve, is far sweeter and more tender than leg, which can be a little tough and dry – at least when I cook it, that is. I never buy expensive loin for the same reason.

I roast shoulder in the same way as I would a piece of belly, but for longer (see recipe for Roast Belly of Pork, page 71.)

TIPS •

For an instant apple sauce, place a whole apple per person (first slice through the skin around the middle to stop them from splitting) around the joint half way through cooking.

Pork makes a rich gravy and, after draining off the fat, serve it the French way: pour the juices from the roasting pan onto freshly cooked pasta (tagliatelle for example).

FILLET OF PORK WITH CREAMED APPLES

1 tbsp vegetable oil (e.g. sunflower oil)
1 tenderloin fillet pork
1 medium onion, sliced
**1 large or 2 small eating apples
(I like Cox's Orange Pippin)**
2–3 sage leaves, chopped
1 glass dry cider or, failing that, white wine
Salt and pepper
1 heaped tbsp crème fraîche or double cream

METHOD

1 In a frying pan (if you have one made from cast iron you can finish the cooking in the oven) pour in the oil and add the onions; stir and cook until they are just showing the merest hint of brown. Remove from the pan and keep to one side.

2 Cut the fillet into medallions a bit thicker than 5mm (¼ inch) but less than 1 cm (½ inch). Heat the pan (adding a little more oil of necessary) and brown the meat, turning it once – about a minute per side. If you are cooking for more than two people, it is best to do this in stages.

3 Wash and cut the apple(s) into quarters and remove the core. Slice thinly but don't peel. When the pork is brown return all of it to the pan, add the cooked onions, sliced apple and sage leaves and stir. Pour on the cider or white wine, and season with salt and pepper. Cover the pan (if you have one the right size – it isn't obligatory) and simmer for about 10 minutes until the apple is soft.

4 Add either the crème fraîche or double cream; stir and serve.

5 This goes equally well with plain boiled rice, fresh pasta or mashed potatoes.

ROAST BELLY OF PORK

This has to be one of the nicest (and most economical) of cuts – remember that it is uncured streaky bacon. Simply roasted, cut into chunky slices, there is not a lot that can beat it. It is equally delicious cold and if there is any left over I can be caught nibbling at cold crackling at seven o'clock in the morning! No real preparation is needed, but I am ridiculously squeamish and remove any hint of nipple, cutting them away with a sharp knife or pair of scissors.

1 strip of belly (depending on how many you are feeding – I allow approx. 5 cm [2 inches] per serving)
1 onion, sliced
1 stick celery, sliced
1 capful cider vinegar
½ tsp salt
1 dessertspoon flour
150–300 ml (5–10 fl oz) water or vegetable stock

METHOD

1 Preheat the oven to gas mark 5 (190°C, 375°F).

2 Get the butcher to score the skin thoroughly. Put the onion and celery into a roasting dish and lay the pork on top. Fill the cap on the vinegar bottle with vinegar and pour over the raw crackling. Sprinkle over the salt and rub well in.

2 Roast for about 30 minutes so that the crackling turns crispy. You don't want it to burn, so loosely place a piece of kitchen foil over the top. Continue cooking a further 20–30 minutes until the juices run clear. In spite of modern trends, I like to eat my pork well done.

3 Remove from the heat and rest in a warm place. Drain off as much fat as possible from the pan, add the flour and mix with all the juices, scraping the bottom and sides of the pan. Put on the heat and stir for a minute. Add either boiling water or vegetable stock (or cooking water from the potatoes – I use 1 dessertspoon flour to 300 ml [½ pint] liquid, plus any juices), stir and bring back to the boil so that the gravy thickens. Either strain the juice into a jug or serve as we do, bits and all.

4 To carve, lift the crackling from the meat and cut into pieces using kitchen scissors. Cut the meat into slices about 5 mm (¼ inch) thick and serve with gravy and the crackling.

5 Serve with apple sauce (see recipe page 173). (We also like bread sauce with roast pork or chops.)

SAUSAGE MEAT PILAF

An inexpensive fork supper for eating in front of the television that can be made in advance and reheated – just make sure that everything is piping hot right through.

SERVES 3–4
Oil for frying
1 large or 2 medium onions, sliced finely
½ green pepper, sliced finely
½ red or orange pepper, sliced finely
115 g (4 oz) mushrooms, diced
1 packet sausages with a high meat content
115 g (4 oz) left-over cooked chicken pieces or 1 cup frozen prawns
115 g (4 oz) frozen peas
salt and pepper

225 g (8 oz) freshly cooked rice (see page 110)
2 large tomatoes, chopped or
6 cherry tomatoes, cut in half
150 ml (¼ pint) water or chicken stock if necessary
½ tsp paprika

METHOD

1 Fry the onions in a little oil until soft and just beginning to colour. Remove from pan.

2 Fry the mixed peppers in the pan (adding a little more oil if necessary). Stir and cook for approximately 5 minutes.

3 Add the mushrooms and mix well. Remove from pan; cover and keep to one side while you deal with the sausage meat.

4 Squeeze the sausage meat from the skins, discarding the latter. Heat the pan in which the onions etc. were cooked (no need to add any more fat – there will be enough in the sausages) and fry the meat, stirring and squashing it so that it browns as much as possible – rather like frying mince. This will take about 5–10 minutes – you want the sausage meat to be cooked and crumbly – not a solid cake-like lump.

5 Mix in the cooked vegetables; add the chicken pieces (not the prawns yet, if using) and raw peas. Season well with salt and pepper. Cook for 5 minutes, adding a little stock or water if necessary, stirring every now and then.

6 Fold in the rice and, if you are using prawns rather than chicken, add them now. Add a little water only if the rice is too dry. Mix well and pile into a gratin dish. Sprinkle in the raw tomatoes and dust with paprika. Cover loosely with foil and warm in the oven (gas mark 5, 190°C, 375°F) for about 15–20 minutes until piping hot.

7 The sausage meat may release more fat while it is heating up – if so, pour it off before bringing to the table.

SAUSAGE TOAD

**2-3 pork sausages per person (choose sausages
with the highest pork content you can find)**
115 g (4 oz) flour
1 large egg
225 ml (¹/₂ pint) milk or 50–50 milk and water mix
¹/₄ tsp salt
1 tsp dried mixed herbs

METHOD

1 Preheat the oven to gas mark 7 (220°C, 425°F).

2 Place the sausages in a roasting dish and bake on the middle shelf for at least 15 minutes, when they will have taken on a little colour and released some fat which will be piping hot by this stage.

3 Whilst the sausages are in the oven, prepare the batter. Sieve the flour into a basin and make a well in the centre into which you break the egg. Gradually work the flour into the egg. Next, slowly add the milk (or milk and water), whisking well to remove any lumps and to create a smooth batter the consistency of single cream. Add the salt and herbs and mix well.

4 Remove the sausages from the oven, and pour the batter around the sausages. Put back into the oven on the middle shelf and cook for a further 20 or so minutes or until the batter is puffed up and golden brown.

6 Serve with an onion gravy (see recipe page 185) and freshly made English mustard. The sweetness of baked beans goes very well with this, but because of the batter there is no need for potatoes – just something green perhaps, like broccoli or runner beans.

APPLE AND SAUSAGE SURPRISE

This quirky, blokey recipe was given to me by our gardener, Mike, and it seemed like fun to try. You will end up with something looking a little rude, but which provides instant apple sauce, gravy and sausage all in one go.

4 good quality sausages
2 apples, dessert or cookers
Salt and pepper to taste

METHOD

1 Brown the sausages under the grill or in a frying pan until they are just more than half cooked.

2 Cut the apples in two and remove the core and pips from each half.

3 Place the flat side of the apple onto a metal baking sheet or tray and stuff the half-cooked sausage upright into the hole. Lightly season and put in a moderately hot oven for about 20 minutes or until the apple is cooked through, along with the sausage.

Offal

I have to admit that out of choice I would pretend offal didn't exist. I can just about face lambs' liver once in a while but only if I cook it myself. Fried with bacon (or sliced pancetta), mashed potatoes and fried onions it is a tasty, inexpensive meal and very good for you. If you prefer, buy calves' liver instead of lambs' but it is more than twice the price and probably comes from abroad. Think of the air miles...

FRIED LAMBS' LIVER WITH ONIONS

When I am buying liver, I watch the butcher slice it and tell him when to stop when I think he has cut enough, regardless of the actual weight.

1 large onion, peeled and sliced
Butter and oil for frying
Sliced pancetta or smoked bacon
Lambs' liver (as many slices as needed)
Flour seasoned with salt and pepper
Milk, enough to cover the raw liver in a bowl
Freshly made English mustard

METHOD

1 When you are ready to eat (liver should be consumed as soon as it is done), first put your onions in a pan with a little oil and water (enough to moisten without drowning them) and simmer until the water has evaporated. Raise the heat and carry on cooking and stirring until the onions are nicely browned. Remove them onto a separate dish and keep warm.

2 Fry the bacon or pancetta until crispy and put aside to keep warm.

3 Take the liver from the fridge, drain off and discard the milk (see Tip below) and pat the slices dry with kitchen paper. Then, take one slice at a time, dip into a bowl of seasoned flour and coat well; put on a separate plate.

4 Heat 2 tablespoons oil (sunflower is ideal) in a pan. Add about 15 g (½ oz) of butter and let this melt whilst swizzling the pan as you don't want it to burn. When the butter has stopped sizzling and has gone quiet, add the liver piece by piece. You may have to do half at a time – if you tip in a lot at once the temperature will be reduced and the liver will not brown evenly. (See Tip below on how long to cook.)

5 There will be some nice juices and gungy bits and pieces left in the frying pan once all the liver is cooked. Add a cup of water or vegetable stock and stir well, scraping up the juices. The residues of flour will thicken the liquid. Add the fried onions and stir again for a minute. Pour this over the cooked liver and serve sprinkled with

the pancetta, and loads of mashed potato and greens – buttered cabbage is lovely.

6 You don't need to go all cheffy by stacking the liver on top of a mound of mash – it may look professional but it will rapidly lose heat and you want to eat it when it's piping hot.

TIPS •

As soon as you get home put the raw liver into a bowl and cover with cold milk. Keep in the fridge until you are ready to cook it. This is not vital but can make the liver sweeter removing any possible bitterness.

If you are cooking a small amount, to save time put the seasoned flour into a bag, add all the liver at once, give it a good shake and then empty the lot onto a plate. Shake off any excess flour prior to frying.

The secret to cooking liver is simple: I was told how to cook it to perfection by (sadly, the late) Thierry Cabanne who used to own Thierry's Restaurant in the King's Road, Chelsea. He advised that, as soon as little pin pricks of blood appear on the upper surface of the liver, turn it over. Cook only for a minute or two longer on the other side, since the slices are thin, and serve at once.

PIG'S CHEEKS

This is a Catalan dish called *galtas*. This is not exactly offal, but as it is not humdrum, every-day pork, I shall include it in this chapter. Please don't run away and hide – this is one of the sweetest cuts of meat, and pig's cheeks (or as they used to be known, bath chaps) are now available at select supermarkets or a friendly butcher's – until recently they were probably put into sausages and other processed dishes. When we used to go to the Catalan region in northern Spain on holiday, this was one of our favourite (and least expensive) choices, served with a bowl of French fries or sauté potatoes.

1 or 2 pig's cheeks per person, depending on size
Olive oil
1 onion, sliced finely
1 carrot, chopped into little cubes
Fresh thyme
2 bay leaves
1 clove garlic, chopped
1 glass red wine (Rioja, being Spanish, is an excellent choice and you can drink the rest with the meal)
Salt and pepper
A little water if necessary
Parsley

METHOD

1 Preheat the oven to gas mark 3 (170°C, 325°F).

2 First, fry the pig's cheeks in a little olive oil in an ovenproof casserole and, when brown, remove and lift them onto a plate.

3 Next, fry the onion and carrot in the juices from the pork for about 5 minutes. Then add the thyme, bay leaves, chopped clove garlic, red wine and season with salt and pepper. Add the pig's cheeks and any juices. Place on a middle shelf in the oven and braise for about an 1½ hours. Check from time to time to see how things are going. You can add a little water if needed, but you want to end up with very little liquid left and the vegetables to have caramelised into a rich, sticky goo. The final test is to see if the meat falls off the bone at the touch of a fork. Drain off any fat and sprinkle with chopped parsley.

4 Savour a mouthful and transport your spirit to Catalunya, the land of rocky cliffs, the scent of pine trees, and the swish of the waves in a crystal clear, turquoise sea...

OXTAIL STEW

This is a much maligned dish and was off limits when we had the mad cow's disease scare, but it is now firmly back on the menu, thank goodness. I am not sure if it is actually classed as offal but we love it, and it is particularly appreciated when the weather is in full winter temper tantrums. If you can, it is far better cooked the day before for two reasons: 1) the flavours develop, and 2) oxtail is a fatty meat and by letting it get cold you will be able to remove the fat the next day when it has congealed.

1 oxtail (cut into thick chunks)
3 tbsp oil or dripping
2 onions, peeled and sliced
1 stick celery, sliced
2 carrots, peeled and cut into chunks
1–2 cloves garlic, peeled and chopped
Salt and pepper
Bouquet garni (bay leaf, thyme, parsley)
1 bottle decent wine (the whole point of cooking with wine in my mind is to use the same wine which you would be drinking later when the dish is cooked)

METHOD

1 Preheat the oven to gas mark 2 (150°C, 300°F).

2 Wash the oxtail and place in a saucepan. Cover with cold water and bring to the boil when it will produce a lot of scum. This will not smell very appetising and could remind you of dog meat but battle on. It removes some of the strong flavour the meat may possess. Let it boil for a couple of minutes then drain the meat in a colander and quickly rinse any residue of scum under the tap.

3 Heat 2 tablespoons of the oil or dripping in a casserole and brown the oxtail several pieces at once, turning them with tongs every now and again. Reserve the meat in a bowl and reheat the pan, adding another tablespoon of oil.

4 Fry the onions, celery and carrots together and let them sweat for a couple of minutes. Add the garlic and tip in the browned oxtail as well as the juices formed in the bowl. Stir the mix and season well with salt and pepper. Snuggle in the bouquet garni and tip in the red wine – you might not need all of the bottle – take this as a cook's perk.

5 Bring to the boil, cover and put in the oven for 3 hours. If you are using an Aga, once the casserole has been brought back to the boil on the hot plate, place in the simmering oven. You will know when it is cooked because the meat will literally fall off the bone.

6 When the dish is cooked, drain most of the liquid into a measuring jug and, when the fat has risen to the surface, pour off as much as you can, then return the juices to the oxtail.

7 Serve with puréed parsnips, mashed by hand (not a blender), some sort of greenery and potatoes.

TIPS •

As I mentioned above, this dish is best cooked the day before you need it and allowed to go cold. I don't generally thicken the gravy because I like it to be runny, but you can do this using a crumbly mix of flour and butter called *beurre manié* (see recipe page 68) – this can be kept in a screw-topped jar in the fridge for use as and when. (Don't use cornflour and water – this will only end up making the juices taste exactly of that: of cornflour and water.) Add it a spoonful at a time, stir and check on the subsequent thickness adding more if necessary.

GOOSE OR DUCK LIVER PATE

When you buy a fresh duck (or a goose at Christmas), use only the neck, heart and gizzard for stock to make the gravy. Don't throw away the liver, but make a tasty (albeit not a large quantity) of pâté.

Liver from the duck or goose
Milk
1 small shallot, peeled and chopped
1 small clove garlic, peeled and chopped
1 tbsp butter
1 dessertspoon brandy or cognac
Salt and pepper

METHOD

1 First take out any sinewy bits from the liver. To do this, put the liver onto a chopping board and hold one end. Take a sharp knife, and run it firmly along the piece of liver, rather like removing the skin from a fillet of fish. The stringy pieces will come away in one go.

2 Put the liver into a small dish and add enough cold milk to cover. Leave this to soak in the fridge for an hour or so – the milk will sweeten it. Remove the liver, rinse away the milk and pat dry in some kitchen paper.

3 Peel and chop the shallot and garlic. Heat the butter in a small frying pan and when bubbling, add the shallot and garlic and fry for about 4 or 5 minutes, stirring to prevent them turning brown.

4 Add the liver and cook until lightly browned, stirring all the while. (This will only take a minute or so.) Allow to cool for a few minutes and tip the mixture into a blender. Add the brandy or cognac and season well with salt and pepper. Whizz until it reaches a paste. Using a plastic spatula, turn the pâté into a ramekin and smooth the surface with a knife. Allow to cool.

5 Melt enough butter to cover the pâté. Take the pan off the heat and pour only the golden liquid into a small jug, leaving behind the white milky residue, which you throw away. Allow to cool a moment or two and pour on top of the pâté. Return to the fridge for the butter to set hard.

6 Eat with plenty of thinly cut toast or, if you have the time, some

elves' toast (see recipe below). Serve with gherkins and a jar of onion jam.

ELVES' TOAST

Don't waste gas or electricity just to make these – make them when the oven is already nice and hot for something else. They will store for a few days in an airtight tin.

METHOD

1 Slice some brown or white bread as thinly as you dare and remove the crusts. I find kitchen scissors invaluable for this task.

2 Place onto a baking tray and put in the hot oven for about 4–5 minutes. Remove when golden brown and crisp. This fragile toast will curl as it cooks into pretty shapes.

Poultry and game

I am very reluctant to eat wild duck for the simple reason that we are visited each spring by a pair of mallards – we named them Oscar and Gwyneth Poultry, because a week or so before they first arrived in our garden Gwyneth Paltrow won an Oscar. It would be like eating our own children!

Once again supermarkets are wonderful hunting grounds for reduced items and it means we treat ourselves to something special which we wouldn't consider buying at full price. If there is a guineafowl going begging, into the basket it goes and then the freezer, as does a really nice organic, free range chicken. If I pay the full price for a chicken, because we don't necessarily fancy eating it for three days running, I cut the breasts off, cook these straight away and freeze the legs and thighs still attached to the carcass to roast in one piece as and when. Doing it this way even an average sized free range (and possibly organic) bird won't set you back hugely giving four to six generous portions plus some useful stock. Not bad value all in all.

Chicken

Before we start **a word of warning**: raw chicken contains salmonella and you must be very careful during preparation. All work surfaces, sink, bowl and taps are vulnerable. Our taps have levers which I can operate with my wrists or elbows – rather like a surgeon when 'scrubbing up'. If you have to turn yours on by hand make sure that you clean the taps each time to remove any traces. I have a chopping board solely for cutting up raw poultry and this is scrubbed with lots of washing up liquid and very hot water. Also, whatever you do, wait until a chicken dish is completely cooked before you taste the sauce or you could end up with a really bad tummy a few hours later.

How to cut up a raw chicken into eight pieces

Ideally, invest in a strong pair of kitchen scissors or poultry shears. First of all, remove the elastic truss. Cut straight through the back bone, then push back the legs and thighs away from the breast. Using a sharp knife, cut the skin between these sections. In order to separate them from the carcass you may have to use the poultry shears again for cutting through any bones which get in the way. Next, take a leg piece in your hands and pull back against the joint until it snaps and relaxes, then you can cut through this knuckly bit and separate the drumstick from the thigh. Repeat with the other leg.

Either cut through the breastbone with the shears or carefully remove the breast fillets from the bones, running the knife as close to the rib cage as you can. Keep the winglet attached or remove with a combination of knife and/or shears. Depending on the size of the breasts and how many pieces of meat I need, I cut each in two or leave whole. Once decided what I am going to cook, any pieces of raw chicken not needed are wrapped individually and put into bags and then frozen for later use.

To make chicken stock

Don't chuck out the stripped carcass, but roast it in a hot oven (gas mark 5, 190°C, 375°F) for 15–20 minutes as this will improve the flavour. Next place it in a large pan with some cut up raw onion (if you don't remove all the outer skin – it will give more colour to the stock), a couple of peeled or scrubbed carrots cut into chunks, any herbs you have to hand, I prefer not to add rosemary or basil as they are too pronounced in flavour, a couple of cloves of fresh garlic, a bay leaf or two and enough cold water to cover. Bring to the boil and simmer for an hour.

Strain through a sieve and either remove the fat immediately by draping pieces of kitchen paper over the surface to mop up the grease, or allowing it to cool, place in the fridge, and then later, lift the congealed fat with a spoon. Use within 2 days or freeze when cold but keep no longer than 3 months.

How to cut up a cooked chicken

I haven't carved a roast chicken for maybe 30 years or more. There is always an argument as to who has the white meat and who has the brown (particularly with young ones). It is one of life's great mysteries that, when it comes to carving the large bird you put into the oven to feed six, it shrinks during cooking to provide barely enough for four if carved the traditional way. Here is the solution: when the chicken has rested, reach for the poultry shears.

First cut through the breast bone dividing the bird in two lengthways. Take each half and remove the whole legs. Separate each thigh from the drumsticks. Next, cut the breasts in two and either remove the winglets to make an extra nibble for someone or leave attached.

SPATCHCOCKED BREADED BIRD

1 free range chicken (organic if possible, although these aren't automatically free range – read the label if concerned)
1 onion, peeled and sliced
1 stick celery, washed and sliced
Salt and pepper
Dried mixed herbs
1 clove garlic, chopped (optional)
$1/4$ tsp chilli flakes (optional)
1 cup toasted breadcrumbs
Olive oil

METHOD

1 Preheat the oven to gas mark 5 (190°C, 375°F).

2 To spatchcock a chicken: cut through the back bone and flatten it out so that it looks like a squashed butterfly. The advantages of doing this are twofold: 1) it cooks more quickly and you therefore consume less energy and, 2) all the skin is facing uppermost and gets crispy in the process.

3 Remove any lumps of fat from around the neck and discard, then rinse the chicken under cold running water. There is no need to pat dry.

4 Put the onion and celery into the base of an oven dish. Put the flattened chicken on top and rub salt, pepper, the herbs and chopped garlic all over it. Add the chilli flakes to taste if wanted.

5 Sprinkle the bird with the breadcrumbs (see recipe below) and drizzle with some standard olive oil (not your expensive cold pressed, virgin oil). Place into a hot oven; there is no need to baste it if you have an Aga, but you may want to do so in a gas or electric oven a couple of times. When the juices run clear, the chicken is done; place it on a separate dish to let it rest and keep it warm.

6 Drain any fat from the roasting dish and add some vegetable stock (if you have it) or boiling water. Scrape around the edges to mix in the baked on juices. I don't thicken the gravy but serve it as it comes together with the gooey bits of caramelised onion and celery.

7 Cut into portions using poultry shears or prise the joints apart with a carving knife.

BROWNED BREADCRUMBS

Depending on which diet I happen to be on at the time, I often end up with a half eaten loaf of bread. Rather than let it go mouldy and waste it, I tear it into pieces onto a roasting tray and bake in the oven until lightly brown and crisp. When cool, blitz it into crumbs (or pass through the hand mincer) and store in an airtight jar. These keep for quite a while, but slip in a piece of paper with the date you prepared them to remind you and sniff before you use them – if they are stale, your nose will tell you.

CHICKEN WITH GREEN PEPPERS AND MUSHROOMS

1 chicken breast with winglet attached per person
115 g (4 oz) button mushrooms
1 green pepper
1 lemon

WHITE SAUCE
150 ml (¹/₄ pint) milk
25 g (1 oz) flour
25 g (1 oz) butter
Salt and pepper

METHOD

1 Preheat the oven to gas mark 5 (190°C, 375°F).

2 Put the chicken pieces into a pan and cover with cold water. Bring to the boil and simmer until cooked (about 15 minutes). When cool enough to handle, remove the skin and discard. Cut off the breast in large pieces, then remove any meat from the winglets.

3 To make a white sauce: melt the butter in a pan with the flour. Stir when hot for a minute or two, then add the milk bit by bit, stirring all the while to prevent lumps from forming. Bring to the boil and cook for further 2 minutes. Remove from heat and season with salt and pepper. Pour a little of the sauce into a cup for later and set both aside.

3 Grate the zest from the lemon and put into a small dish. Cut the lemon in two and squeeze one half.

4 Rinse the mushrooms, cut in half, and cook in a pan with a little water and the juice from one half of the lemon. When cooked, strain the mushroom juices into the larger quantity of white sauce and keep the mushrooms warm on a separate dish.

5 Cut the pepper in half and remove seeds and any white core. Slice finely and cook in a little butter until soft.

6 Add the lemon zest and the juice from the other half to the white sauce. Fold in the cooked green peppers and smaller pieces of chicken and pour into a gratin dish. Lay the larger pieces of chicken

on top and cover with the reserved cup of white sauce.

7 Place the mushrooms around the edge of the dish and heat up in the oven for about 10–15 minutes until bubbling.

8 Serve with plain boiled rice and a green vegetable.

CHICKEN BREASTS WITH PANCETTA OR PARMA HAM

I have stopped buying bacon and use only sliced pancetta (not the packets of cubed meat) as I find the flavour is not only superior to the average slice of smoked bacon but there is no nasty milky residue in the pan when it is cooking.

1 chicken breast per person (although sometimes 2 breasts will be enough for three people if you slice them when cooked)

Approx. 1 tbsp per breast of any sort of cheese you fancy or have handy (e.g. mozzarella, feta, Brie, Camembert, Stilton, dolcelatte)

1 packet Parma ham or pancetta (in slices, not chopped)

1 clove garlic, peeled and chopped, per 2 breasts

1 tsp fresh or dried herbs of your choice (e. g. thyme, mixed Italian seasoning, oregano)

Salt and freshly ground black pepper

Juice 1 lemon

1 glass white wine

METHOD

1 Preheat the oven to gas mark 5 (190°C, 375°F).

2 Remove the skin from the breasts and discard. Find the opening in the fillet and fill this with the cheese(s) of your choice. Wrap each breast in either Parma ham or strips of pancetta, tucking the ends under. Place in a gratin dish.

3 Sprinkle the garlic along with the herbs over the chicken. Season with only a little salt (as the pancetta/ham will be quite salty), and lots of pepper.

4 Pour over the lemon juice and white wine and bake for about 20

minutes, basting a couple of times, until the chicken juices run clear. You may need to add a little water or more wine during cooking to prevent the dish from drying out.

5 Serve with plain basmati rice and vegetables of your choice.

TIPS ••

For a change, grate a small amount of fresh unwaxed lemon zest and mix into the cooked rice. This gives a lovely, unusual tang.

You can also substitute the herbs with paprika (smoked or hot).

LEMONY CHICKEN BREASTS

Quick, simple, perfect!

1 chicken breast per person
1 lemon
Salt and pepper
Butter

METHOD

1 Preheat the oven to gas mark 5 (190°C, 375°F).

2 Put the chicken breasts with skin intact onto a flat oven dish. Squeeze over the lemon juice, then season with salt and pepper. Dot with butter (half a teaspoon per breast).

3 Place in the oven and bake for 20–25 minutes until the juices run clear and the skin is golden brown and crispy.

4 Serve with buttered pasta and petits pois or another green vegetable.

SPICY CROQUETTES

I always used to get muddled as to what constitutes a croquette or a rissole: according to the *Good Housekeeping Cookery Book* (1944), a rissole is meat or poultry wrapped in pastry and shaped like a Cornish pasty and a croquette is when the meat is shaped like a sausage and egg and breadcrumbed. Both are fried. In the recipe below, thighs are used rather than the breasts, as these have more flavour.

2 chicken thighs per person
2 slices fresh brown bread, made into crumbs
2 eggs, beaten separately
1 tbsp finely chopped parsley
1 tbsp fresh tarragon, if available
1/2 tsp grated nutmeg
1 onion, peeled and chopped finely
Salt and pepper
Pinch of chilli flakes (optional)
2 tbsp flour for coating
Fresh breadcrumbs for coating

METHOD

1 Remove the skin from the chicken pieces and take the flesh off the bones. Either put the chicken into a blender and blitz on the pulse method – try to avoid overdoing it as you don't want a purée – or pass through a mincer.

2 Place the minced chicken in a bowl and add the brown breadcrumbs, one of the beaten eggs, the parsley, the tarragon if available, grated nutmeg and onion. Season well with salt and pepper and add the chilli flakes if using.

3 Set out three bowls, one containing the flour, one with the other beaten egg and the third with the fresh breadcrumbs. Wet your hands under the tap and take a small quantity of the chicken mixture. Roll into a sausage shape. Take each one and roll it in the flour, then dip into the egg and then finally coat it with the breadcrumbs. Set aside on a plate and keep in the fridge if not cooking immediately.

4 You can either shallow fry them in a pan on the stove, or oven bake them. If you choose to fry them, pour half an inch of oil such as maize or sunflower into a frying pan and heat until the tip of a wooden spoon sizzles when immersed. Cook each croquette for about 5 minutes on each side, turning once. Drain on kitchen paper and serve immediately.

5   For oven cooking, place the croquettes onto a greased baking sheet and drizzle with a little oil. Put into a moderately hot oven (gas mark 5, 190°C, 375°F) and bake for about 20–25 minutes until they are golden brown and cooked through thoroughly.

6   Serve with mashed potato and creamed sweetcorn.

FRENCH ROAST CHICKEN

This is truly one of the simplest and nicest ways of eating chicken – it is perfect for a summer lunch, or a cosy one in the middle of winter. The diet is put on the back burner for this dish.

115 g (4 oz) butter
Juice 2 lemons
2 large cloves garlic, peeled and chopped
1 free range organic (if possible) chicken
Salt and pepper
**Some lettuce leaves for serving (these are
solely for decoration so use the raggedy outer
ones from the salad, washed first of course)**

METHOD

1   Preheat the oven to gas mark 5 (190°C, 375°F).

2   Melt the butter with the lemon juice and garlic in your roasting dish. Place the lemon halves inside the cavity of the chicken and place in the roasting dish. Spoon over the sauce. Sprinkle with a generous amount of sea salt and freshly ground pepper. Put in the oven to roast, basting every now and again, until the juices are clear (use a fork to prod the breast and legs). A medium to large bird (1. 3–1. 8 kg [3–4 lb]) usually takes 1¼ to 1½ hours to be on the safe side. When done, put on a separate plate and keep warm. Drain off the fat and keep for roasting potatoes.

3 Use poultry shears to cut up the beast into eight portions (see page 84).

4 When you are ready to serve, decorate a large serving dish with the lettuce leaves, pile on the cooked chicken pieces, drain off the fat, then pour over the juices from the pan, scraping as much of the sticky bits from the edge as you can.

5 A bowl of new potatoes and a crispy green salad, mixed with a light oil and vinegar dressing (see page 180), go well with this, and a sliced baguette or crunchy, rustic bread is essential to mop up the juices.

OVEN COOKED, BREADED CHICKEN BREASTS

Baked bananas go well with this recipe. Give the stripped cobs from your corn to your chickens to play with or put on your compost heap (hopefully not for the rats...).

1 chicken breast per person (on or off the bone) but with winglets attached
Plate of flour, seasoned with salt and pepper
1 or 2 eggs, beaten
Freshly made white and/or wholemeal breadcrumbs
Oil
1 banana per person
1 fresh corn on the cob per person
1 or 2 lemons cut into wedges

METHOD

1 Preheat the oven to gas mark 5 (190°C, 375°F).

2 Pull off any skin from the chicken pieces and discard. Coat each piece of chicken with the seasoned flour. Shake off any excess then slide it into the beaten egg. The flour helps the egg to stick to the chicken. Be warned, this is apron country and you may wish to rinse your hands every now and again during the process because they will get clogged. Once the egging is done, put the chicken into the bowl of breadcrumbs and coat it well, rolling it around so that as much of the surface area as possible is crumbed. Lift carefully and place onto a baking tray ready to put in the oven.

2 Drizzle a little oil over the chicken pieces and bake for a good 30 minutes – it's surprising how long it takes to get to the 'clear juice' stage – much will depend on the size of your chicken pieces. Check by prodding with a pointed knife or skewer to allow the juices to flow.

3 Half way through cooking, peel the bananas and place on the same dish (if there is room) or on a separate one and place in the oven.

4 Now for the sweetcorn: while the chicken and bananas are cooking, peel off the outer leaves and silky tassels and then, holding the cob upright on a steady board, run a sharp knife downwards, slicing off the niblets. Put these into a pan but don't add any salt (this toughens the grains) and just enough boiling water to cover. The fresher the corn, the less time it will take to cook.

5 These take little more than 3–4 minutes to cook. Drain, add a good knob of butter (about one tablespoon) and season with salt and pepper.

6 I don't think any other vegetables are necessary, but it's your choice. Serve with lemon wedges.

ALTOGETHER BAKED CHICKEN

$1/2$ chicken (cut a fresh one in two
and freeze the other half)
1 lemon
2 large red onions
1 red or green pepper (the red ones are sweeter)
350 g ($3/4$ lb) ripe tomatoes
350 g ($3/4$ lb) new potatoes (if you can get them, Jersey
Royals have lots of flavour)
3 tbsp olive oil
1 glass white wine
1 or 2 cloves garlic
Salt and pepper
2 lemons: 1 cut into slices or wedges, 1 squeezed for juice
$1/4$ tsp dried chilli flakes or 1 red chilli (optional)
Fresh thyme
2 bay leaves

METHOD

1 Preheat the oven to gas mark 5 (190°C, 375°F).

2 Separate the breast, leg and thigh joints from the carcass using a knife and/or poultry shears. Cut the drumstick from the thigh and cut the breast in two. You will have four pieces of chicken. Keep the skin on if you wish, or remove and discard.

2 Peel the onions and cut into quarters. Cut the pepper in half; remove the pips and pith and cut into rough chunks. Scrub the new potatoes (keeping the skin on for flavour) and cut into wedges or in half if they are small. Peel and chop the garlic.

3 Put the above into a shallow roasting tin and pour on the olive oil and white wine. Add the lemon juice. Season well with salt and pepper and add the chilli if desired. Mix everything well in the pan and scatter with sprigs of fresh thyme; tuck in the bay leaves and lemon wedges/slices.

4 Bake in the hot oven until the chicken is cooked, basting every now and again. Before serving, spoon off any extra fat – there won't be much if you have removed the skin from the chicken – and serve on its own or with a green salad and some watercress.

TIP •

Once you have stripped a carcass of its meat, don't throw it away. Make a stock with the skin, bones etc. It makes a good base for soup.

YUMMY LEFTOVER CHICKEN WITH GREEN PEPPERS

No one would ever dream this dish was made from leftovers.

About 2 cups leftover roast chicken
1 green pepper
55 g (2 oz) butter
1 dessertspoon flour
150 ml (5 fl oz) milk (approx.)
1 lemon
Salt and pepper
1 tbsp crème fraîche or cream (optional)

METHOD

1 Start by stripping any meat from the cold chicken carcass – you will be surprised how much you can find! Put this to one side. Place the bones, skin etc. in a pan and add about 225 ml (½ pint) water. Cover and bring to the boil. Simmer for about 10 minutes. Strain the stock into a bowl and throw away the bones. Skim off any fat with some kitchen paper.

2 Cut the green pepper in half and remove the seeds and core. Slice thinly. Melt half the butter in a saucepan and add the pepper. Stir and simmer for about 10 minutes. Add the chicken pieces.

3 Add the remaining butter and flour to the chicken and peppers, put back on the heat and stir for a minute. Add the stock and stir again, bringing it up to the boil. Pour in a little milk at this stage and stir well. Grate the zest of ½ lemon, cut the lemon in two and squeeze one half into the chicken mixture. Season with salt and pepper and cover. Simmer for 10 minutes (you want the chicken to be piping hot). Add the cream or crème fraîche now if you want to.

4 Serve immediately with plain boiled rice.

PINAR'S TURKISH CHICKEN

Pinar Shaw is married to my cousin Chris, and this delightful dish always causes a stir.

1 free range chicken
1 onion (for the stock), peeled only
1 bay leaf
Sprig rosemary
1 cup walnuts pieces – no need for expensive, whole ones
2–3 cloves garlic
1 cup fresh breadcrumbs
1 small onion, chopped roughly
Salt and pepper to taste

METHOD

1 Put the chicken into a large pan and add the onion and herbs. Cover with cold water and bring to the boil. Allow to simmer for about an hour or until the chicken is cooked through and tender.

2 Remove from the stock and put aside to rest and cool enough to handle. Bring the stock back to the boil and reduce by a half.

3 Meanwhile take the cooked chicken from off the bones, discarding any skin and bones.

4 Allow the stock to cool. Put one cup of stock, the walnuts, garlic, breadcrumbs, chopped onion, salt and pepper into a blender and whizz until smooth.

5 Pour this sauce over the chicken.

6 When ready to serve, decorate a platter with some lettuce leaves and carefully arrange the chicken pieces and sauce on top.

TIP •

If you prepare this dish the day before, the flavour will improve by keeping it in an air tight container in the fridge.

Guinea Fowl

I like to think of guinea fowl as poultry with 'O' levels or the result of an illicit union between a chicken and a pheasant – with more flavour than one and less than the other. The meat is low in fat and very tasty. As they are marginally more expensive than a chicken I only buy them when they are on special offer.

GUINEA FOWL BREASTS WITH APPLES AND SHALLOTS

2 breasts guinea fowl
1 dessertspoon oil
20 g (³/₄ oz) butter
1 large shallot or 1 red onion, peeled and sliced
1 sharp eating apple (e.g. Cox's Orange Pippin)
Salt and pepper
1 good sized glass white wine
1 good sized dessertspoon crème fraîche
or ¹/₂ cup double cream

METHOD

1 Cut up the bird and separate the breasts, legs and thighs from the carcass. Bag up the walking parts for the freezer for another day. Remove the skin from the breasts if you want to be healthy and discard.

2 Heat the oil with the butter in a frying pan and fry the shallots/onion until soft (about five minutes) on a medium heat. Push these to one side of the pan, raise the heat and brown the breasts on both sides for about 5 minutes.

3 Whilst these are cooking, wash and cut up the apple, removing the core but not the skin and cut into thin slices. Place these in the pan around the breast and mix with the shallots. Season with salt and pepper and pour over the white wine. Cover if you have a lid which fits and simmer until the breasts and apple are cooked (approximately 8–10 minutes). Add a little water if the juices evaporate too much.

4 Now add the crème fraîche or double cream, stir and warm through without boiling.

5 Serve with mashed potato, plain boiled rice or some sort of pasta, e.g. tagliatelle.

GUINEA FOWL LEGS WITH MUSHROOMS

This wonderfully comforting dish uses up the walking parts of the previous recipe. For your choice of mushrooms, button mushrooms look pretty but don't have much flavour – chestnut ones do, but are more expensive. All chefs say, 'Never wash a mushroom' but I do – I know what they grow in. A wipe with a damp cloth ain't sufficient for me and so under the tap they go.

2 legs and thighs from a guinea fowl
Oil for frying
1 red onion, peeled and sliced
1 clove garlic, peeled and sliced
1 packet of pancetta, sliced
1 packet mushrooms, washed and chopped
Salt and pepper
1 glass red wine
150 ml (5 fl oz) water (approx.)
Juice 1 lemon
2 tbsp crème fraîche or double cream

METHOD

1 Preheat the oven to gas mark 5 (190°C, 375°F).

2 Brown the legs and thighs in a little oil in a cast-iron enamel casserole (if you have one – if not use a frying pan and transfer to an ovenproof dish with a lid). Remove and put on a plate.

3 Fry the onions, garlic and pancetta in the pan juices until the pancetta is beginning to turn from floppy to just crispy (about 6 minutes). Add the chopped mushrooms and lemon juice.

4 Put the legs and thighs back into the casserole and season with salt and pepper. Pour in the red wine and the water. Cover and place in the oven for about 25 minutes. Check every now and again to see that it hasn't dried out – if this is the case, add a glass of water. At the end, stir in the cream or crème fraîche.

5 Serve with mashed potato, pasta or one of the Irish dishes like colcannon (see page 135) or champ (page 136) and a vegetable of your choice.

TIP •

The first time I cooked this, although we ate all the meat there was quite a lot of the mushrooms, onions and gravy left over. Too good to throw away, the next day I poured in 600 ml (1 pint) of water, tipped in the left-over vegetables (in this case courgettes, mashed potato and broccoli), brought it to the boil and let it simmer for about 15 minutes. I tasted it for seasoning and then bashed away with the potato masher to break up the mushrooms and vegetables. It made a hearty, flavoursome soup.

Pheasant

One of my main gripes about eating pheasant is that they are more attractive alive than dead. If roasted (and only use young ones for this method), the breast cooks long before the legs and tends to become dry and unpalatable. My recipe for roast pheasant achieves good results for both parts of the anatomy, regardless of age.

CHEAT'S ROAST PHEASANT

This recipe first appeared in my book, *A Compost Kind of Girl*. A close friend told me that when she read the following sentence, 'By cooking pheasant this way you will always end up with tender, moist legs and thighs and a succulent, juicy breast', she thought it referred to the cook...

1 young pheasant (old birds have long spurs and are tough)
2 onions, peeled and sliced
2 carrots or mixture of root vegetables of your choice, peeled and sliced
40 g (1½ oz) butter
1 dessertspoon oil
Salt and pepper
1 glass red wine
300 ml (½ pint) chicken stock
1 stick celery, sliced
150 ml (¼ pint) stock or water

METHOD

1 Preheat the oven to gas mark 5 (190°C, 375°F).

2 Start by cutting the legs and thighs away from the carcass, keeping the breasts on the bone.

3 Place the onion, root vegetables and celery in an ovenproof casserole. Sweat these on the stove in half the butter and a splash of oil. Add the legs and thighs and brown on both sides. Season with salt and pepper, pour on the wine and the stock or water. Cook in the oven for about 30 minutes.

4 Twenty minutes or so before you are due to sit down to eat, melt the remaining butter in a small roasting dish and coat the breasts with it (leave the skin on). Season with salt and pepper and put into the oven to roast – about 15–20 minutes until the juices run clear. This can rest in a warm place while you are dealing with the legs.

5 Remove the pheasant pieces from the casserole, separate the thighs and legs and place attractively onto a serving dish. Next carve the breasts into slices from the carcass and arrange next to the legs and thighs and keep warm.

6 You now have a choice as to what to do with the vegetables. You can pour the lot over the carved bird as is or you can lightly crush them with the juices and serve separately. It is up to you.

7 A combination of mashed potato and celeriac make a lovely accompaniment as does puréed parsnip, only don't blitz this in a blender – it turns into wallpaper glue – use a potato masher or fork. Serve with baked apples for savoury dishes (page 172).

Quail

Quail are tiny, fiddly little birds, but are well worth the effort of extricating the sweet meat from the bones. I try to buy free range birds for flavour.

QUAIL WITH GRAPES

If you can buy Muscat grapes in season (summer to autumn), their delicious perfume elevates this dish into sheer heaven.

25 g (1 oz) butter
1 packet sliced pancetta, chopped
2–3 shallots, peeled and chopped
1–2 quail per person depending on appetites
1 glass white wine
150 ml (¼ pint) stock (chicken or vegetable)
or plain water
Salt and pepper
85 g (3 oz) green seedless grapes

METHOD

1 Preheat the oven to gas mark 5 (190°C, 375°F).

2 Heat the butter in a casserole and cook the pancetta and shallots until both take on a hint of colour. Remove from the pan and put to one side to keep warm.

3 Heat the casserole again and brown the quails, turning them from time to time, in order to seal the outside.

4 Add the browned shallots and pancetta, the white wine and a quarter of a pint of stock or water, salt and pepper and put on the lid. Simmer gently either on a medium to low hot plate or place in a moderate/hot oven (see temperature above) for about 15 minutes.

5 Add the whole grapes and mix with the other ingredients, basting the birds at the same time. With the lid off, let this bubble away for a further 5–6 minutes to cook the grapes.

6 Serve one or two birds per person with the juices and grapes, mashed potato and vegetable(s) of your choice.

Duckling

We love duckling as it is very easy to cook – the only recommendation I can give is to place the bird on a wire rack in the roasting dish to keep it away from the large quantity of fat it is going to release. Carefully drain this fat into a bowl during cooking – about two or three times and keep for roasting potatoes. If you don't have a rack, scrunch up a large piece of tin foil and rest the bird on top. Another trick is to cut up a couple of oranges into quarters and place these underneath the duckling, then once cooked, remove the bird, drain off any extra fat and squash the oranges with a potato masher to squeeze out the juice, remove the skins and you have instant duck à l'orange.

Michel Roux (of Waterside Inn fame) allegedly never pricks the outside of a duck and puts salt only inside, not on the skin. I used to do the reverse until I read this. Try both ways and decide which you prefer. Other people like to put the raw duck on a rack over the sink and pour a kettle of boiling water over it, then pat it dry with a tea towel before putting it in the oven. This is meant to loosen the skin and fat and make for really crispy skin.

I don't like to be over-fussy with duckling as the meat is really succulent, so I alternate between doing nothing other than salting it, to putting an orange or an apple cut in half, or perhaps an onion in the cavity. On other occasions I have sprinkled the whole thing with dried mixed herbs and a crushed clove of garlic, rubbing this (with salt) into the skin. It tasted more like goose when cooked.

Insofar as the gravy is concerned, sometimes the giblets are included and I use these to make a stock. If I am not cooking the duckling until the next day, as soon as I get it home I remove them from inside the bird and make the stock as in the recipe below.

Once again I like to butcher a duckling so that I can freeze half – a whole bird is too much for Jimmy and me on our own. I remove the legs and thighs and these will be very simply seasoned and baked on a metal tray in a hot oven – they will almost taste as though they were preserved in fat like *confit de canard*. Either I remove the breasts to be grilled as *magret de canard* (this must be served pink – the longer you cook it the duller and tougher the meat) or I leave them on the carcass and roast in the oven in one piece. This is sold commercially as a crown of duckling. Turkey breast is also often sold like this.

I tend not to mess around with vegetables – we grow most of our own and frankly nothing beats the flavour of a really fresh cabbage, sprouts or carrots cooked within minutes of being harvested – short of the addition of a knob of butter and some chopped herbs like chives, parsley or chervil and possibly a squirt of lemon juice. Having said that, *petits pois à la française* complements duck and chicken an absolute treat (see page 126)

To make stock

Wash the giblets (neck, gizzard and heart) and put into a small pan (but leave out the liver). Add a peeled, sliced onion, one sliced carrot, a few sprigs of parsley, a stick of chopped celery and a bay leaf. Cover with water, bring to the boil and simmer for about an hour. When ready to make the gravy, strain this stock through a sieve into the roasting pan and heat through, mixing it with the cooking juices, having drained off the fat beforehand.

An average duckling takes about 1½ hours to cook – don't overdo it or the flesh will become tough. Let it rest in the warm on a separate dish.

Sometimes I make a gravy using a couple of tablespoonfuls of redcurrant jelly and whisk this with the stock to dissolve it. My mother used to put in a good tablespoon of Oxford marmalade. I chop up and freeze a few Seville oranges when they are available in January and February so that I can add a spoonful to the duckling gravy later on in the year – a little honey, maple syrup or sweet fruit jelly must be added at the same time to sweeten the bitterness of the orange. It will need to cook for a further 10 minutes as the orange is raw.

Goose

Order your fresh Christmas goose well in advance or take your chance at the supermarket. (I have never tried a frozen bird.) Either roast it plain or with a stuffing of your choice (see recipes page 184).

As soon as you get home, remove the bag of giblets from inside the bird. It will be in a plastic bag tucked probably inside at the neck end. To make the stock for the gravy see recipe below. Don't include the liver – once trimmed and cleaned this will make a delicious pâté (see page 81).

TO MAKE STOCK
1 large onion, peeled and quartered
1 large carrot, scrubbed and cut into large chunks
1 stick celery, sliced
1 bag goose giblets (1 use only the neck, gizzard and heart)
Bouquet garni made from parsley, thyme and a bay leaf
600 ml (1 pint) water

METHOD

1 Put the vegetables into a saucepan, add the washed giblets, bouquet garni and the water. Bring to the boil and simmer for a good 1–1½ hours. I don't season as there will be plenty in the roasting juices when the time comes to finish the task.

2 Pour through a sieve and once cold, keep in the fridge until needed. Remove any fat if necessary.

TIP •

One brilliant trick (but a little fiddly to do) is to remove the wish bone before you cook the goose (or turkey) – this makes carving so much easier. You will need a sharp knife and strong hands. Feel where the wish bone is at the neck end and cut into the flesh as close to the bone as you can. Using brute force, winkle your fingers up and under and behind the bone – this is where strength comes into play. Pull for all you are worth, wriggling and twisting and eventually it will loosen and come free. It's worth the effort, believe me and he (or she) who carves will thank you for it. Add the wishbone to the pan and it can be pulled later with the one you love.

ROAST GOOSE

METHOD

1 Preheat the oven to gas mark 7 (220°C, 425°F).

2 Lift the flappy skin around the neck end of your goose and work your way lifting and pushing the skin away from the breast meat – do this very carefully so as not to rip the skin. Once this is done, take handfuls of your chosen stuffing and squish it into the pocket you have made. You may have a little stuffing left over. If you do, put it to one side and bake separately in a small dish. Tuck the flap of skin underneath the bird and secure with skewers – these are easily obtained from your butcher.

3 Once again, I don't prick the bird. Although a goose can release well over 600 ml (1 pint) of fat during cooking (which makes the best ever roast potatoes), it is in fact quite a lean meat. With this in mind I smear the whole thing with 115 g (4 oz) of soft butter before I season it with salt and pepper. The bird will be quite heavy at this point and you may need an extra pair of hands to lay it on the rack in the roasting dish.

4 After the first half hour, reduce the oven temperature to gas mark 4 (180°C, 350°F) and cook for a further 1½–2 hours. You don't want the meat to shrink away from the bones on the drumsticks, but make sure the juices run clear. Lift out the bird (see Tip below). Cover it with a sheet of tin foil and then something thick (a towel for example) to keep the heat in while it rests.

5 Now for the gravy: this is the same virtually as for roast duckling. Drain off any excess fat and add 1 tablespoon flour to the remaining juices in the roasting pan. Mix this well with the gorgeous residue, at the same time scraping the sides of the dish, and then add the stock (see recipe above) – you may not need all of it. Stir and either thicken on top of the stove, or for those of you with an Aga, put it back in the top oven for about 8–10 minutes. Check for seasoning. I don't add any other flavours to the gravy such as red wine, port or sweet jelly but, again, it is a matter of personal choice.

6 Jimmy is fond of braised red cabbage with goose and I get cracking with this the day before (see page 127). To go with this I do something green – *the petits pois à la française* (see page 126) perhaps. We also adore sprouts.

TIPS •

A cooked (and stuffed) goose is cumbersome to lift and this is a good tip: put on a clean pair of rubber gloves and quickly remove the bird from the roasting dish and put it onto a serving plate. It will be very hot but if you move fast enough the heat will not penetrate the gloves.

Remember that goose meat is very rich, so don't overdo things or else indigestion tablets will become part of the menu.

Fish and seafood

I like fish but I am always careful when buying it in its raw state, making very sure about its freshness – it must smell of the sea and not of ammonia. There's no knowing how long it may have been languishing on ice but, if you check to see that the eyes are bright and clear and that the gills are nice and red, it should be absolutely fine. A friend who was once a chef in the army told me that he and his fellow chef mates only ever buy frozen fish (unless they know of its actual source), since it is chilled on the boats within a very short time of being caught, thus preserving the quality.

For everyday use I always keep a good supply of frozen North Atlantic, line-caught haddock – most supermarkets sell this. It never smells nor tastes fishy and can be cooked without having to be defrosted. Insofar as prawns are concerned, once again I buy only those from cold northern seas, never from the Far East or South America.

REFRESHING PRAWN AND MELON STARTER

Imagine for a moment that you are eating this revamped prawn cocktail in dappled shade under a willow tree with the tinkling of a fountain nearby. In the real world, it will probably be inside, the wind and rain beating against the windows. We had this recipe as a starter on our wedding day, blizzards blowing outside, back in January 1991 and not a smidgen was left. We have also enjoyed a similar dish at a local restaurant where they add a little cream and fresh crab.

1 bag good quality frozen prawns

1 ripe melon (preferably Cantaloupe or Ogen – something perfumed rather than a bland, honeydew type)

350 g (3/4 lb) jar good quality bought mayonnaise

2 tbsp tomato ketchup

Juice 1 lemon

3–4 shakes Tabasco sauce

Salt and freshly ground black pepper

Paprika for garnish

1 packet mustard and cress

METHOD

1 It's best, if you have time, to thaw the prawns at room temperature but they can always be defrosted quickly using several dunkings in cold water, draining well in a sieve afterwards.

2 Use a special implement for making melon (or butter) balls if you have one, but if not, cut the melon into segments, remove the pips and pare off the skin. Cut each slice into smaller chunks and put into a bowl. Add the thawed, drained prawns.

3 In a separate bowl, tip in the jar of mayonnaise, ketchup, lemon juice, Tabasco, a little salt and a good grinding or two of pepper and mix thoroughly before incorporating into the melon and prawns. Keep in the fridge until needed.

4 Decorate a serving dish with some shredded lettuce leaves and pile the prawn and melon mixture on top. Dust with some paprika, sprinkled through a fine sieve, for effect, and scatter the washed mustard and cress.

5 Very thinly sliced brown bread and butter, retro style.

TIP ••

When choosing a melon, do what the continentals do – don't push your thumb into the flesh to see if it gives, sniff the fruit first. If it is ripe and ready to eat you will smell the sweetness of the melon. If it has no scent, put it back and leave it for another day.

_____

MY SIMPLE KEDGEREE

Kedgeree (or kitcheree) used to be a regular feature at the Victorian breakfast table but is equally welcome at any time of the day, notably a fork supper in front of the television. It can be prepared in advance and frozen, but, if you do this, do not include any eggs at this point – they go rubbery – add them freshly cooked when the kedgeree has been thawed, re-heated and is piping hot.

2 eggs

**1 fillet (about 225–350 g [8–12 oz])
of naturally smoked haddock**

300–350 ml (10–15 fl oz) milk

15 g (1/2 oz) butter

1 bay leaf

Freshly ground black pepper

115 g (4 oz) rice (I like basmati)

Salt

1 large onion, peeled and sliced

1 dessertspoon oil

**3 tbsp parsley, washed and chopped
(flat leafed parsley has more flavour than curly)**

1 lemon

Cayenne pepper

**25–30 g (a generous 1 oz) of extra butter
to add at the end**

METHOD

1 To hard-boil the eggs, boil them for 10 minutes. Take off heat, drain and cover with cold water. Tap each egg on the work surface, roll it around in the palms of your hands and the shell will loosen and come away more easily.

2 Meanwhile rinse the fish under the tap and put into a shallow dish. Pour on enough milk almost to cover it. Dot with butter (about half an ounce), and slip in a bay leaf if you have one handy. Do not add any salt because the fish will have enough, but give it a good dose of ground pepper. Cook in a medium/hot oven for about 8–10 minutes.

3 While the fish is cooking, prepare the rice: pour into a pan half full of cold water. Squidge the grains in your hand and you will see that the water turns milky. Tip this away but keep the rice in the pan. Repeat the process a couple of times more. This is to remove some of the starch and will help your cooked rice to be fluffy and not something with which you could re-grout your bathroom tiles. Cover the rice with twice as much cold water as it says on the packet, a pinch of salt and bring to the boil. Stir once only to separate the grains. My rice always boils over if I leave the lid on, but it does need some cover so I leave the wooden spoon in the pan and prop the lid against it. Simmer for about 10 minutes and test. It should retain a little bite – *al dente* – like pasta.

4 At this stage, remove from the heat and you will see that most of the water has been absorbed. Fill the pan containing the rice with fresh cold water from the tap and strain immediately in a sieve. Replace the sieve containing the rice back on top of the saucepan (into which you add about an inch of water), put the lid on top and return to the boil. The rice will continue to cook and dry out above the hot water, remaining nice and fluffy.

5 Back to the haddock – drain off the cooking milk and keep this to one side. With a knife and fork flake the fish and discard the skin and any bones.

6 Place the onion in a frying pan, cover with a little water and add a splash of oil. Bring to the boil and then simmer, stirring every now and again. Once the water has evaporated you want the onions to cook for a further few minutes until they are nice and brown but not burnt.

7 Get a large mixing bowl and carefully combine the fish, rice, parsley, grated zest from half the lemon, a good pinch of cayenne (depending on how brave you are, maybe even as much as a quarter of a teaspoon), and lots of freshly ground pepper.

8 Put this mixture into a gratin dish big enough for the job. Cut the hard-boiled eggs into quarters and scatter over the rice mix. Next, put the browned onions on top, spreading them randomly. Dot with masses of butter. Last but not least pour on a cup of the cooking liquor from the fish – enough to moisten.

9 At this stage, either you can put it to one side to heat up later (but note the warning about heating up rice on page 154) or put it immediately into a medium/hot oven (gas mark 5 [190°C, 375°F]) to heat through thoroughly for about 15–20 minutes.

10 Just before serving, cut the lemon in half and squeeze the juice over the dish.

TIP •
I have never worked out what to drink with kedgeree but, funnily enough, as it used to be a classic breakfast dish, a cup of decent tea is very pleasant, or just plain water, or a cold lager perhaps? For you to experiment.

GREAT UNCLE ALEC'S FISH PIE

This can be cooked as easily for one person as for six. This is the list of ingredients for two people.

2 fresh or frozen fillets of white fish

225 g (8 oz) new potatoes, washed with skins left on, sliced to about the thickness a pound coin

2 medium onions, peeled and sliced

225 g (8 oz) ripe tomatoes, sliced

1 clove garlic, peeled and finely chopped

$^{1}/_{2}$–$^{3}/_{4}$ tsp fennel seeds (optional)

Scant $^{1}/_{4}$ tsp (depending on taste) dried chilli flakes (optional)

Salt and pepper

2 tbsp olive oil

1 glass white wine

1 lemon, sliced

METHOD

1 Preheat the oven to gas mark 5 (190°C, 375°F).

2 Lay the potato slices onto the bottom of a buttered gratin dish followed by the onions and then the tomatoes. Scatter the garlic on top. Add the fennel seeds and chillies, if using.

3 Season well with salt and pepper and drizzle over some good olive oil. Bake in the oven for about 15–20 minutes until the potatoes are almost done.

4 Remove from the oven and snuggle the fillets (even if still frozen) amongst the vegetables. Pour in the wine and baste the fish with the juices. Slice the lemon and place over the top. Give a final drizzle of olive oil and put back into the oven. The fish should be cooked in about another 15 minutes.

5 Serve immediately. There is no need to have any other vegetable, but if you want something green to look attractive on the plate, fine French beans fit the bill.

GREAT-GRANNY'S FISH RAGOUT

**2 large tomatoes or 4–6 smaller ones, sliced
2 small onions, peeled and sliced
2 cloves garlic, peeled and chopped
2 tbsp olive oil
2 tsp Worcestershire sauce
2 fillets frozen or fresh fish
Salt and pepper**

METHOD

1 Heat the oil in a saucepan and add the onions. Cook until soft and then add the tomatoes, garlic and Worcestershire sauce. Stir and cook a further 10 minutes or until the liquid is reduced and the sauce quite thick.

2 Add the fish to the pan and cook gently for 5 minutes without stirring – you don't want the fillet(s) to disintegrate. Season well with salt and pepper and serve immediately with plain, boiled rice.

A FISH DISH FOR SOMEONE WHO HASN'T BEEN VERY WELL

My mother trained as a nurse in New Zealand before the War and taught me a huge amount about caring for and feeding a sick person – the tips she passed on have proved invaluable over the years. She always made this simple baked fish when we were children after our temperature had returned to normal and we were ready to eat something but nothing too ambitious because, as she put it, 'We didn't have the strength to punch the skin on a rice pudding'. Even if you aren't poorly, there are times when this dish is welcome in its own right.

Completing the picture of how my mother looked after us when we were unwell, she would run us a warm bath (never too hot - if you are weak you can feel faint and risk a fall). She added a capful of inexpensive eau de cologne to the bath water. Her reason for this is the following: when you have a fever, your skin becomes tender to the touch making washing uncomfortable; by the addition of eau de cologne, psychologically you will feel clean and fresh without actually having to use soap.

While we were soaking, Ma would air the bed, fluff the pillows and slip in a warm hot water bottle. Once patted dry (with help), dusted in talcum powder, clean pyjamas donned, we collapsed, exhausted but relaxed into a feathered heaven. Nine times out of ten, we fell instantly asleep.

SERVES 1
1 fresh or frozen fillet of haddock
Enough milk to cover the fish
1 tsp butter
Little salt and pepper
1 piece white bread sliced very thinly, with a scraping of butter cut into 8 tiny triangles, crusts removed

METHOD

1 Preheat the oven to gas mark 6, (200°C, 400°F).

2 Place the fish in a small dish and cover with milk. Dot with butter and season with a very little salt and pepper. Bake in the preheated oven for about 6 minutes only – fish cooks quickly, even from frozen.

3 Serve a little of the fish on a small, pre-warmed plate. Spoon on some of the buttery milk. By not overwhelming the patient with a large portion and by giving them a small amount, not only might they manage to eat this, but they might even want a second tiny helping. The whole point is not to overwhelm the invalid.

4 Arrange the bread and butter on a matching or smaller plate.

5 Put these onto a tray laid with a proper napkin and pretty tray cloth – presentation is essential as hopefully it will encourage them to eat something – however small.

TIPS •

When someone has been ill and not eating, nothing cleanses the mouth better than fresh pineapple. Once again, the quantity is all important. Select a small wine or sherry glass. Prepare a slice of the fruit by removing the outer skin and the dark pippy bits. Cut into tiny segments and put only two or three into the glass. Take it to the sick room on a tray with a child's fork to eat it with. The patient may only eat one piece but if they do, they will feel a huge sense of achievement.

Try serving other fruits in a similar fashion: one quarter of an apple, peeled and cut into tiny, bite-sized pieces, some pear or melon. Strawberries may be too acidic, as are oranges, except when served as freshly squeezed juice, diluted with water and sweetened with sugar plus natural glucose. If they have had little food intake, glucose provides vital energy reserves. This can be bought over the counter at the chemist's.

THE NICEST FISH PIE

2 frozen or fresh haddock fillets (or cod if you prefer)
Milk, enough to cover the fish
20 g (³/₄ oz) butter
Salt and pepper
2 eggs
450 g (1 lb) potatoes, peeled and cut into small pieces
2 tbsp freshly chopped parsley
Zest and juice of 1 lemon
Tabasco sauce
6 small mushrooms (optional)
2 tbsp grated cheese (Cheddar, Gruyère or Emmental)
4 tbsp fresh breadcrumbs (white or brown)

WHITE SAUCE
25 g (1 oz) butter
25 g (1 oz) flour
Liquid reserved from cooking fish

METHOD

1 To poach the fish, pour enough milk to cover, add the butter and season with salt and pepper. Cook either in a shallow pan on the stove on a gentle simmer or bake in a preheated oven set at gas mark 6 (200°C, 400°F) for 6–8 minutes. Reserve the cooking liquid.

2 Boil the eggs for 8 minutes and then drain, cover with cold water and remove the shells.

3 Boil the potatoes, covered, until soft. Drain, add three quarters of the butter and enough milk to make it into a soft but not sloppy mash.

4 Make a white sauce: melt the butter with the flour and stir until it bubbles. Add the fish liquor and stir constantly to prevent lumps from forming. (If you don't mind the possibility of removing the non-stick lining to your milk pan, use an egg whisk which guarantees no lumps. You can then abandon this and return to your wooden spoon for the final stages.) Once the sauce has thickened taste for seasoning and adjust accordingly.

5 Flake the fish into chunks and add to the white sauce along with the parsley, lemon juice and zest and a couple of shakes of Tabasco. Stir very gently.

6 Cut the eggs in half and then in quarters and carefully add to fish mixture. Pour into a buttered gratin dish and top with the mashed potato. Level it slightly and decorate using the back of a fork – do a wiggly pattern like an inebriated farmer dragging a plough.

7 Mix together the grated cheese and breadcrumbs and scatter these on top of the potato. Dot with a little extra butter, but not too much – 1 teaspoon will do.

8 Either keep to one side until you need to heat it up, or put into a hot oven (gas mark 5 [190°C, 375°F]) for 15 minutes, until it is bubbling and the top golden brown.

9 You can freeze this pie, but, if so, leave out the hard-boiled eggs at this stage and add them when you reheat it.

10 I like to serve this with lashings of tomato ketchup or a dish of oven-baked sliced tomatoes.

TIP •

If you are poaching a whole fish, remove the gills before cooking. If left, they make the flesh taste bitter.

FISH CAKES

I buy only organic salmon. Although not a patch on wild, it has a better consistency and flavour than ordinary farmed fish, which can be very fatty and have a flabby texture.

SERVES 4
1 frozen haddock fillet, frozen or fresh
1 serving fresh organic salmon
Milk and/or water, to cover
20 g ($^3/_4$ oz) butter
2 tbsp freshly chopped parsley
Tabasco sauce
Zest and juice one lemon
115 g (4 oz) cold mashed potato
Flour for coating
1 egg, beaten
Fresh white breadcrumbs (approx. 3–4 slices bread, crusts removed, blended or processed)
Salt and pepper

METHOD

1 Preheat the oven to gas mark 6 (200°C, 400°F).

2 Put the frozen haddock and salmon into the same dish, cover with milk or water and dot with butter. Cook in the oven for about 10 minutes.

2 Remove and drain, then flake the fish into smallish pieces. Put into a mixing bowl.

3 Add parsley, lemon zest and juice, two or three shakes of Tabasco, the mashed potato and seasoning to taste, and mix.

4 When the mixture is cool enough to handle, shape into round patties or sausage-shaped torpedoes. Roll each one individually in the flour, dip into the beaten egg and then into the breadcrumbs.

5 Cook them in a frying pan in a little mixture of oil and butter, or in the oven. If the latter method is chosen, place them on a metal tray, drizzle with a little olive oil and bake in a hot oven for about 10–15 minutes – you want the outside to be crisp and crunchy, the inside soft and hot.

6 Serve with a green salad and an extra wedge of lemon.

TIP •
When dividing mixtures for fish cakes, rissoles, meat balls, etc., first spread the raw mixture into a round. Cut it into equal portions, like a clock face, and then each one will weigh the same.

GOOD FRIDAY FISH

A Danish friend gave me this traditional Scandinavian recipe, which she used to have every year as a child on Good Friday. It is a very delicate, gentle dish, good for the soul and body, and welcome any time of the year. The combination of cold vegetables, hot fish and potatoes with the richness of melted butter is most pleasing.

**1 small tail of a young cod – if this
isn't available, 2 cod steaks
350 g (12 oz) new potatoes – as it's Easter, try
and get hold of some Jersey Royals
4 small to medium cold cooked beetroots, chopped
2 hard-boiled eggs, chopped
2 small shallots or 1 red onion, chopped
1 tbsp capers, chopped
2 large gherkins, chopped
1 tbsp chopped parsley
1 tbsp fresh dill, chopped
85 g (3 oz) melted butter**

**FOR COOKING THE FISH
1 small onion, sliced
1 bay leaf
6 peppercorns
$\frac{1}{2}$ tsp salt**

METHOD

1 Preheat the oven to gas mark 5 (190°C, 375°F).

2 Scrub the new potatoes but leave the skins on and put them on to boil or steam.

3 Cooking the fish: Place the cod on a piece of aluminium foil. Add the sliced onion, bay leaf, peppercorns and salt. Wrap up in the foil and place on a baking tray, then into the hot oven until the fish is cooked – about 8–10 minutes. Keep warm.

3 Put the beetroot, hard-boiled eggs, onions or shallots, capers, gherkins and parsley either into individual dishes or arranged decoratively on a large platter.

4 Lift the fish from the foil, take off the skin and remove the bones. Put the fish onto a warmed dish. Decant the potatoes into a bowl and scatter the dill on top.

5 Each person then helps themselves to fish and potatoes and spoonfuls of the beetroot, etc. Finally drizzle the hot melted butter over everything, plus a couple of twists of pepper.

BREADED SALMON FILLETS

In this recipe I suggest using salmon because the combination of the colours, flavours and added crunch are very appealing and it is a different way from the usual method of cooking this increasingly good value fish. Of course, you can use fresh or frozen (thaw first) cod or haddock. I like the flat, triangular-shaped pieces of salmon, called 'Caledonian' fillets rather than the thick, chunky steaks, but this is a matter of choice.

2 pieces salmon (cod or haddock fillets)
Flour for coating
1 egg, well beaten
Browned breadcrumbs
1 unwaxed lemon
50/50 oil and butter mix (about 1 tbsp)
Salt and pepper
Scant 1/2 tsp dried chilli flakes (optional)

METHOD

1 If you are using salmon, first remove the skin by carefully separating it from the flesh with a sharp knife then pulling it back and off the fillet – it should come away easily. Rinse under cold water and pat dry in some kitchen paper. Check for any bones by running your fingers across each piece and tug out, either with tweezers or by pinching it between the tip of a knife and your thumb.

2 Get out three small dishes: in the first pour in enough flour to coat the fish, in the second the beaten egg, and in the third, the browned breadcrumbs (see page 86). Wash the lemon, then grate the zest into the breadcrumbs and mix. Dredge each fillet of fish in the flour, shake off any surplus, then dip it into the raw egg, making sure they are thoroughly coated. Finally, put into the breadcrumbs and again, coat evenly.

3 Once all the fish has been bread-crumbed in this way, you can leave them in the fridge for a while until you wish to cook them. I like to bake them in a hot oven as this uses far less fat (you can control how much is absorbed by the breadcrumbs), but by all means shallow fry them in a pan in the mixture of oil and butter (see point 5 below).

4 If you choose to bake the fish, preheat the oven to gas mark 5 (190°C, 375°F). Place the breaded fillets onto a greased baking sheet (or a non-stick one), season with salt and a couple of twists of ground pepper and the chilli flakes if you want some extra heat. Drizzle a little oil or dot with a little butter. Put on the middle shelf and cook for about 8 minutes.

5 If you are frying the fish, heat the oil (about 1 tablespoon) in a pan and carefully drop in the fish. Cook for 2–3 minutes and then turn over using a fish slice. Now is the time to add a knob of butter if desired, shaking the pan as it melts to spread it about – butter will impart a lovely flavour. Cook for a further 2 minutes. If you are using thicker steaks of salmon, you may need to cook them a little bit longer – check by cutting one carefully to expose the middle: if it is still darker than the outside, it means it needs a couple more minutes of frying/baking.

6 Serve with mashed potato, green vegetables (for colour), possibly some carrots to match the salmon and the lemon (the one with the zest removed) cut into wedges.

TIP •

To remove bones from your fingers when you are preparing raw or cooked fish, have handy a bowl of warm water in which to dip your fingers as you work – the bones will drop off into the water.

SMOKED SALMON TERRINES

115 g (4 oz) thinly sliced smoked salmon
200 ml (7 fl oz) cream cheese
1 tbsp fresh dill
1 tbsp horseradish cream
½ cucumber, peeled and diced
Pepper
Paprika (optional)

METHOD

1 Either use individual ramekins or one larger dish. First moisten the inside of the dish(es) and then line with cling film, making sure that there is enough to fold over the edge of the pot – this will help you remove the terrines later. By wetting the inside it will help the cling film to stick.

2 Line the pots with the smoked salmon. If there are any trimmings, chop these finely and add to the cream cheese mixture later.

3 Put the cream cheese into a bowl and beat with a fork to make it smooth. Chop approximately a tablespoon dill and along with the horseradish and cucumber add it to the cheese. Season well with ground pepper and mix again. You can add a pinch or two of paprika as well if you like.

4 Pour into the moulds and place in the fridge to chill and set. When ready to serve, ease the cling film from around the edge and turn onto a plate. Peel off the cling film and decorate the salmon moulds with a sprig of dill and a wedge of lemon.

Mussels

A girlfriend of ours told me of the occasion she had invited some friends to supper, two of whom were professional chefs. She decided to cook *moules à la marinière*. They were proving a huge success and just as she was beginning to relax, half-way through the meal, one of her guests picked up something very odd from the centre of his plate. It was the black, rubber plug from her sink! Unfortunately, when she had finished cleaning the mussels and was lifting them into the saucepan, the bung came too!

Buy rope-grown mussels as they will be free of sand. They are generally sold in bags of varying weight so check with the fishmonger as to the quantity you require. Keep them in the fridge until you are ready to cook them.

MOULES A LA MARINIERE

Mussels (enough for your requirements – generally speaking, a bag is enough for two people as a main dish)
55 g (2 oz) butter
1 clove garlic, crushed
1 large shallot, peeled and chopped
2 glasses white wine (drink the rest with the mussels)
Salt and pepper
200 ml (7 fl oz) crème fraîche
1 heaped tbsp flat-leafed parsley, roughly chopped
1 crusty loaf or baguette

METHOD

1 *Preparation is all important.* Tip the mussels into a bowl full of cold water and have a good sort through: any which are cracked or broken or which are open and don't close immediately when given a sharp tap with a knife, chuck out. If any mussels float to the top of the water, discard these as well – they are also wrong'uns! Then the real work begins as you clean them one by one. First of all, with a knife, grip the hairy bits (called the beard) sticking out of one side

of the shell. Tug this away. Scrape off any remaining bits of barnacle and put the clean mussels into a fresh bowl of water and rinse well.

2 Heat the butter in a good sized pan with a lid and add the chopped garlic and the shallots. Cook for a couple of minutes, giving the pan the odd shake.

3 Next, tip in the mussels, add the white wine and season with salt and pepper. Stir a couple of times and put the lid on. The shells will open almost on hitting the heat and only take 2–3 minutes to cook – don't overdo it or they will become tough.

4 Stir in the crème fraîche.

5 Have some warmed soup bowls ready plus an empty receptacle for the discarded shells. Before serving, have a look to check if there are any mussels which haven't opened. A closed mussel in this instance is a dead one – pick any out like this and discard. Serve in a large bowl and sprinkle with the chopped parsley.

6 The only way to eat a mussel is to use a complete shell as a pincer. You can also use one half to scoop up the creamy sauce. Lots of crisp, French bread is vital to mop up any remaining juices. Finger food at its best!

TIP •

If a recipe requires only a 'squeeze' of lemon juice, rather than cut one in half and waste some, cut out a slice and put it through a garlic press. The juice will be easily extracted along with the zest, giving extra flavour.

Vegetables and Savoury Dishes

In general I don't do much to vegetables apart from maybe adding a little butter and/or fresh herbs, but sometimes it is fun to experiment and give the dish a twist - they can then be a main course in their own right.

TIPS ••

When I need to purchase an individually priced item, such as celery, prepacked courgettes or tomatoes (they are sometimes cheaper sold this way as against loose), I weigh them in the scales available to shoppers – there can be quite a difference. Every penny counts!

This is a very useful tip when preparing broad beans: use a vegetable peeler and run the knife down one rib of the pod. The 'seam' opens and you can remove the beans in a matter of seconds.

I never cut my runner beans into large, diagonal diamond shapes. Instead, I take a very sharp knife and once the beans have had the stringy side bits removed, I slice the bean into very thin, 5–8 cm (2–3 inch) strips – a bit like green, flimsy pasta. Cook the beans in a saucepan with a sprinkling of salt and the tiniest pinch of bicarbonate of soda – this keeps them bright green and the flavour is out of this world. Add just enough boiling water to the pan to make the beans wet, but not so much that they are swimming in water. It will then quickly come back to the boil. Stir the beans so that they have all had contact with the boiling water, then let them cook for no longer than 3 or 4 minutes. Drain and serve plain, or heat with a knob of butter, squeeze of lemon juice and some chopped summer savory.

PETITS POIS A LA FRANCAISE

In a perfect world, use your own freshly picked garden peas – I never buy them at the supermarket as they could be days old: peas start turning to starch immediately they leave the plant (as does corn on the cob). If you don't have your own supply, frozen petits pois are a very close second – they are frozen within hours of being harvested. This dish can be cooked in advance and reheated either in a microwave oven or in a pan on the cooker.

450 g (1 lb) peas in their pods or 350 g (^{3}/$_4$ lb) frozen peas
25 g (1 oz) butter
**1 bunch slim spring onions (cut into 2. 5 cm [1 inch]
pieces) or 3 bulbous, larger ones (cut into quarters)**
**2 hearty Little Gem lettuces, cut into quarters
(again, if possible your own home grown
or organic ones from the supermarket)**
1 tsp sugar
^{1}/$_4$ tsp salt

METHOD

1 Begin by shelling the peas (if you are using frozen, don't bother to defrost them).

2 In a saucepan, melt the butter and add the spring onions. Stir for a minute or so and then add the washed little gem lettuces cut into quarters. Stir, cover the pan and simmer for 3 more minutes.

3 Add the peas, sugar and a pinch of salt, stir and cover. If you are using fresh peas, add a small glass of water at this stage – the frozen peas will have enough moisture of their own. Simmer gently for about 15 minutes.

BRAISED RED CABBAGE

This dish is better prepared the day before, then reheated.

650 g (1½ lb) red cabbage, finely shredded
1 medium onion, sliced
25 g (1 oz) butter
2 cooking apples, peeled and chopped
2 tbsp red wine vinegar
1 rounded tbsp demerara sugar
Salt and pepper
**25 g (1 oz) flour kneaded into a paste
with 25 g (1 oz) butter**

METHOD

1 Preheat the oven to gas mark 2 (150°C, 300°F).

2 Put cabbage into a large pan and add some boiling water. Blanch for 1 minute and drain.

3 Cook the onion in the butter until soft. Add the apple and continue cooking a further 2 minutes. Turn onto a plate. Pile into an ovenproof casserole, alternating layers of cabbage and apple/onion mixture sprinkling with vinegar as you go. Add 2–3 tablespoons of water, the sugar and some salt and pepper.

3 Lay a buttered paper over the cabbage, replace the lid and cook in a slow oven for about 2 hours. Stir from time to time and moisten, if necessary, with a little water.

4 When the cabbage is very tender, stir in the butter/flour mix. Heat for a few minutes to cook the flour and thicken the juices.

LITTLE GREEN CABBAGE BUNDLES

This is a great way to stretch a small cabbage to feed more mouths than planned – the cabbage cooks without disintegrating into a mush.

1 green cabbage, a Savoy ideally
Butter
Salt and pepper
$1/2$ lemon

METHOD

1 Begin by removing the tough outer leaves of the cabbage – put them in the compost or give to the chickens if you have any. Peel off half a dozen of the remaining outer leaves and wash well – if the rib is large, carefully cut this away and discard, keeping the rest of the leaf intact. Blanch these leaves in boiling water for a minute or two, then drain and refresh with cold water - this will make them much more pliable and easier to fold once filled with the raw, shredded cabbage.

2 Cut the cabbage into quarters, and remove the core by cutting it out with a knife. Wash the cabbage, drain in a colander and shred very thinly.

3 Take a large, whole leaf and put some of the shredded cabbage on top. Add a tiny bit of butter, and season with salt and pepper. Fold the outer leaf around the filling to make a sausage shaped bundle. This doesn't have to be particularly tidy or closed up – enough to keep the filling inside. Place in a steamer, and repeat with the other cabbage leaves, packing the parcels closely together – this will stop them from bursting open. Squeeze over the lemon juice and season with a little more salt and pepper.

4 When the water is boiling in the steamer, cook the cabbage for about 6–7 minutes or until tender. Lift carefully with a spoon and a fork and serve.

TIP ••
If you have some raw cabbage left over, keep it fresh in a plastic bag and cook the next day, stir-fried with lemon juice and butter (see page 129).

CABBAGE WITH LEMON JUICE AND BUTTER

**1 cabbage (Savoy or Sweetheart –1/2 will be
enough for 2 people)
40 g (1 1/2 oz) butter
Juice 1/2–1 lemon
Salt and pepper**

METHOD

1 Cut the cabbage in two and remove the tough core, plus any tatty outer leaves. Shred the rest of the cabbage very thinly.

2 Melt the butter in a saucepan and throw in the shredded cabbage, stirring well. After a minute add the lemon juice and a little salt. Stir and allow to cook in the steam from the juices, without a lid. This won't take long if you like your cabbage to have a bit of crunch.

3 Give a good two or three twists of pepper, stir and serve immediately.

CREAMY BAKED POTATOES

This goes well with cold roast meat or hot gammon.

**450 g (1 lb) floury potatoes (not new ones)
1 large clove or 2 small cloves garlic, peeled and chopped
Salt and pepper
225 ml (1/2 pint) milk
200 ml (7 fl oz) crème fraîche
1/4 tsp nutmeg**

METHOD

1 Preheat the oven to gas mark 6 (200°C, 400°F).

2 Peel and slice the potatoes thinly into a bowl of cold water. Butter a gratin dish. Drain the potatoes and place in a dish with the chopped garlic. Season well with salt and pepper.

3 In a bowl, mix the milk with the crème fraîche and pour over the potatoes. Using a fine grater, dust the top with a little nutmeg – you don't want people to think they are eating rice pudding!

4 Bake for about 30–40 minutes until the potatoes are cooked and the top a bubbling brown. If you have an Aga, put it in the top oven until it is brown and finish off the cooking in the simmering oven.

BAKED POTATO WEDGES

For some reason, potatoes cooked this way seem to go a lot further than if boiled and mashed; in fact one large potato is more than enough for two people, even with decent appetites.

1 medium sized potato per person (not large baking ones)
1 clove garlic, peeled and chopped
2 small red onions, peeled and quartered
1 tsp finely chopped rosemary
1 tbsp olive oil
Salt and pepper

METHOD

1 Preheat the oven to gas mark 6 (200°C, 400°F).

2 Scrub the potatoes but don't peel them. Cut them in half and then into boat-shaped wedges and put into a bowl.

3 Add the garlic, onion and rosemary to the potatoes, add the olive oil, season with salt and pepper and mix thoroughly, coating everything. Place in a roasting dish.

4 Position on the middle shelf of the oven and bake for about 25–35 minutes.

5 These are delicious with virtually anything and equally good eaten in your fingers with a pot of mayonnaise to dip into.

CHEAT'S TOMATOES A LA PROVENCALE

**225–450 g (¹/₂–1 lb) large, ripe tomatoes cut
in half – enough to fit in a gratin dish
1 packet luxury bread sauce
2 tbsp parsley, chopped
1 clove garlic, peeled and crushed or chopped
Salt and pepper
1–1¹/₂ tbsp olive oil**

METHOD

1 Preheat the oven to gas mark 5 (190°C, 375°F).

2 Arrange the tomatoes in an ovenproof dish, cut side upwards.

3 In a bowl mix the dried bread sauce with the parsley and the garlic. Spoon the mixture onto the tomatoes. Season with only a little salt (the bread sauce will have plenty) and several good grindings of black pepper. Drizzle with olive oil and bake for 10 minutes on the middle shelf.

4 Serve with grilled or barbecued lamb chops – or as a light lunch or supper dish, serving the tomatoes on slices of toast.

TIP •

We love proper bread sauce with roast chicken but I rarely buy white bread which is an essential ingredient. However, instant luxury bread sauce is a very good substitute for the real thing. To make it appear as though I have made it myself, I add some freshly grated nutmeg, a tablespoon of single cream or a teaspoon of butter and a twist of black pepper.

PAN CON TOMATE
(BREAD WITH TOMATOES)

This is another Catalan dish, which the Spanish serve as part of a tapas meal along with olives, fresh anchovies, clams, cured meats and sausages, etc. It is also a wonderful filler/nibble/blotting paper to be handed out at a barbecue while the meat is cooking. It tastes of summer.

When we used to go on huge family holidays to the Costa Brava, Jimmy was always in charge of making this dish. He got the preparation down to a fine art and invented the word GATSO to remind him of the order in which to use the ingredients: first the garlic, then the tomato, salt and the oil at the end.

MAKES PLENTY FOR 8 HUNGRY PEOPLE
1 large crusty, rustic loaf (a baguette is too thin)
Several large ripe, beef style tomatoes
150 ml (5 fl oz) olive oil
Salt
Garlic – as many cloves as you need

METHOD

1 Slice the bread and toast both sides – but don't stack the slices or the steam will make them soggy.

2 Peel the garlic and rub the clove over one side of the toasted bread. Cut a tomato in half and rub the fleshy side onto to the bread. Don't throw away the remaining skin – add it to the stock pot. Sprinkle some sea salt on top, finishing each slice with a drizzle of good olive oil. Arrange on a large platter and continue until you have enough to feed the hordes.

TIP •
The Catalans like to drape a few thin shreds of anchovies on top (salted or fresh). If you try this, then cut out the salt.

INDIAN CARROTS

I love the flavour of sweet, buttery carrots with cardamom. These can be prepared in advance and reheated.

450 g (1 lb) carrots, peeled and sliced diagonally
1 tbsp cardamom pods
25 g (1 oz) butter
$^1/_2$ tsp sugar
Salt
150 ml (5 fl oz) water (approx.)

METHOD

1 Put the carrot slices into a pan with the cardamom pods, butter, sugar, salt and water. Cover with a lid and bring to the boil for 5 minutes, shaking the pan every now and again. Remove the lid, reduce the heat to a fast simmer and continue cooking so that the water can evaporates, for a further 10 minutes. The carrots will be soft and glistening, glazed with the butter and sugar.

2 You can either amuse yourself for a few minutes and remove the cardamom pods one by one or leave that to your guests – these are mostly for flavour although some people do eat them.

CARROTS WITH SPRING ONIONS

4 medium carrots per person, peeled and sliced diagonally
Bunch of large spring onions, trimmed and quartered
1 dessertspoon butter
$^1/_4$ tsp salt
$^1/_2$ tsp sugar
150 ml (5 fl oz) water
Freshly chopped parsley

METHOD

1 Melt the butter in a saucepan and add the vegetables. Add the salt and sugar and about a cup of water. Bring to a boil and let it bubble so that some of the water evaporates.

2 When you are ready to serve, sprinkle with the fresh, chopped parsley.

TIP •

If onions are added raw to a mixed salad or sandwiches, sometimes they can have a bitter, harsh taste. In order to sweeten them, peel and slice them thinly and soak them for 20–30 minutes in cold water. Drain and dry in kitchen paper before using.

CARROT AND PARSNIP GRATIN

2 large parsnips, peeled
450 g (1 lb) carrots, peeled
25 g (1 oz) butter
1-2 large shallots, peeled and sliced
300 ml (8 fl oz) double cream (or half fat crème fraîche)
Salt and pepper to taste
Nutmeg

METHOD

1 Preheat the oven to gas mark 3 (170°C, 325°F).

2 Cut the parsnips and carrots into thin strips – if you have one, use the julienne blade on your processor. Blanch in a pan of boiling water for 2 minutes and drain well.

3 Melt the butter in a frying pan and cook the shallots until they become transparent but not brown. Tip into a shallow dish and add the parsnips and carrots. Season with salt and pepper and pour over the cream/crème fraîche. Mix well and grate a little nutmeg over the top.

4 Cover with foil and bake in the oven for about 1-1½ hours until soft.

5 Serve with a roast – they can be cooked at the same time.

COLCANNON (MASHED POTATO WITH CABBAGE AND SPRING ONIONS)

The Irish amongst us will know this dish well. It was the forerunner of the English 'Bubble and Squeak'.

450 g (1 lb) floury potatoes
225 g (8 oz) cabbage, curly kale or Tuscan kale
55 g (2 oz) butter
6 spring onions, trimmed and roughly chopped
150 ml (5 fl oz) milk
150 ml (5 fl oz) cream
Salt and pepper

METHOD

1 Peel and cook the potatoes and then mash them, removing any lumps. If you have a potato ricer use this, but do not put in a food processor.

2 Slice the cabbage (or curly kale) finely and steam until soft, about 5 minutes. Tuscan kale will take twice as long.

3 Heat half the butter in a pan and add the onions. Cook for 3 minutes, stirring now and then so they don't burn.

4 Heat the milk and cream. Fold the cabbage/kale and onions into the mashed potato and mix in the warmed milk and cream – don't pour in the whole lot in one go, do half first and add any extra if necessary.

5 Spoon into a dish and make a small hollow in the centre into which you place the remaining butter. It will melt with the heat from the vegetables and form a golden puddle. Serve as a side dish with a roast or eat as a meal on its own.

CHAMP

This is similar to colcannon but has no cabbage in the recipe. There are lots of other lovely names for this dish, such as *bruisy*, *cally* and *pandy*. It used to be prepared especially for the festival of Hallowe'en.

6 spring onions, trimmed and sliced
225 ml (¹/₂ pint) milk
450 g (1 lb) floury potatoes, peeled and chopped into smallish pieces
Salt and pepper
55 g (2 oz) butter

METHOD

1 Warm the onions with the milk in a saucepan, cooking until they are soft.

2 Boil the potatoes and mash, making sure there are no lumps. Don't use a food processor as it changes the texture of the potatoes. Add two-thirds of the milk to begin with, and spring onions, and season well with salt and pepper, mixing well, adding more of the milk if necessary.

3 Turn into a serving dish, make an indentation in the centre and drop in the butter. It will melt into the potatoes. Serve piping hot.

VEGETABLE BAKE

This can be prepared in advance and heated up later in the oven.

1 courgette, sliced
2–3 tomatoes, sliced
2 red onions, sliced
3 new potatoes in their skins, sliced
1 clove garlic, chopped
4 tbsp olive oil
2 tbsp fresh basil
1 dessertspoon oregano
Salt and pepper

1 packet sliced pancetta, chopped
25 g (1 oz) grated cheese (Cheddar, Emmental, Gruyère)
55 g (2 oz) fresh brown breadcrumbs

CHEESE SAUCE
25 g (1 oz) butter
25 g (1 oz) flour
225 ml ($1/2$ pint) milk
55 g (2 oz) grated cheese (Gruyère, Emmental,
Cheddar – your choice or you can mix and match)
1 tsp Dijon mustard
100 ml ($3^1/_2$ fl oz) crème fraîche
Salt and pepper

METHOD

1 Preheat the oven to gas mark 3 (170°C, 325°F).

2 Put all the prepared vegetables into a baking dish, add the chopped garlic, drizzle with the olive oil, sprinkle with the herbs, season with salt and pepper and bake on the middle shelf of the oven until the vegetables are soft but not burned. You may have to cover them loosely half way through with a piece of foil to protect them from the direct heat.

3 Put the chopped pancetta into a frying pan and cook until crisp, stirring every now and then. Remove from the pan and keep warm.

4 Make the cheese sauce: melt the butter with the flour and when hot, stir and cook for a couple of minutes. Pour in the milk, stirring briskly, and bring to the boil. Cook for a further 2 minutes, remove from heat and add the grated cheese and mustard. Mix well and add the crème fraîche, salt and pepper.

5 Remove the vegetables from the oven, pour over the cheese sauce. Scatter the cooked pancetta. Mix the rest of the grated cheese with the breadcrumbs and sprinkle over the dish.

6 Put under the grill until the topping bubbles and is turning a nice golden brown.

TIP •••
Add a beaten egg to the cheese sauce to give a fluffy, light topping like that of a moussaka.

VEGETABLE STIR-FRY

1 packet dried or fresh egg noodles

4 tbsp sunflower oil

4 tbsp good quality soy sauce

1 bunch of spring onions

Any combination of the following vegetables – as few
or as many as you wish (you will need in total about
650 g ($1^1/2$ lb) of vegetables):

$^1/2$ green pepper, de-seeded and sliced finely

1 large leek, washed and sliced finely

1 courgette, sliced finely

1 stick celery, washed and sliced

1 carrot, peeled and sliced finely

115 g (4 oz) mushrooms, washed and sliced

115 g (4 oz) bean shoots

1 large clove garlic, peeled and crushed

1 red or green chilli, de-seeded and chopped finely

2. 5 cm (1 inch) piece fresh ginger, peeled and grated

Toasted sesame oil for serving

METHOD

1 First of all, prepare the noodles according to the instructions. Then, heat half the oil in a wok, add the noodles and stir constantly for about 2 minutes. Add half the soy sauce and continue stirring for a further 2 minutes. Take off the heat and put in a dish to keep warm while you are cooking the vegetables.

2 Trim and wash the spring onions. Have ready a bowl of cold (or iced) water. Using a pointed knife, cut lengthways through the white part of the onion, roll it over and make another cut so that the bulb end is in quarters but still attached to the green stalk. Put them all into the water, cut end immersed for later. After a time, the cut onions will splay out like a champagne swizzle stick. Scatter them raw over the stir-fry when ready to serve.

3 Prepare the vegetables.

4 Heat the wok and add the remaining oil. Add garlic, chilli and ginger, stirring for 30 seconds and tip in the vegetables. Stir for a minute and cover. Stir every now and then for a couple of minutes and add the remaining soy sauce. Add the noodles, stir, then add another splash of soy. Serve immediately. A splash of toasted sesame oil at this point is a nice touch.

5 A pot of weak jasmine tea is a refreshing drink to serve with this.

TIPS •

You can always incorporate leftover cooked turkey, duck or chicken into this dish – toss in a little hot oil before adding the vegetables as this must be reheated thoroughly.

Frozen (thaw first) or fresh prawns make a good alternative to meat, but do not overcook or they will toughen.

Instead of noodles, cook some rice and serve it separately.

ZUCCHINI (COURGETTE) BAKE

This recipe was given to my mother by the son of some very dear friends. He became Australian Ambassador in one of the South American countries and his wife told me the following story. The elegant Embassy mansion had a serving hatch between the dining room and kitchen but in spite of this, the staff insisted on carrying everything along the corridors. This took quite a time and the food inevitably arrived cold. Some time into their stay, they were due to give a formal dinner to a gathering of important dignitaries; Linda tactfully suggested that the hatch might come into play.

All was going according to plan until the first course was about to be served. To her horror, through the opening to the kitchen a leg appeared, then an arm, precariously holding a dish. Her staff had taken her instructions literally!

SERVES 4
1.3 kg (3 lb) courgettes, top and tailed and grated
1 large onion, peeled and grated
Salt and pepper to taste
1 cup freshly chopped parsley
3–4 tbsp flour
2 eggs, beaten lightly
115 g (4 oz) strong grated cheese (such as mature Cheddar)
1 large tomato
25 g (1 oz) butter
1 tsp paprika

METHOD

1 Preheat the oven to gas mark 4 (180°C, 350°F).

2 Mix together the onion and courgettes and add the parsley, salt and pepper to taste, flour, eggs and half the grated cheese.

3 Butter a shallow dish and pour in the mixture – it should not be more than 5 cm (2 inches) deep. Place the sliced tomato around the edge and sprinkle the top with the remaining grated cheese; dot with the butter and dust with the paprika.

4 Bake in the oven for an hour or until set and lightly browned.

TIPS •

It is easy to halve the quantities for two people but cook for only 30-40 minutes.

Instead of baking all the mixture in one go, shallow-fry spoonfuls of the mixture to make fritters.

COURGETTE SALAD

**Several small courgettes, about 6 if they're
roughly the size of a sausage
2 tbsp freshly chopped mint
Oil for pan-frying
1 tbsp white wine vinegar
Salt and pepper to taste**

METHOD

1 Cut the courgettes into slices the thickness of a pound coin. Heat a little oil in a frying pan and sweat the courgettes for a few minutes, turning them now and again. They must neither turn brown nor be cooked through – you are aiming at al dente style with a bit of crunch. Remove from the heat.

2 Add the mint to the pan, then a tablespoon of vinegar, salt and pepper. Mix and turn into a dish to cool. Serve at room temperature.

ORANGE, OLIVE AND RAISIN SALAD

**6 oranges
85 g (3 oz) black olives
25 g (1 oz) seedless raisins**

**FOR THE DRESSING
115 g (4 oz) olive oil
55 g (2 oz) dry sherry
1 tbsp freshly chopped mint
2–3 sprigs thyme**

METHOD

1 Remove the zest from one of the oranges with a vegetable peeler, trying not to include any pith. Cut into very fine strips and blanch for a couple of minutes in a pan of boiling water. Drain and cool.

2 Using a sharp knife, remove the peel from the remaining oranges and the pith from the original orange and slice.

3 Add the olives and raisins.

4 Make the dressing by combining the oil, sherry, mint and thyme (can be done quickly in a screw-top jar) and add to the other ingredients. Stir, put into an attractive dish and chill before serving.

ORANGE SALAD

This goes well with wild duck.

1 orange per person
1 tbsp salad oil (grapeseed, rapeseed, sunflower, etc.)
Splash brandy
1 tsp caster sugar
1 tsp finely chopped chervil (for an aniseed taste) or tarragon

METHOD

1 Remove all the skin and pith from the oranges with a sharp knife. Cut into slices between the sections, removing any skin. Place onto a decorative plate.

2 Mix the salad oil with the brandy and caster sugar, and toss the oranges in the dressing.

3 Scatter the chervil or tarragon over the salad and serve.

MOCK FONDUE BAKED CHEESE

SERVES 4 AS A STARTER

**1 round soft cheese (Camembert for example)
in a wooden box**
1–2 cloves garlic, peeled and sliced
2–3 small sprigs rosemary
1 tbsp Calvados
French stick

METHOD

1 Preheat the oven to gas mark 6 (200°C, 400°F).

2 Take the cheese out of the wooden box and remove any paper wrapping. Replace it in its wooden box, but not the lid.

3 Pierce the cheese with the point of a knife and insert a piece of garlic in each slit, along with a small sprig of rosemary.

4 Drizzle with a little Calvados (but don't drown the cheese) and place the box on a metal sheet in the hot oven, middle shelf, for about 20–30 minutes.

5 Serve with sliced baguette to dip into the hot, melted cheese.

MACARONI CHEESE WITH MUSHROOMS AND LEEKS

This can be done in advance and, if you are feeding a vegetarian, the mushrooms provide a bit more substance. Serve on its own or with a green salad.

Before I give you the recipe, I wish to relate a little story concerning an elderly relative, now aged 96, ('I'm not looking forward to growing old…') and mushrooms. We used to take her out to lunch now and again and one day we went to The Mermaid pub in Rye. The dining room in this beautiful ancient building is narrow, intimate and peaceful. We settled down with a chilled bottle of Sauvignon to study the set lunchtime menu.

One of the starters included organic mushrooms. After a few moments, our companion boomed, 'Organic mushrooms? Organic? What's the difference? They're all grown in s**t!'

The dining room ground to a halt, freeze-framed, and you could have heard a pin drop. Unperturbed and certainly not in the slightest bit embarrassed, my mischievous relative looked at me over her glasses and gave the tiniest of winks. Ah, the joys of reaching maturity and allowing oneself to say exactly what one thinks...

115 g (4 oz) uncooked macaroni

1 leek

85 g (3 oz) mushrooms

25 g (1 oz) butter

1 tbsp flour

225 ml (¹/₂ pint) milk

85 g (3 oz) cheese (Emmental, Gruyère or Cheddar – or mix and match)

1 tsp Dijon mustard

Salt and pepper

Scant ¹/₄ tsp nutmeg

1–2 slices brown breadcrumbs

About 6 cherry tomatoes

METHOD

1 Preheat the oven to gas mark 6 (200°C, 400°F).

2 Begin by boiling a saucepan of water. Add half a teaspoon salt and throw in the macaroni. Give this several stirs during cooking – there is no need to add any oil to the water to prevent the pasta from sticking. The macaroni will take about 8 minutes to cook – sometimes a bit longer. Taste and if still al dente (with a little 'bite') remove from the heat and strain in a colander and put back into the saucepan, lid on, to keep warm.

3 Meanwhile, prepare the leek by removing the root end and trimming some of the dark green leaves. Cut the length of the leek and remove the outer leaves. Wash thoroughly and slice finely.

4 Wash the mushrooms, trim the ends of the stalks and slice finely.

5 Melt three-quarters of the butter in a pan and add the leek and mushrooms together. Let them cook on a medium heat (stirring

now and then) until almost cooked. Spread this mixture onto the bottom of a buttered oven dish.

6 Make the cheese sauce: put the flour and remaining butter into a non stick milk pan and stir whilst the butter is melting. Boil for a minute and then add the milk, stirring (or whisking) to incorporate it with the butter and flour so that there are no lumps. Bring to the boil, stirring all the time and once it is bubbling, cook for a further minute.

7 Remove from the heat and add all but 1 tablespoon of the grated cheese. Mix with the sauce and add the mustard, pinch of salt (not too much because the cheese will be salty) and a good grind or two of pepper. Grate a little fresh nutmeg into the sauce and stir well into the mixture. Add the sauce to the cooked macaroni, mix, then pour over the leek and mushrooms.

8 In a bowl, combine the breadcrumbs with the extra cheese and sprinkle over the cheesy macaroni.

9 Cut the cherry tomatoes in half and position around the edge of the dish.

10 Dot the top with the extra butter. Either bake on the top shelf of the oven for about 15 minutes until brown and bubbling and the tomatoes are cooked, or keep to one side for heating later.

TIP ••

If you want to cook some mushrooms but without any fat, either slice them or leave them whole and cook them in a saucepan with a little water and a good squeeze of lemon juice. Simmer until the liquid has evaporated (about 5–6 minutes) and the mushrooms are tender. Season with salt and pepper.

SAVOURY SUPPER SNACKS

MUSHROOM BAKE

450 g (1 lb) mushrooms, cleaned and sliced
85 g (3 oz) butter
2 cloves garlic
6 tbsp double cream
2 tbsp chopped parsley
Salt and pepper
Paprika to dust

METHOD

1 Preheat the oven to gas mark 7 (220°C, 425°F).

2 Lay the mushroom slices in a shallow baking dish.

3 Melt the butter, add the garlic, cream and parsley, and mix. Season well with salt and pepper and pour over the mushrooms.

4 Bake in the oven for about 15-20 minutes until bubbling and the mushrooms are cooked.

5 Sprinkle with a dusting of paprika and serve.

———————————————

SOFT AND TASTY AUBERGINES

This is a very quick and easy way of cooking aubergines without them mopping up gallons of oil.

1 to 2 aubergines, cut lengthways into slices
about a quarter of an inch thick
Olive oil
Zest and juice of 1 lemon
Dried mixed herbs
Salt and pepper

METHOD

1 Place the aubergine slices in a colander (over a bowl) and sprinkle them liberally with salt. Allow to drain for three to four hours.

2 Rinse the slices thoroughly under cold running water and dry them in a clean tea towel. Lay the aubergines onto a sheet of kitchen paper to continue drying in the air for about another thirty minutes.

3 Brush the upper surface of each slice with some olive oil. Heat a griddle pan until smoking hot and position the slices oild side down. Depending on how many aubergines you have prepared, you may have to do this in stages. While the first side is cooking, brush the other side of the aubergine slice with olive oil and, after about three minutes, turn the slices over to cook for a further three minutes.

4 Place the aubergine slices in a dish. Add a clove of peeled and crushed garlic, salt and pepper, the lemon zest and juice, a sprinkling of dried Italian mixed herbs and a good slug of olive oil. Stir carefully so as not to break up the aubergines and leave to cool.

5 These can be eaten immediately as a side dish or kept for later, but they are best served at room temperature. Remember that, if chilled, the olive oil will harden, but it will melt after half an hour out of the fridge.

STEAMED MISH-MASH

This looks like a very odd list of ingredients and an even stranger way of cooking them but bear with me. A dear friend (Bridget Köllerström) used to cook it for me when I rented her basement flat. She lived upstairs, but there was a connecting door and we saw each other daily. In the mid-seventies, Bridget had two jobs: one was as a dancer with the Royal Ballet, the other as choreographer for the fight scenes in the scandalous stage show, *Oh! Calcutta!* She loved the irony of working in the traditional atmosphere of the Opera House in Covent Garden in the morning, ending up in the Duchess Theatre in the afternoon – from the sublime to the ridiculous. Incidentally, that play's enigmatic title came from the French phrase, *Oh! Quel cul t'as!* which loosely translates (politely) as 'Oh! What a backside you have!' Now you know!

FOR 1 HEARTY SERVING
1 medium sized or 2 small tasty new potatoes – Jersey Royals if possible
2 strips smoked back bacon
2 large open (field) mushrooms
¼ cabbage (about 115 g [4 oz])
Fresh dill weed
Salt and pepper

METHOD

1 Scrub the skins of the potatoes, cut in half and place in a steamer.

2 Wash the mushrooms and snuggle these on top of the spuds.

3 Cut the cabbage into wedges and pile onto the rest. Drape the bacon on top of everything. Scatter over a couple of sprigs of the dill weed – this gives a nice, quirky taste. Season with salt and pepper. Steam for about 30 minutes or until the potatoes are cooked.

4 Lift everything onto a warm plate, dot with butter and some more freshly ground pepper. The smoky flavour of the bacon filters through and permeates the vegetables.

TIP •

Anything leftover can be fried in a little dripping or oil as an exotic bubble and squeak bolstered by the addition of a fried egg. Great for a hangover...

CAULIFLOWER AND BROCCOLI CHEESE

I do this for lunch very often instead of soup – it is always commented on and nothing is ever left. The cheeses used here are more delicate and less greasy than Cheddar which can be a bit heavy.

SERVES 4

1 large head cauliflower (choose one with nice tight, white curds and check that the outer leaves are not tired and wilting)

1 head broccoli (about 450 g [1 lb])

1 packet sliced pancetta, chopped

2 slices brown bread, made into crumbs

FOR THE CHEESE SAUCE

$1^1/_2$ tbsp flour

40 g ($1^1/_2$ oz) butter

425 ml ($^3/_4$ pint) milk

55 g (2 oz) grated Gruyère cheese

55 g (2 oz) grated Emmental cheese

1 tsp Dijon mustard

Salt and pepper
Scant 1/4 tsp freshly grated nutmeg
100 ml (3 1/2 fl oz) crème fraîche

METHOD

1 Preheat the oven to gas mark 6 (200°C, 400°F).

2 Prepare the cauliflower by cutting off the outside leaves, keeping any of the young, green inner ones and slice them finely. Cut it in half and slice the florets from the main trunk; the latter you add to your compost bucket. Wash the broccoli and as with the cauli, cut the florets away from the stem.

3 Fry the pancetta until really crispy. Drain off the fat.

4 Either steam or boil the vegetables until they remain slightly firm – al dente, like pasta.

5 Meanwhile, make your cheese sauce: put the flour and butter into a non-stick pan to melt. Cook for a minute to burst the flour molecules, stirring all the time. Gradually add the milk, using an egg whisk to avoid lumps. Continue until the sauce boils. Cook for another minute, remove from the heat and mix in the cheeses. Add the mustard, season with salt and pepper and half a dozen gratings of nutmeg. Finally, stir in the crème fraîche.

6 Drain the vegetables and put in a large gratin dish – a lasagne dish is ideal. Cover with the cheese sauce and scatter over the crispy pancetta.

7 Sprinkle the breadcrumbs over the top and dot with a small knob of butter (not more than a teaspoon).

8 Either put under a hot grill for 5 minutes to eat immediately, or keep for later and re-heat in a hot oven for about 15 minutes, or until the top is bubbling and brown.

TIP ••

You can add extra bulk and protein by hard boiling a couple of eggs, chopping and scattering them on top of the cheese sauce.

ONION QUICHE

280 g (10 oz) ready-made flaky pastry
450 g (1 lb) onions, peeled and sliced
25 g (1 oz) butter or goose fat
3 eggs, beaten
150 ml ('/4 pint) crème fraîche or double cream
1 tsp mixed, dried herbs (optional)
Salt and pepper

METHOD

1 Preheat the oven to gas mark 4 (180°C, 350°F).

2 Line a 25-cm (10-inch) quiche/tart mould with the pastry. Prick the base with a fork, line with baking parchment and scatter a packet of dried butter beans to weigh it down. These can be stored (once cold) in a jar to be used repeatedly and they are considerably cheaper than the special ceramic beads made for the purpose. Bake for about 10 minutes. Remove from the oven, shake off the beans, peel off the parchment and bake a further 5 minutes.

3 Meanwhile, cook the onions in a frying pan in the butter or goose fat. Cool slightly before pouring into the prepared pastry case.

4 Beat the eggs with the cream and season well. Stir in the mixed herbs at this point if you are including them. Pour this custard on to the onions and bake for 20–30 minutes or until the quiche is puffed up and golden and the pastry cooked.

LEFT-OVER CHEESEBOARD QUICHE

When we have friends in for a meal I always buy far too much cheese. Somehow it never seems to taste as nice the following day and invariably it ends up on the bird table. This is an excellent way of dealing with the problem. Also, don't throw away the pastry scraps – give these to the birds as they adore raw pastry.

1 packet ready-rolled flaky pastry
25 g (1 oz) butter
3 good sized leeks, washed and sliced finely

3 eggs
100 ml (3^1/$_2$ fl oz) crème fraîche
Salt and pepper
About 175 g (6 oz) leftover cheese, broken into bits
(Gorgonzola, Camembert, Brie, goat's, Stilton, etc.)

METHOD

1 Preheat the oven to gas mark 4 (180°C, 350°F).

2 Remove the pastry from the fridge 30 minutes before using so that it reaches room temperature. Then, take off the cellophane wrapping and unroll it into a buttered flan dish. Push the pastry into the sides. There may be a gap or two where the pastry hasn't reached the edge, so cut off any trimmings, moisten the areas which need to be filled in with a little water and attach the spare pastry, fixing it in place by pushing gently with your fingers. Once again, trim away any excess and prick the bottom with a fork. Put the flan case back into the fridge to chill for 30 minutes.

3 Melt 25 g (1 oz) butter in a large frying pan and add the leeks. Let them sweat for about 5–6 minutes, stirring every now and again.

4 Beat the eggs in a bowl (cracking them separately to check they are fresh and have no bits of shell); mix in the crème fraîche, and salt and pepper to taste.

5 Take the pastry case out of the fridge and spread the leeks over the base. Then disperse the cheese morsels over the leeks and pour on the egg custard.

6 Bake on middle shelf for at least 30 minutes. The filling should rise and be a lovely golden brown but you want to make sure that the pastry is cooked. Turn down the heat to medium, cover the quiche loosely with a piece of foil and bake a further 15 minutes.

7 Serve either hot, cold or warm with a green salad.

TIPS •

Instead of always using plain pastry for a topping, when I make this myself, sometimes I add a teaspoon of mixed dried herbs to the flour to add a little twist of flavour.

If you are being health-conscious, use half-fat crème fraîche.

ROQUEFORT BITES

1 packet ready-made flaky pastry
1 egg
1 packet Roquefort cheese

METHOD

1 Preheat the oven to gas mark 7 (230°C, 425°F).

2 Roll out the pastry to about 3 mm (⅛") in thickness and cut into squares just over an inch in size. Beat the egg with a little water and paint the edges of half the squares. Drop a little lump of Roquefort (about the size of a large hazelnut) into the centre of each square. It is a very strong cheese and a little goes a long way.

3 Take a pointed knife and slash three little parallel cuts in the centre of the remaining squares. Lift these 'lids' carefully and place on top of the cheese halves, pressing down on the edges to seal the bundles. Glaze with more beaten egg and put in the fridge until you are ready to bake them. Bake on a high shelf for about 5–6 minutes until puffed up and golden and serve warm (or at room temperature) as a nibble with a drink.

TIP •

If you make larger packets (5–8 cm [2–3 inches] square or even in rounds), they make a perfect light lunch course, served individually with a green salad.

TOMATO CUSTARD BAKE

650 g (1$^1/_2$ lb) sweet, ripe tomatoes or cherry tomatoes
4 eggs
25 g (1 oz) plain flour
200 ml (7 fl oz) pot crème fraîche
4 tbsp milk
Salt and pepper
85 g (3 oz) freshly grated Parmesan
Fresh herbs: basil, oregano or summer savory

METHOD

1 Preheat the oven to gas mark 5 (170°C, 190°F).

2 Butter a flan dish. Slice the tomatoes and place on the bottom or scatter the cherry tomatoes.

3 Beat the eggs and add to the flour, whisking well to remove any lumps. Beat the crème fraîche with the milk and add to the flour and egg mixture to make a smooth batter.

4 Season well with salt and pepper and add 55 g (2 oz) of the grated cheese (the equivalent of 2 tablespoons). Mix and pour over the tomatoes. Sprinkle the remaining cheese over the top and add the torn basil leaves and/or other chopped herbs.

5 Bake for approximately 20 minutes or until it is puffed up and golden brown. Serve warm with a salad.

RICE SALAD

This easy, fresh-tasting salad can be made the day before but make sure that the rice is cooled quickly and put straight into the fridge – bacteria grows alarmingly in cooked rice and, if you contract food poisoning after an Indian or Chinese meal, the chances are it comes from the rice.

As long as you are vigilant in your preparation, there should be no problems, but if there is any left over then throw it away. Better to be safe than sorry.

1 cup rice (uncooked)
$\frac{1}{2}$ cup salad oil
Salt and pepper to taste
$\frac{1}{3}$ cup white wine vinegar
1 green pepper, de-seeded and chopped
1 red apple, cored and chopped
3 spring onions, sliced
1 clove garlic, peeled and crushed
1 dessertspoon curry powder
115 g (4 oz) cashew nuts
2 tbsp raisins
2 tbsp sultanas
2 tbsp chopped parsley

METHOD

1 Rinse the rice thoroughly in cold water and cover with at least two inches of water. When cooked, rinse again in cold water, drain and allow to cool. (See method in recipe for Kedgeree, page 109)

2 In a bowl whisk the oil, salt and pepper and vinegar and add to all the other ingredients. Mix well and put into a plastic container with a lid and then into the fridge until needed. This will allow the flavours to develop.

3 Serve with cold meats and other salads.

CORN FRITTERS

1 large tin sweetcorn
2 tbsp soft brown sugar
3 eggs, beaten
55 g (2 oz) melted butter
4 tbsp grated Parmesan
Salt and pepper
150 ml (5 fl oz) corn oil for frying

METHOD

1 Put the sweetcorn in a bowl and add the sugar, eggs, butter and cheese. Season with salt and pepper. Mix thoroughly.

2 Heat the oil in a pan (about a cupful). Using a tablespoon as a measure, carefully spoon the mixture into the hot oil and fry for 2 minutes. When golden, flip over and fry the other side for a further minute or two. Lift out with a fish slice, drain on a piece of kitchen paper. Serve immediately.

3 Serve these with oven-baked breaded chicken (see page 92–3).

SWEETCORN SIDE DISH

I have used colourful bell peppers in this recipe. Green peppers are not as sweet as the other colours.

15 g (1/2 oz) butter
1 large can sweetcorn
1 small green chilli (or red if you prefer more heat), de-seeded
1 red, yellow or orange pepper or a mixture, de-seeded and sliced
Salt and pepper
Handful of flat leafed parsley, chopped

METHOD

1 Melt the butter in a saucepan and add the drained sweetcorn. Heat gently.

2 Add the chilli and peppers to the pan. There's no need here to cook them thoroughly – you want a bit of crunch.

3 Season with salt and pepper and remove from the heat. Add the parsley or, if you wish, some chopped dill or chervil, both of which taste faintly of aniseed.

4 Serve alongside any sort of grilled meat, chicken or fish.

Lentils, beans and pulses

I once knew a girl who fancied anything if it had a pulse. As for me, I fancy a pulse with anything! Along with lentils and beans, they have to be the most magical ingredients in the store cupboard, providing a treasure trove of inspiration. Not only are they extremely good for us (they are riddled with fibre and protein), but they also have the added bonus of being very low in fat – brilliant if you are on a diet. To be honest, I am far more likely to open a can of lentils or beans, as I am, like the majority of us, up against the clock, never thinking ahead in time to soak the dried ingredients in time for when I need them.

Tinned pulses and beans are a perfect addition to cold salads, retaining all their goodness and most of their flavour. They can also be mashed into hummus (butter beans are a delicious alternative to chick peas), but if you prefer to eat them hot, tip them into casseroles, soups, or transform them into a Brit version of Boston-baked beans. They can even be chucked in as a spontaneous ingredient to an omelette or a frittata (using leftover, cold roast potatoes).

Some lentils, the orange ones for example, and Puy lentils, have the advantage that they do not need any soaking and cook relatively quickly. Why not try Puy lentils mixed with yoghurt and fresh herbs for a summer salad served alongside cold poached salmon.

TIP •

Do not add salt to the cooking water as this will toughen lentils – add it last thing when they are thoroughly cooked.

WHITE BRAISED BEANS

This can be prepared the day before and goes very well with both lamb and pork.

**1 tin white haricot beans (or dried ones, soaked overnight
and cooked according to the instructions on the packet)**
2 slices smoked bacon, cut into pieces
1 shallot, peeled and chopped
**2 large tomatoes, cut into chunks
or 1 small tin chopped tomatoes**
1 tbsp concentrated tomato purée (approx.)
1 tsp freshly chopped thyme
1 small sprig rosemary
1 stick celery, sliced
2 bay leaves
1 clove garlic, chopped

METHOD

1 Rinse and drain the tinned beans or drain the cooked dried beans.

2 Fry the bacon in a casserole until brown. Add the shallot, stir for a minute and then add the tomatoes, skin and all (I never bother with peeling and de-pipping as it's too much effort). Pop in all the other ingredients, add enough water to cover, stir and simmer for approximately 45 minutes to 1 hour. Check every now and then, stirring as you go, to make sure it's not getting too dry.

TIP

To give more bulk to this dish and turn it into an inexpensive main course, leave out the smoked bacon and use fresh belly of pork. One strip should be more than enough per person (if they are large, two strips will easily feed three people). Cut the belly into chunks and brown in some oil, then add it to the above ingredients. Bring to the boil and simmer for at least $1\frac{1}{2}$ hours until the meat is tender. Mop up the fat with some kitchen paper and then sprinkle with chopped parsley. Serve with new potatoes and something green.

CURRIED LENTILS (DHAL)

This is a quick and easy dish either to eat with plain boiled rice and a salad of tomatoes and onions or as an accompaniment to a curry. This caters very much for English tastes using ready made curry powder as against a combination of individual spices. Similar recipes would have been served in British households in India at the time of the Raj.

1 cup red lentils (in their dry state)
1 onion, peeled and sliced
600 ml (1 pint) water or stock
1 tbsp curry powder (always fry any spices
before adding the liquid)
Salt and pepper

METHOD

1 Wash the lentils to remove any dust and pick through to remove any small stones.

2 Fry the sliced onions in a little oil until browned. Remove from the pan.

3 Fry the lentils until they change colour from orange to yellow, then add the curry powder and fry for a further minute, stirring all the while. Return the onions to the pan with the lentils and add either water or stock. Don't season at this stage. Bring to the boil and simmer until cooked – about 20 minutes. You may have to add a little more water during cooking as you don't want it to be too solid – dhal should have the consistency of slightly sloppy porridge. Season with salt and pepper.

TIP •
You can add a little more tang to this lentil dish by adding some raw chopped tomato (or half a tin of chopped tomatoes) at the beginning when you add the stock or water.

SPLIT YELLOW LENTILS

This is an easy-to-prepare dhal dish and can be done in several stages, in your own time. It can be eaten on its own with rice, naan bread or poppadoms or instead of potatoes with a meat dish.

225 g (8 oz) dried split yellow lentils
1 tbsp sunflower oil
1 large red onion, peeled and sliced
**2.5 cm (1 inch) piece of fresh root ginger,
peeled and finely grated**
**225 g (8 oz) fresh tomatoes, roughly chopped,
or 1 tin chopped tomatoes in juice**
1 red chilli
**2 tbsp fresh coriander leaves or 1 tbsp from
a jar of coriander in sunflower oil**
Salt and pepper

METHOD

1 Soak the lentils overnight in a basin with plenty of cold water. The next day, drain away the water and put the lentils into a large saucepan. Cover with lots of fresh cold water (at least a pint) and bring to the boil. Do not add any salt or this will toughen the lentils and prevent them from breaking down into a purée. Simmer for at least 40 minutes (it can sometimes take nearly an hour) until most of the water has been absorbed and the lentils are very soft and mushy. You may need to add a little water during the cooking if the lentils have absorbed the original water and remain slightly raw. Once they are cooked and soft, remove from the heat and spoon into a dish and put to one side. You can either carry on with the recipe, or leave the next stage until later.

2 Heat the oil in a frying pan and add the onions. Cook on a medium heat for 5 minutes, stirring every now and again. Add the ginger to the pan.

3 Split the chilli in half and remove the seeds and the whitish ribs. Chop very finely and add to the other ingredients. Stir.

4 Add the fresh tomatoes or tip in a tin of chopped tomatoes. Add the coriander and give everything a good stir. Cook for a further 5 minutes on a medium heat.

5 Tip in the cooked lentils and season well with salt and pepper. The lentils (if you did them in advance) will now be a solid mass like cold mashed potato but the heat from the pan will loosen them enabling you to mix everything well. Simmer for about 20 minutes, stirring every now and again to prevent it sticking to the bottom of the pan. Taste for seasoning and adjust accordingly. This can sit quite happily in a warm oven until needed.

TIPS •

If, when you are making a curry, the sauce splits or curdles, add a small quantity of water and stir – it should make it join together again.

An easy way to remove the seeds from fresh chillies: cut off the stalk end and roll the chilli in the palms of your hands. Tap onto your chopping board and they should fall out of the end. You can then slice it into rounds. Wear Marigold or surgical gloves to protect your skin.

EMERGENCY PICKY-PICKY LUNCHES

I relish the challenge of cooking on the hop and, so that I can cater for emergency mouths, I try to keep a selection of the following in the fridge and larder:

Packet of organic smoked salmon
Packet of parma ham
Organic eggs
Cherry or large tomatoes
Cucumber
Celery
Carrots
Onions: ordinary, red and spring
Tins of mixed salad beans
Tins of sweetcorn

Tins of good quality fish like sardines in olive oil, smoked tuna slices, etc.
Jar of marinated sweet herrings (in the fridge)
Lump of good Parmesan cheese
Sweet and sour gherkins
Good quality mayonnaise (Hellmann's with olive oil or Delouis fils French mayonnaise are two of the best)
Cold water-caught frozen large prawns
Cooked beetroot
Melon
Fresh herbs, such as basil, parsley and coriander
Lettuce

Depending on how many I am having to feed, I hard-boil some eggs (one per person); as soon as they are cooked immerse in cold water. As soon as they are cool enough to handle, tap the egg on the work surface and roll it around in the palm of your hands – this will loosen the shell.

Over the years we have collected several large Victorian platters and these are ideal for this sort of lunch as you can lay everything out like a mixed hors d'oeuvres – letting people help themselves to whatever they want.

TIP •
I keep a few part-baked baguettes in the freezer for such unplanned meals.

Here are some suggestions for quick lunches:

A **tomato salad** is quick and easy: slice the tomatoes, lay them on a dish. Slice a red onion in rings and add to the tomatoes. Drizzle some olive oil and vinegar (plus a dash of balsamic vinegar) and a good squirt of lemon juice. Sprinkle some sea salt and a couple of grinds of pepper and a few torn basil leaves.

Cut a **melon** into small boats (removing the skin and pips) to serve alongside the **Parma** ham.

Hard-boil the **eggs**, cut in half. To keep them from rolling over, shred a little lettuce and snuggle in the eggs. If you really want to show off, put some mayonnaise into an icing bag with a decorative nozzle and pipe a swirl on top of the yolks. Sprinkle with a dusting of paprika.

Thaw some **frozen prawns** and mix with **pink sauce** (page 181) or serve plain with lemon wedges and a jar of mayonnaise.

Open a tin or two of **fish** (sardines in various sauces or plain olive oil, smoked and ordinary tuna, etc.) and decorate with parsley and lemon wedges.

If you have some cooked **beetroot**, chop it up and mix with **half mayonnaise/half natural yoghurt**. Decorate with chopped chives. Serve this separately or everything will turn puce coloured!

Finely grated **carrot** mixed with oil, vinegar, lemon juice and salt and pepper is always welcome and easy to prepare.

A delicious salad (which keeps for a day or two in the fridge if not eaten all at once) is made from a tin of **mixed salad beans**. You can add **sweetcorn** as well to bulk it out. Rinse the beans thoroughly under running water, drain and put into a bowl. Chop up a **shallot** or **red onion**, add any fresh, chopped **herbs** such as parsley, chives or chervil. You can add **chopped walnuts**, **pumpkin** and **sunflower seeds** for more crunch. Pour on some vinaigrette and mix thoroughly. This bean salad is even better if a tin of **tuna** is added and perhaps a stick of **celery**, finely sliced.

Make a platter of salad with the **lettuce**, torn into pieces and then (using a vegetable peeler) dot it with shavings of **Parmesan**. Add a few **cherry tomatoes** cut in two, some chopped **spring onions**, perhaps a few slices of **celery** and dress with **vinaigrette** (page 180). If you have any **walnut** pieces or halves, break these into little bits and dot about for a bit of extra crunch. Once again, **sunflower** and **pumpkin seeds** or toasted **pine nuts** all make good additions.

Wash and trim a bunch of fat, juicy and very fresh **radishes**. Pile them into a bowl of iced water. Eat them the French way: have a pat of **unsalted butter** and a little dish of sea salt; dip the end of the **radish** in the salt and attach a tiny nugget of butter on the end. Crunch into it and eat it in one piece, along with some baguette. The peppery flavour of the vegetable harmonises beautifully with the creamy butter and salt.

Once assembled, put the dishes and platters on the table alongside jars of pickled gherkins, mayonnaise, chutney and lots of crusty bread, and let everyone tuck in.

TIP ••

I don't cook risottos as I don't have the patience to cope with all that continual stirring. However, if you want to have a go, a useful tip is the following: put the washed rice onto an oven tray, drizzle with a little oil and bake in a hot oven for 2 minutes. Then cook it with stock, but poured on in one go. Bring to the boil and stir, then reduce the heat to a gentle bubbling simmer and continue cooking for 30 minutes or until the rice is cooked and most of the liquid is absorbed. You will still need to give a stir now and again.

Party Buffet Salads

These can all be prepared in advance.

BULGUR WHEAT SALAD

Any leftovers of this dish will be absolutely fine the next day, if kept in the fridge overnight.

FOR 6 SERVINGS
1 packet organic bulgur wheat
1 cucumber, cut into small dice
6 tomatoes, chopped roughly into small pieces
1 handful (about 4 tablespoons)
of fresh mint, chopped finely
1 handful (about 4 tablespoons) of parsley, chopped finely
6 spring onions, chopped finely
Juice 2 lemons
4 tbsp good olive oil
1 tsp sea salt
6 twists of freshly ground pepper

METHOD

1 Begin by cooking the bulgur wheat according to the instructions on the packet, but add an extra amount of water – it makes cooking the grains easier and any excess, when they are ready, can be drained away; better than allowing it to stick and burn to the pan. Allow to cool.

2 To the cold bulgur wheat, add all the other ingredients, stir and serve in a pretty bowl. This can keep safely for a day or two in the fridge.

MIXED BEAN SALAD

In the winter, I add a handful of sultanas to this salad, which injects a subtle sweetness.

SERVES 4
1 tin mixed salad beans (organic if possible)
1 tin kidney beans
1 large tin sweetcorn niblets
2 sticks celery, sliced finely
1 large red onion, peeled and chopped finely
1 good handful of chopped parsley, chives or whatever herb is to hand
1 sharp apple, skin on, chopped finely
Chopped walnuts and/or seeds of any sort: pumpkin, sunflower, etc. (optional)
$^1/_3$-$^1/_2$ packet feta cheese

FOR THE DRESSING
1 tsp Dijon mustard
100 ml (3$^1/_2$ fl oz) olive oil
60 ml (2 fl oz) vinegar (red, white wine or cider)
Salt and pepper
1 clove garlic (optional)

METHOD

1 Begin by rinsing the tinned beans and corn under a running tap. Drain and place into a mixing bowl.

2 Add all the other vegetables and seeds and nuts if required. Scatter the salad with some crumbled feta cheese.

3 For the dressing: in a jar, combine the mustard, oil, vinegar, salt and pepper. Peel and chop the garlic, add if wanted. Shake till blended.

4 Incorporate the dressing into the salad; put into a serving bowl and cover with cling film before putting into the fridge until needed.

TIP •

This salad lasts 2–3 days and any leftovers, if combined with a tin of tuna or other tasty fish, makes a really nice lunch accompanied by some crusty bread – which can also be from the day before and refreshed in the oven. Waste not, want not!

CUCUMBER A LA CREME

1 cucumber, peeled and thinly sliced
150 ml (5 fl oz) crème fraîche
1 tbsp white wine vinegar
1 tbsp olive oil
Salt and pepper

METHOD

1 Place the cucumber slices in a colander on top of a bowl. Sprinkle with some salt. Cover and allow to stand for about an hour. This is to remove some of the liquid in the cucumber. Rinse thoroughly under running cold water, drain and squeeze out as much of the water as you can. Finish off by drying in a clean tea towel.

2 Mix the cream with the vinegar, oil, salt and pepper and mix with the cucumber. Put into a pretty bowl and refrigerate until needed.

3 Serve with hot herb or garlic bread.

TIP •

You can refine this dish by peeling the skin, cutting the cucumber in half and removing the pips before sprinkling with the salt, but the end quantity will be slightly less.

Sauces and accompaniments

A sauce can make or break a dish – I have never gone in for complicated lengthy preparations, preferring to whisk up something with what's in the fridge or cupboard, counting on the ingredients to speak for themselves. Varying combinations of good butter, lemons and cream are about all you need to transform a simple fillet of fish or an overripe banana into something special. The old adage 'less is more' is the perfect benchmark.

NO-FUSS TOMATO SAUCE FOR PASTA

**1 tin chopped tomatoes in juice or 450g
(1 lb) ripe tomatoes (pips, skin 'n' all)
2–3 cloves garlic, peeled and chopped finely
3 tbsp olive oil
$\frac{1}{2}$ tsp sugar
Salt and pepper
Pasta of your choice
Basil leaves**

METHOD

1 If you are using fresh tomatoes chop them roughly.

2 Heat the oil in a pan and add the garlic and cook for half a minute. Add the tomatoes, sugar, salt and pepper and stir. Leave to simmer, stirring from time to time. You want the tomato sauce to be thick and slightly jammy in consistency.

3 While this is under way, cook the pasta. When the pasta is cooked, strain through a sieve, pour the tomato sauce into the pasta pan, tip in the pasta, add a drizzle of olive oil, twist or two of black pepper and mix well.

4 Serve in a large bowl and scatter torn basil leaves over it. Have a block of Parmesan and a cheese grater handy for everyone to help themselves.

EASY PEASY PESTO

**2 tbsp pine nuts
2 handfuls of fresh basil leaves
1 large clove garlic
150 ml (5 fl oz) olive oil
$\frac{1}{4}$ tsp dried chilli flakes
Salt and pepper
2 tbsp freshly grated Parmesan, plus more to serve
Pasta of your choice**

METHOD

1 Place the pine nuts on an oven tray and roast under the grill for barely a minute until just golden, watching closely so that they don't burn – you only want a whisper of colour.

2 Put these into a measuring jug and add all the other ingredients. Blitz with a hand-held electric blender.

3 When your pasta is cooked al dente, drain in a colander, put back into the saucepan and add the sauce. Stir for 30 seconds on the hotplate and serve immediately with some more freshly grated Parmesan.

TIP •

If you find the above quantity of pesto too much for two people, any leftover can be stored in a screw-topped jar in the fridge for about a week, first covering the surface with a little olive oil. It is also delicious added to a bowl of vegetable or cabbage soup (see page 21–22).

BROCCOLI PESTO

Sometimes it is nigh on impossible to get children to eat a vegetable let alone a green one, but this is in disguise – most children love pasta and this should do the trick!

1 head of broccoli
1 tbsp pine nuts
1 large clove garlic, peeled
70 g (2¹/₂ oz) freshly grated Parmesan cheese
Freshly ground black pepper
150 ml (5 fl oz) olive oil

METHOD

1 Wash the broccoli and cut the florets from the main trunk. Keep this for later to add to a soup. Steam the florets for 5 minutes until nearly cooked – you want them to have a little 'bite' to retain as much of the goodness and flavour as possible.

2 You can roast the pine nuts if you want to – this gives them a nuttier taste. Either put them under the grill (see Easy Peasy Pesto, page 168) or heat a dry frying pan and add the pine nuts. Shake the

pan to turn them, watching carefully. In a short space of time they will turn a light golden brown. When this stage is reached, remove immediately from the heat or they will burn.

3 Put the garlic into a blender with the broccoli, cheese, pine nuts, a few twists of black pepper and a little olive oil. Blend the ingredients for a moment then add the remaining oil in a drizzle through the opening of the blender lid as you continue to whizz. If it is too thick, then slacken with a little cold water. It is now ready to use.

FRESH TOMATO KETCHUP

3. 6 kg (8 lb) ripe tomatoes, chopped, skins and pips included
6 onions, peeled and sliced
2 large red peppers, de-seeded and sliced
2 large cloves garlic, peeled and crushed
115 g (4 oz) soft brown sugar
1 tbsp salt
450 ml (16 fl oz) red wine vinegar
Enough water to cover the vegetables in the pan

SPICES
½ tsp dried chilli flakes
2 bay leaves, torn
1 tbsp dried celery seed (not celery salt)
1 tbsp yellow mustard seed
1 tsp black peppercorns
1 stick cinnamon

METHOD

1 This must be cooked in a large preserving pan, made from anything other than copper, which will react with the vinegar.

2 Put the tomatoes, onions, red peppers and garlic into the pan and add enough cold water to cover. Bring to the boil and simmer until everything is soft.

3 Using the electric hand blender, give a light whizz to break up the ingredients and then pass everything through a sieve. This will take a little time because you can only do small amounts in one go. Discard the skin, pips, etc. as you go.

4 Wash the preserving pan, and pour back in the tomato mix. Put the spices into a piece of muslin and secure well with a piece of string. Add this to the pan.

5 Bring to the boil and simmer until nice and thick, stirring every now and again. You want it to be like commercial ketchup. This process could easily take 45 minutes to 1 hour. Note that the sauce will thicken a little further as it gets cold.

6 Pour into sterilised bottles or jars and cover when cold. Store in the fridge.

TIP •
This tomato sauce goes very well with fried fish and also as an accompaniment to shepherd's pie.

QUICK BBQ SAUCE

1 tbsp brown (demerara) sugar
4 tbsp tomato ketchup (see page 170)
2 tbsp soy sauce

METHOD
1 Mix all the ingredients together thoroughly.

BAKED APPLES FOR SAVOURY DISHES

These are an elegant alternative to apple sauce and complement roast pheasant perfectly.

SERVES 4
4 dessert apples (such as Cox's Orange Pippin)
55 g (2 oz) sultanas
2 tbsp Calvados or brandy
25 g (1 oz) butter

METHOD
1 Core the apples and cut through the skin of each fruit in a circle with a sharp knife, around two-thirds of the way up each apple. This will stop them exploding as they cook.

2 Soak the sultanas in the alcohol for about an hour (any left over can be stored in a screw-topped jar and kept for another day).

3 Pile the drunken sultanas into the cavities in each apple, top with a knob of butter and bake in the oven to gas mark 6 (200°C, 400°F) for about 15–20 minutes, or until soft in the centre.

TIP •
Put these apples in the oven at the same time as a breast of pheasant as they will take the same time to cook.

APPLE SAUCE

2 large cooking apples, peeled and sliced thinly
75 g (1¹/₂ oz) butter
55 g (2 oz) sugar
4 tbsp water

METHOD

1 Place the apples in a pan with the butter, sugar and a little water. Simmer until soft and mash with a fork.

UNUSUAL SAUCE FOR FISH OR COLD ROAST MEAT

This spicy sauce should be served cold and goes well with yesterday's roast, or with fish cooked in a court bouillon (see Tip on page 116).

6 tbsp olive oil
3 medium onions, sliced
55 g (2 oz) tomato purée
4 tbsp cider vinegar
3 tbsp dry white wine
1 tbsp Worcestershire sauce
3 sprigs thyme
1 bay leaf
2 cloves garlic, peeled and crushed
4 tbsp runny honey
1 tsp Dijon mustard
Salt and pepper
Dash of Tabasco sauce

METHOD

1 Heat the oil in a pan and cook the onions until very soft and begin to take on some colour. Add the concentrated tomato purée, then the vinegar. Bring to the boil and cook for 2 minutes, stirring all the while.

2 Add the wine, Worcestershire sauce, thyme, bay leaf, garlic, honey and mustard. Leave to simmer for 15 minutes until the sauce becomes slightly thickened and creamy in texture.

3 Season with salt and pepper and add the dash of Tabasco.

SAUCE TARTARE (1)

Serve this sauce with fried fish or scampi.

1 onion, peeled and sliced
2 tbsp olive oil
Yolks from 4 hard-boiled eggs (see Tip below)
Salt and freshly ground black pepper
1 tbsp white wine vinegar
2 small gherkins, chopped
1 dessertspoon capers, chopped
1 tbsp chopped parsley

METHOD

1 Fry the onion in a little oil until soft and just beginning to take on some colour. Put to one side to cool.

2 In a bowl, mash the egg yolks with a fork into a paste. Add a good amount of freshly ground pepper and a pinch of salt. Gradually drop in the oil (as though you were making a mayonnaise) beating all the time, then add the vinegar and mix well.

3 Beat the fried onions to turn them into a purée or put into a small blender, and add this to the egg mixture.

4 Finally, mix in the gherkins, capers and parsley.

TIP •
Don't throw away the whites – chop them and add to a salad of cold asparagus or green (French) beans, some chopped parsley and chives, and an oil and vinegar dressing.

SAUCE TARTARE (2)

I include this second recipe because it can be done in the shake of a nanny goat's tail!

2 medium gherkins
1 dessertspoon capers
1 shallot or 2 spring onions
2 tbsp good ready-made mayonnaise
1 dessertspoon freshly chopped parsley
Freshly ground pepper

METHOD

1 Chop by hand as finely as possible (no need to dirty the blender for this) the gherkins, capers and shallot/spring onions. Mix in the mayonnaise and parsley and several twists of pepper.

TIP ••

You can make an equally tasty sauce by substituting a finely chopped green pepper for the gherkins and capers.

SPECIAL FISH DIP

55 g (2 oz) can anchovies in olive oil
225 g (8 oz) cream cheese
150 ml (5 fl oz) fresh single cream
Pepper

METHOD

1 Drain the anchovies and soak them in a bowl of cold milk for 30 minutes.

2 Beat the cheese with the cream until light and fluffy.

3 Drain the anchovies, pat dry with kitchen paper and chop finely. Add to the cheese mixture and freshly ground black pepper to taste.

4 Spoon into a serving bowl and chill in the fridge. Serve with crudités such as small fingers of celery, carrot, cucumber, peppers or savoury biscuits and crisps.

JUST-RIGHT SIMPLE SAUCE FOR FISH

This goes perfectly with any sort of steamed or fried fish.

55 g (2 oz) butter
Juice 1 lemon
Pinch cayenne pepper

METHOD

1 Melt the butter in a pan (don't let it boil), add the lemon juice and cayenne; mix.

2 The only vegetable served should be plain boiled or steamed potatoes. Drizzle the buttery sauce over everything.

SAUCE PIQUANTE

1 cup ready-made mayonnaise
1 tsp French or English mustard
4–6 small gherkins, chopped
1 tsp anchovy essence
1 tbsp chopped chives or 4 spring onions

METHOD

1 Mix all the ingredients together and serve with fried fish.

EGG SAUCE

This old-fashioned but delicious accompaniment to fried fish smacks of traditional golf clubs (the sort where women are *persona non grata* and are only allowed to play on a Tuesday when the kitchen is closed – you know the kind I mean). It is so quick to make and is great with pan-fried fillets of fish.

2 medium sized hard-boiled eggs
Salt and pepper
1 tbsp freshly chopped parsley (optional)
Cayenne pepper (optional)

WHITE SAUCE
25 g (1 oz) butter
1 tbsp flour
300 ml (¹/₂ pint) milk

METHOD

1 Chop the hard-boiled eggs into little pieces.

2 Make the white sauce: melt the butter and flour in a non stick pan, stirring for a minute when it begins to boil. Add the milk in one go and stir using an egg whisk to avoid lumps. Bring to the boil and cook for a further minute, stirring all the while.

3 Remove from the heat, season with salt and pepper; gently incorporate the eggs, and parsley if desired.

4 Serve in a dish with a ladle or in a jug – it should be neither solid nor runny – something in between. A pinch of cayenne peps it up with extra heat.

MARINADE FOR CHOPS

Use with grilled or barbecued chops, sausages, etc.

ENOUGH FOR ABOUT 8 CHOPS OR CUTLETS
2 tbsp ordinary olive oil
1 tbsp Worcestershire sauce
Juice 1 lemon
2 tbsp soy sauce
1 clove garlic, peeled and crushed
Lots of freshly ground black pepper
A little salt (the soy is usually salty enough)
Herbs (optional) – thyme, rosemary, marjoram, etc.

METHOD

1 Mix all the ingredients together.

2 Put the chops in a bowl and pour over the marinade, turning them with a spoon. Cover with cling film and keep in the fridge until needed. They don't need a long time to marinate and can if necessary be used immediately.

HOT LEMON DIP

This is a tasty dip for barbecued sausages.

115 g (4 oz) butter
1 clove garlic, peeled and crushed
4 level tsp flour
2 level tbsp sugar
$1/2$ level tsp salt
Freshly ground pepper
$1/2$ level tsp dried thyme
$1/2$ tsp Tabasco
Grated rind of 1 lemon and juice of 2 lemons (about 4–6 tbsp)
150 ml ($1/4$ pint) chicken stock

METHOD

1 Melt the butter, add the garlic and stir in the flour. Cook for 2 minutes stirring all the while.

2 Add all the remaining ingredients and stir. Cover and simmer for 15 minutes. Put into a bowl and allow to cool.

PRAWN DIP

Another BBQ sauce, especially good for serving with giant prawns.

1 tbsp horseradish sauce (ready made)
Juice 1 lemon
1 tbsp tomato ketchup
2 tbsp mayonnaise
1 tbsp crème fraîche (optional)

METHOD

1 Mix all the ingredients in a bowl using a whisk to a smooth cream.

GREAT-GRANNY'S NO OIL SALAD DRESSING

This tastes like commercial salad cream and is handy if you have a friend or member of the family who can't take too much oil. It makes a classic sauce for a coleslaw or potato salad.

1 cup vinegar
2 tsp made mustard – English or Dijon
3 tbsp sugar
1/4 tsp salt
2–3 eggs, beaten
1 tsp butter

METHOD

1 Boil the vinegar and pour over the mustard, sugar, pinch of salt and eggs. Beat together and strain into a double boiler. Add small piece of butter.

2 Stir over the hot water until it thickens. Once cool, refrigerate and it will keep for 2 weeks.

PERFECT FRENCH DRESSING

Just like the one you have at the motorway stops in France – no sugar, no garlic, no nonsense. Use a clean 450 g (1 lb) jam jar to mix the dressing in – half fill it with oil and then add the vinegar and other ingredients. A butterhead lettuce is ideal for this dressing.

**Twice as much oil
(sunflower, rapeseed, corn, for example)
as vinegar – red wine is the classic choice
1 heaped tsp Dijon mustard
1/4 tsp freshly ground black pepper
1/4 tsp salt**

METHOD

1 Put all the ingredients together in the jar. Use what you need for one salad and keep the rest for another day.

OLIVE OIL DRESSING

**1 tsp Dijon mustard
4 tbsp good extra virgin olive oil
2 tbsp red or white wine or cider vinegar
1 small clove garlic, peeled and chopped
Salt and pepper
Juice 1/2 lemon**

METHOD

1 Put the mustard into the salad bowl and add the remaining ingredients except the oil. Mix thoroughly then add the oil slowly, blending as you go.

TIP •

Don't add the salad to the bowl until you are ready to eat it or it will absorb the oil and go transparent and slimy. However, you can almost get away with it if you put salad servers in the bowl, crossing them over each other. Drop the leaves on top and the servers will keep most of the salad away from the dressing, until ready to be tossed. An American friend of ours (an excellent cook) made a pretty good gazpacho (chilled tomato soup) using up left over, dressed salad.

HARD-BOILED EGG MAYONNAISE

A good substitute for those who should not eat raw egg, such as the elderly and very young.

4 eggs
1 tbsp vinegar
1 tbsp Dijon mustard
200–225 ml (7–8 fl oz) oil
1 dessert spoon chopped parsley and/or chives
Salt and pepper

METHOD

1 Separate the yolks from the whites of the eggs. Mash the egg yolks with a fork and add the vinegar and mustard. Mix well and pour in the oil, little by little, beating as you mix.

2 Stir in the chopped egg whites, then add the chopped chives and/ or parsley.

PRAWN COCKTAIL SAUCE

150 ml (¼ pint) lightly whipped cream
**Enough tomato ketchup to colour it
light pink (about 1 tbsp)**
Couple of dashes of Tabasco
1 tbsp lemon juice
1 tsp sherry (optional but nice)

METHOD

1 Lightly combine all the ingredients into a smooth sauce using a hand whisk.

MUSTARD SAUCE

To serve with fish.

2 tbsp butter
2 tbsp fish liquor if handy, or plain water if not
1 dessertspoon chopped parsley
1 tsp lemon juice
2 tsp Dijon mustard
1 egg yolk

METHOD

1 Melt the butter in a pan and heat until it just begins to brown. Remove from heat and add the fish liquor or water, the parsley, lemon juice and mustard. Mix well and add the egg yolk.

2 Return to the stove and heat gently, stirring constantly until thick enough to coat the back of the spoon – don't boil or the egg will scramble.

3 Serve with steamed or fried fish and lemon wedges.

QUICK AND EASY HUMMUS

I love hummus but given the chance, I would always make it myself because it is so quick and easy. The recipe should contain tahini, which is a rich paste made from sesame seeds. However, since you only need a very small amount (about a tablespoon) and once opened, the jar should be consumed within a month, it is nearly always wasted – even with my appetite. This is a tasty alternative which takes only minutes to produce.

1 410 g (14 oz) can of organic chick peas
1 large clove of garlic, peeled
Juice 1 or 2 lemons
$\frac{1}{2}$ cup olive oil
$\frac{1}{2}$ tsp salt and freshly ground pepper
Water
Paprika

METHOD

1 Drain and thoroughly rinse the chick peas and put into a small blender.

2 Add the garlic clove to the chick peas along with the juice of one lemon to begin with, half a cup of olive oil, and seasoning. Blend until it reaches a purée. If it is very firm, add a little cold water. Blend again and taste. This is when you may wish to add extra lemon juice and/or seasoning.

3 Scrape out of the blender into a pretty bowl and pour on a drizzle of olive oil. Sprinkle the surface with some paprika and serve with raw carrots, cucumber and peppers cut into strips, bread sticks or hot pitta bread, toasted and cut into triangles.

SIMPLY WONDERFUL STUFFING FOR DUCKLING

85 g (3 oz) butter
115 g (4 oz) white breadcrumbs
450 g (1 lb) cooking apples, peeled and sliced thinly
Salt and pepper
2 tsp sugar
$1/4$ tsp ground cinnamon

METHOD

1 Fry the breadcrumbs in the butter in a frying pan until golden.

2 Add the apple slices to the pan. Stir, cover and cook on low heat until soft.

3 Add salt and pepper, sugar and cinnamon.

3 When cool, use it to stuff a duckling under its skin (see recipe for roast goose, page 105). If you fill the cavity of the bird, add an extra 15 minutes to your cooking time.

PICKLED WALNUT STUFFING FOR CHRISTMAS GOOSE

1 large onion, peeled and chopped finely
1 large cooking apple, peeled and chopped finely
2 tsp chopped sage and thyme
Grated rind and juice 1 lemon
6–8 pickled walnuts, chopped finely
225 g (8 oz) fresh brown or white breadcrumbs
Salt and pepper
55–85 g (2–3 oz) butter
1 egg, beaten

METHOD

1 Sweat the onion in the butter until soft then mix in all the other ingredients, except for the egg, and cook for about 5 minutes.

2 Remove from the heat and when cool enough, add the beaten egg which will bind the stuffing. Once cold, use to stuff a goose (see page 105).

TIP •

When you want to cook cranberries at Christmas time for the sauce to go with the turkey or goose, never add sugar until the fruit is well and truly cooked. If you do, the skins toughen. To 450 g (1 lb) of cranberries, add 150 ml (5 fl oz) liquid (this can be a mixture of orange juice, port and/or water). Then, when the fruit is soft, add 225 g (8 oz) sugar. Heat gently, stirring until the sugar has dissolved. Boil for a couple of minutes and set aside to cool to be used later.

ONION GRAVY

25 g (1 oz) butter
3 or 4 red onions (about 225 g [8 oz]), peeled and sliced into rings
150 ml (¹/₄ pint) chicken stock
¹/₂ cup red wine
1 tsp demerara sugar
1 tsp Worcestershire sauce
Salt and pepper

METHOD

1 Melt the butter in a solid frying pan and when hot, add the onions. To get the most flavour, long and gentle cooking is the best, but if you are in hurry, pump up the heat and halve the cooking time.

2 When the onions are soft and beginning to take on some colour, add the stock, the wine, sugar and Worcestershire sauce. Season with salt and pepper, stir and bring to the boil.

3 Simmer for as long as it takes for half the liquid to have reduced. Check for seasoning and adjust accordingly.

FAIL-PROOF YORKSHIRE PUDDING

SERVES 4
2 eggs
Flour
Milk and water mixed
PLUS:
1 tsp vinegar
2 tbsp dripping
Pinch salt and pepper

METHOD

1 Preheat the oven to gas mark 6 (200°C, 400°F).

2 Put the dripping into a small roasting dish and allow to get to a smoking heat in the oven.

3 Meanwhile, break the eggs into a cup and note how far up the cup they go. Tip them into a separate container and beat lightly with a fork.

4 Next, measure the same volume of flour as for the eggs into the cup and put into a dish. Do the same with the milk (or a milk and water mix for a lighter batter).

5 Sieve the flour into a mixing bowl, make a 'well' in the centre and pour in the beaten eggs. Work in the flour, using a whisk and then gradually add the milk. Mix until the batter is smooth.

5 Add the vinegar, season with salt and pepper and give a final whisk.

6 Carefully pour the batter into the hot, smoking dish and cook for about 20 minutes until risen and a crusty golden brown.

BRANDY SAUCE FOR PLUM OR CHRISTMAS PUDDING

115 g (4 oz) unsalted butter
115 g (4 oz) caster sugar
1 small wine glass of good brandy
$\frac{1}{2}$ to $\frac{3}{4}$ glass of sherry

METHOD

1 Partially melt the butter and heat with the sugar until it looks like double cream.

2 Gradually stir in the brandy and the sherry, mixing well.

3 Serve in a small jug with hot plum or Christmas pudding.

EASY SIDE DISHES TO GO WITH A CURRY

TOMATO AND ONION SALAD

Mix together 2 sliced tomatoes (or 8 cherry tomatoes cut in half) and 1 sliced small red onion. No need for any dressing.

CUCUMBER RAITA

Pour 150 ml (5 fl oz) of natural yoghurt (whichever one you like) into a bowl and add to it about 15 cm (6 inches) of cucumber (grated), $1/4$ tsp ground cumin and the same of coriander, approximately 1 tablespoon chopped fresh mint and finally season with a pinch of salt and lots of pepper. Mix well together and tip into a small bowl.

COCONUT TO SPRINKLE

I like to have a small bowl of desiccated coconut rather than use coconut cream in my cooking. It goes particularly well with an old fashioned, Raj-style beef or lamb curry.

BANANA

For 2 people: slice 1 (not over-ripe) banana into a dish and cover with the juice $1/2$ lemon – this not only goes well with the fruit but prevents it from going brown.

EMERGENCY CHUTNEY

If you have run out of chutney, you can make an emergency version and no one will notice that it wasn't made from mangoes. Take half a jar of some good apricot preserve, and add about 2 tablespoons of Worcestershire sauce. Mix well and put in a pretty glass bowl.

Puddings

I wonder sometimes if it wouldn't be a good idea to start the meal with a pudding simply because, by the time we reach this stage in the proceedings, my appetite has waned. Having said that, with encouragement I can usually find a little space tucked away.

I certainly don't make puddings on a daily basis, but always have a go when we entertain and, for this reason, I do use proper cream. However, if you have a growing family and enjoy finishing with something sweet, then to avoid piling on the pounds double cream can generally be substituted by a light crème fraîche, low fat yoghurt or fromage frais.

Most of the puddings included here are ones we have for a special occasion or a treat; therefore the ingredients I have chosen are with that in mind.

RICH SWEET PASTRY

225 g (8 oz) plain flour
1 level dessertspoon icing sugar
Pinch of salt
1 egg yolk
$^1/_2$ tsp lemon juice
$1^1/_2$–2 tbsp water
125–140 g ($4^1/_2$–5 oz) unsalted butter, cubed

METHOD

1 Sift the flour, icing sugar and salt into a large bowl.

2 Beat the egg yolk with the lemon juice and water in a separate dish.

3 Add the butter to the flour and rub in with your fingertips, or blitz in the food processor until it resembles breadcrumbs.

4 If you are using the processor, reduce the speed of the blender and add the egg/water/lemon mix and process until the pastry comes away from the sides and forms a ball. Stop processing immediately. If you are mixing by hand, pour in the egg mix and work into the flour and butter using a fork and then, as lightly as possible again, with your hands, form a ball. Cover with cling film and leave to rest in the fridge for an hour.

5 When it is needed, take the ball from the fridge and allow to reach room temperature before rolling out – 30 minutes should suffice.

TIP •

This pastry is ideal for tartlets and for lining a flan ring. The pastry cases can be cooked in advance and then filled with whipped cream and strawberries. Melt a couple of tablespoons of redcurrant jelly in a pan and pour over the fruit as a glaze. Chill in the fridge so that the jelly sets.

NO-ROLL SWEET PASTRY CASE

115 g (4 oz) hazelnuts
115 g (4 oz) chilled unsalted butter
140 g (5 oz) plain flour
1 tbsp icing sugar

METHOD

1 Pre heat the oven to gas mark 3 (160°C, 325°F).

2 Heat a pan on the stove and brown the hazelnuts. This won't take long, but be careful not to burn them.

3 Cut the butter into small cubes and put into a blender. Add the flour, sugar and toasted hazelnuts. Blitz until it resembles breadcrumbs. Pour the mixture into a buttered flan dish and press it into the sides and the base. It doesn't have to be very even.

4 Bake in the oven for about 20–30 minutes until golden brown. Once cool, fill it with whatever you wish, for example stiffly whipped cream or custard topped with fresh fruit.

QUICK CHOCOLATE TART *SERVES 4-6*

This recipe is not for you if you are practising girth control!

1 200gm (½ lb) bar dark chocolate with high content cocoa solids
225 ml (½ pint) cream
Small glass Irish cream liqueur
1 ready made, cooked (all-butter if possible) pastry case or prepare your own (see page 190)

METHOD

1 Break the chocolate into small pieces and put into a bowl. Gently heat the cream and pour onto the chocolate, stirring while it melts.

2 Add the cream liqueur and pour the mixture into the cooked pastry case. Put in the fridge and allow to set – this could take an hour or so – then it's ready to eat.

TIPS •

For a change and added crunch, mix in a couple of tablespoons of toasted, chopped hazelnuts with the chocolate cream.

When cutting a chocolate tart, first dip the knife into a bowl of hot water, then dry it. The heat will prevent the tart from breaking up.

CHOCOLATE SAUCE

FOR EACH SERVING
1 tbsp golden caster sugar
100 ml (3¹/₂ fl oz) water
1 bar good quality dark chocolate

METHOD

1 Make a sugar syrup from the sugar and water. Bring to the heat, stirring all the while until the sugar has dissolved.

2 Break the chocolate into a bowl and pour on the hot syrup (off the heat). Stir until it has melted and it is ready to use. Don't add cream as this will make the glossy sauce dull.

TARTE A L'ORANGE *SERVES 4-6*

This recipe was given to me by a friend I met in France in the early seventies and we recently met up again after more than thirty years – she hadn't changed a bit, and the tart was just as good!

Pastry (see page 190)
85-115 g (3-4 oz) melted butter,
depending on what size egg you use
1 egg
115 g (4 oz) sugar
Zest and juice 1 orange
Zest and juice ¹/₂ lemon

METHOD

1 Line a flan ring with a very thin layer of your own pastry or buy ready-made, all-butter flaky pastry. Let it rest in the fridge for a good half hour.

2 Preheat the oven to gas mark 6 (200°C, 400°F).

3 Melt the butter (but do not boil) and allow to cool slightly.

4 Beat the egg thoroughly and pass through a tea strainer into another bowl containing the sugar – you don't want any traces of white of egg or stringy bits when the tart is cooked.

5 Add the melted butter, lemon and orange zest and the juices to the egg. Mix well.

6 Take the pastry out of the fridge, prick the base with a fork and pour in the custard mix.

7 Bake for approximately 20 minutes on the middle shelf of the oven, then reduce the heat to gas mark 2 (150°C, 300°F) and continue cooking for a further 10–15 minutes.

8 This is best served at room temperature with either double cream or crème fraîche.

TIP

When you are baking pastry in a flan ring or dish, use one made of metal if possible, rather than one made from china – the metal conducts the heat and will cook the pastry on the bottom more efficiently.

CHEAP TARTS *SERVES 4-6*

1 packet ready-made all-butter short crust pastry
Double cream
Some runny strawberry jam
Berries: blueberries, raspberries,
strawberries, etc. of your choice

METHOD

1 Preheat the oven to gas mark 6 (200°C, 400°F).

2 Roll out the pastry thinly and cut into rounds to fit the hollows on a Yorkshire puddings baking tray. Prick the base of each tart with a fork and leave in the fridge for 30 minutes. Any leftover trimmings can be used the following day for Bananas in Pyjamas (see page 214).

3 Remove the tray of pastry cases from the fridge. Cut sufficient squares of baking parchment approximately the size of the pastry circles, lay one on each circle and drop a spoonful of dried beans or baking beads to hold the paper down. This will prevent the pastry rising during cooking. Bake in the centre of the oven for 5 minutes. When the outer pastry begins to take on a little colour, remove from the oven, and lift off the baking parchment and beans/beads. Cook for a further 5 minutes making sure the pastry doesn't burn. They may not need very long, so have a look after 3 minutes. Set aside until ready to serve.

4 Whip the cream so that it is quite stiff and fold in enough of the runny syrup from the jam to give a little sweetness. Don't mix thoroughly – you want a marbled, rippled effect. Spoon some of this onto the base of each pastry case and arrange the fruit on top. You can either leave them as they are with a dusting of icing sugar (put a spoonful in a sieve and shake it over the top), or drizzle some more jam syrup over the fruit.

STRAWBERRY BRICKS *SERVES 4-6*

1 packet all-butter flaky pastry
1 egg yolk
300 ml (10 fl oz) double cream
450 g (1 lb) strawberries (or other fruit of your choice)
Icing sugar for dusting

METHOD

1 Flour your board and roll out the pastry very thinly (see Tip below). Cut into squares or rectangles and place on an oven tray covered with baking parchment. Put in the fridge for 30 minutes to chill.

2 Mix the egg yolk with 1 dessertspoon cold water. Remove the pastry from the fridge and glaze with the egg mixture. Bake on the middle shelf of a hot oven until the pastry is golden and risen – about 10 minutes. Remove and allow to cool.

3 Slice the strawberries into a bowl and sprinkle with caster sugar and mix well.

4 Whip the cream until stiff. When ready to serve, spread the whipped cream onto half the pastry squares/rectangles and carefully pile the fruit on top. Add another small layer of whipped cream and place a naked pastry square/rectangle on top. Dust liberally with icing sugar and serve.

TIP •

To economise on flour, roll out the pastry between two sheets of cling film.

VERY USEFUL CRUMBLE MIXTURE *SERVES 4-6*

This is handy to make in advance and keep in a screw-top jar in the fridge for emergencies.

225 g (8 oz) flour
140 g (5 oz) butter
Pinch of salt
1 heaped dessertspoon sugar (caster, demerara or golden caster)

METHOD

1 Whizz everything bar the sugar in a blender until it has the texture of breadcrumbs. Add the sugar and give the mix one more quick whizz – it's now ready for action.

MY ALTERNATIVE CRUMBLE MIX *SERVES 4-6*

Adding the ground almonds gives a different dimension to the crumble and goes very nicely with plums and apricots.

140 g (5 oz) flour
2 tbsp ground almonds
115 g (4 oz) butter
Pinch of salt
2 tbsp sugar

METHOD

1 Whizz everything bar the sugar in a blender until it resembles breadcrumbs. Add the sugar and give the mix one more quick whizz.

APPLE AND STRAWBERRY CRUMBLE
SERVES 4-6

450 g (1 lb) apples, peeled and sliced
About 6 strawberries (frozen will do and they don't need to be thawed)
3 tbsp sugar
Crumble mixture of your choice (see above)

METHOD

1 Preheat the oven to gas mark 4 (190°C, 350°F).

2 Put the apple in a baking dish and dot with the strawberries. Spoon over the sugar and then the crumble mix. It doesn't have to be too tidy but try to get it to the edge of the dish.

3 Bake for about 30-40 minutes until the top is a light golden brown.

HONEYCOMB MOULD *SERVES 4-6*

This is a simple, delicate pudding – as children we were always fascinated by the way the custard separated from the jelly beneath. Ma invariably served it with bottled raspberries from our own fruit when we couldn't afford to buy double cream.

2 large eggs
15–20 g ($^{1}/_{2}$–$^{3}/_{4}$ oz) powdered gelatine
(or sufficient leaves for a pint of liquid)
600 ml (1 pint) milk
35 g (1$^{1}/_{2}$ oz) sugar
$^{1}/_{2}$ tsp extract vanilla

METHOD

1 Separate the egg yolks from the whites. Prepare the gelatine according to which type you use – the method is different depending on whether you use leaf or powdered gelatine so refer to the manufacturer's instructions on the packet.

2 Make a custard: heat the milk and sugar up to scalding point (don't allow it to boil). Gradually add about 1 tablespoon of milk to the raw egg yolks, stirring to prevent the milk from cooking the egg. Add another spoonful or two and by this time the egg will be hot enough to mix with the hot milk in the pan. However, add this gradually, still stirring to avoid disaster. Add the vanilla extract.

3 Stand the pan in a frying pan half filled with hot water (called a bain marie) and allow it to thicken stirring constantly to prevent the milk from getting too hot and scrambling the egg. Use a double boiler if you have one. It will be ready when you can coat the back of the wooden spoon with the custard. Remove from heat and allow to cool.

4 When the custard is cold, whisk the egg whites until very stiff and fold into the egg custard. Rinse the jelly mould with water (this will help with de-moulding later), drain and pour in the cold custard. Put it back in the fridge to set, preferably overnight.

5 The next day, choose a pretty plate, rinse it under the tap and drain. Run the tap until it is hot and quickly flash the jelly mould underneath to loosen the pudding. Place the plate on top and turn over. By wetting the plate first, if it has not landed in the middle you can slide the mould into position before giving it a tap and lifting it away.

TIP •

Never use fresh pineapple or kiwi fruit in a jelly – these fruits contains enzymes that prevent the jelly from setting. Curiously, this does not apply to tinned pineapple.

SUMMER STRAWBERRY ICE CREAM *SERVES 4-6*

550g (1¼ lb) strawberries
225 ml (½ pint) double cream
175 g (6 oz) sugar

METHOD

1 Carefully rinse the strawberries and remove the hulls. Blitz them in a blender.

2 Whip the cream until firm but not too stiff.

3 Place the sugar in a bowl and add the puréed fruit. By doing it in this order, the sugar will dissolve on contact with the fruit.

4 Finally, add the whipped cream and fold in. Pour into your ice cream maker and follow the manufacturer's instructions. If you do not have a machine, pour into a plastic container and allow to freeze, but not into a solid lump. Remove and beat thoroughly. Replace the ice cream mix into a clean container and put back in the freezer. Take out 10 minutes before serving to soften slightly. Do not re-freeze.

STRAWBERRY LIQUEUR ICE CREAM *SERVES 4-6*

450 g (1 lb) strawberries
225 ml (¹/₂ pint) double cream
115 g (4 oz) caster sugar
¹/₂ tsp vanilla extract
2 tbsp rum or maraschino

METHOD

1 Carefully rinse the strawberries and remove the hulls. Blitz in a food processor and pass through a sieve to remove the pips.

2 Whip the cream until firm but not too stiff and add to the strawberry purée.

3 Fold in the sugar, vanilla and rum or maraschino.

4 Pour into your ice cream maker and follow the manufacturer's instructions (or see previous recipe instructions, page 198).

TIP •

When you are serving ice cream, first dust the plate with some icing sugar sprinkled through a sieve – once the ice cream is placed on the plate it will not melt around the edges.

FAST AND SAFE VANILLA ICE CREAM *SERVES 4*

Since the original salmonella scare some years ago, I remain reluctant to eat anything containing raw eggs. Thus, sadly, I have given up making chocolate mousse, tiramisu and fresh mayonnaise as they can cause tummy upsets, particularly in young children or the older generation. This recipe tastes brilliant and removes my fear.

225 ml (¹/₂ pint) double cream
Fresh vanilla pod (or 1 tsp vanilla extract)
500 g (1 lb 2 oz) best quality, ready-made vanilla custard
3 generous tbsp icing sugar

METHOD

1 Lightly whip the double cream to a bit stiffer than sloppy.

2 Slit open the vanilla pod lengthways with a sharp knife and scrape out as much of the sticky, black seeds as you can. Mix these with the custard. Vanilla extract can be used instead if you don't have a vanilla pod handy. Don't throw the empty pod away – put it in a small jar filled with sugar to use later, sprinkled in sponge cakes, for example.

3 Sift the icing sugar and fold it into the mixture together with the whipped cream.

4 Pour into your ice cream machine and follow the manufacturer's instructions (or see previous recipe instructions, page 198).

TIP •••

Do not re-freeze uneaten ice cream if it has thawed.

For a speedy, scrumptious sauce which will instantly give plain ordinary vanilla ice cream a zing and with the minimum of fuss, do the following: keep a bag of individually wrapped, fun sized Mars Bars in the fridge and when needed, remove one per person and melt it in a saucepan over a medium heat with a teaspoon of strong black, instant coffee and 1 tablespoon of water. Do not boil. The mallow part of the Mars Bar will struggle to dissolve completely, but don't worry – this adds a pleasant toffee-like, chewy consistency to the sauce. Pour over the ice cream and serve immediately. To peg it up yet another notch, sprinkle some chopped toasted hazelnuts on top. I defy you to keep to one helping...

SAGO PLUM PUDDING *SERVES 4*

Sago, along with tapioca (which we called frog spawn as children because that's exactly what it looked like), seems to have disappeared off the shelves but I am sure you can still find it. It's worth the search. These simple, high carb puddings have more and more value in our current diets: slow release energy and cheap to make, providing central heating in a bowl. If, on the other hand you don't like puddings, turn down the thermostat, put on another pullover and polish the furniture for half an hour. Alternatively, if you hate doing housework (or making puddings), go to the (warm) public library and read the papers. It works for me! Send me a postcard to let me know that I am not completely off my trolley!

3 tbsp sago
55 g (2 oz) fresh breadcrumbs
115 g (4 oz) mixed fruit (currants, sultanas, etc.)
Grated rind of an orange
85 g (3 oz) cup sugar
1/2 tsp bicarbonate of soda
55 g (2 oz) butter
Pinch of salt

METHOD

1 Soak the sago in a cup of water for about 1 hour.

2 Mix everything together and pour into a greased pudding basin. Cover with foil and secure and steam for at least 2 hours.

3 Serve hot with cream.

TIP •
Before steaming a pudding, butter the bowl thoroughly and put it into the fridge to harden for an hour before cooking. It will then tip out easily onto a plate once cooked.

GRANNY'S ALL-IN-ONE PAVLOVA *SERVES 6*

This recipe was given to my grandmother by a Jehovah's witness in 1938 when she lived in New Zealand. Cast aside all the recipes you may have read on how to create a classic pavlova and follow these simple instructions. With my catholic tastes, I like to top my pavlova with passion fruit and whipped double cream, but only if the passion fruits are very ripe – the wrinkly, crinkly ones are the best. If they are still smooth-skinned they won't be sweet enough. Of course, you can add any fruit (tinned or fresh) which tickles your fancy: fresh mango, strawberries (cut into pieces), blueberries and bananas are a balanced combination.

FOR THE BASE
3 egg whites
225 g (8 oz) caster sugar
3 tsp cornflour
1 tsp vanilla extract
1 tsp vinegar
3 tbsp warm water

FOR THE TOPPING
225 ml (¹/₂ pint) double cream, whipped
Fruit of your choice

METHOD

1 Preheat the oven to gas mark ¹/₄ (110°C, 225°F).

2 Pile all the ingredients except the cream and fruit into a squeaky clean, grease-free mixing bowl and whisk until you have firm, stiff peaks – you should be able to turn the bowl upside down over your head without the mixture falling out. Never fear, even though at the beginning it looks as though it will never work. It takes quite a time to achieve, but persevere and in a few minutes you will have a perfect, glossy meringue.

3 Lay a piece of baking parchment onto a flat oven tray and spoon out the meringue roughly in the shape of a circle. Don't be too much of a perfectionist and leave peaks and troughs. Place in the oven and cook for 1 hour – it will take on a little colour but this is normal.

4 Don't add the cream and fruit until the last minute or the meringue will go soggy.

5 To save time, the cream can be whipped in advance and kept in the fridge, along with the prepared fruit ready for assembly later.

TIP ••

To use up your leftover egg yolks, see page 206.

STICKY TOFFEE COFFEE PAVLOVA *SERVES 4-6*

This recipe uses the same ingredients as for the pavlova but with a slight coffee flavour for interest.

FOR THE BASE
3 egg whites
225 g (8 oz) caster sugar
3 tsp cornflour
2 tsp vanilla extract
1 tsp vinegar
3 tbsp warm water
1 tsp instant coffee
FOR THE TOPPING
2 or 3 ripe but still firm bananas
Juice 1 lemon
225 ml (¹/₂ pint) double cream
55 g (2 oz) caster sugar

METHOD

1 Make the pavlova as per the previous recipe, adding the coffee to the mixture with the other ingredients.

2 Just before serving, peel and slice the bananas and cover with the lemon juice.

3 Whip the cream to a soft peak.

4 Put the sugar into a heavy bottomed pan and add 1 tablespoon of cold water. Place on a high heat and it will bubble away. The water will evaporate. Keep a close eye on this – you need to get it to

caramel stage, i.e. the syrup turning from colourless to dark honey.

5   Assemble your pavlova by piling the whipped cream onto the meringue base and scattering it with the sliced bananas.

6   As soon as the sugar has caramelised – this will be very hot indeed – take great care as you drizzle it over the pudding. Try not to tip the caramel out in one large splodge! The caramel will harden almost on contact and will give a smashing crunch.

TIP •

Eton Mess: Another lovely, easy summer pudding is Eton Mess (or as a young friend thought I said, 'Eaten Mess'). Make the pavlova and when cold, crumble it into rough pieces. Whip 225 ml (½ pint) double cream until it is a bit stiffer than sloppy. Trim and cut some ripe strawberries and fold them into the broken meringue and whipped cream. Pile into pretty glasses or dishes and serve at once. This can also be put into a container and frozen straight away as a quick fix ice cream. Remove from the freezer 15 minutes before serving to soften slightly.

FLOATING ISLANDS
(*OEUFS A LA NEIGE*) *SERVES 4-6*

175 g (6 oz) caster sugar
1 litre (1¾ pints full cream milk)
6 eggs
1 tsp vanilla extract

METHOD

1   Put the sugar and milk into a large frying pan and heat, stirring so that the sugar dissolves.

2   Separate the eggs one by one into a dish to check that there is no shell and that they are fresh. Whisk the egg whites until very stiff.

3   When the milk is simmering, but not boiling, using a large spoon, scoop up the meringue mixture and drop it onto the hot milk. Depending on the size of your pan you could probably cook four meringues in one go. They will swell and, after 30 seconds, turn them over using a slotted spoon to cook the other side for a further 30 seconds, no longer. They will puff up a little more. Remove them

from the pan and put to one side on a plate. Continue cooking the meringue mixture in this fashion until it is used up.

4 Now make the custard: beat the egg yolks in a large bowl and gradually pour on a little of the hot sweet milk, stirring fast so that the eggs do not cook. Pour in a bit more, beating all the time and then gradually add the rest of the milk, mixing well. Add the vanilla extract and stir.

5 Strain the custard through a sieve into a clean pan. Ideally this should be placed inside a larger pan half-filled with hot water (a bain marie) so that the egg and milk mixture is not in direct contact with the heat. **Do not let it get too hot**, otherwise the eggs will scramble. Cook the custard, stirring all the while, until it coats the back of the spoon.

6 Once you are satisfied with the thickness of the custard (it can take quite a while to reach this stage and cannot be rushed), pour into a bowl to cool. It will continue to thicken slightly. When the custard is cold, pile the meringues on top and chill in the fridge until ready to serve.

TIPS •

The secret to making a good custard is to remove it before it comes to the boil – if it reaches this point, you will probably have to start again. Having said that, if you notice that the custard has begun to change from a smooth liquid to a granular one, remove it instantly from the heat and pour into the food processor or a blender and whizz it very quickly. You may be lucky and save it in time.

Alternatively, as I was taught in France, grab an empty (clean) wine or Perrier bottle and using a funnel, pour the custard into it. Screw on the cap and shake the bottle like mad for a minute and the custard should miraculously come together again. Breathe a sigh of relief, and pour it into a waiting basin.

To add a crunch to this delicate pudding, make a caramel by putting 55 g (2 oz) of sugar and 1 tablespoon water into a thick-bottomed pan and put on to heat. The sugar will dissolve in the water and will gradually begin to change colour as it caramelises. Remove from the heat when it looks like dark honey and drizzle this immediately over the assembled floating islands. Do this just before serving – if you do it in advance, the caramel will dissolve.

COFFEE CREME CARAMEL *SERVES 4*

This is a nice way to use the egg yolks left over after making the pavlova. Do it the day before so that the caramel will have time to melt.

FOR THE CARAMEL
55 g (2 oz) sugar
2 tbsp water

FOR THE CUSTARD
600 ml (1 pint) full cream milk
55 g (2 oz) sugar
3 egg yolks
1 extra whole egg
1 tsp instant coffee, dissolved in a little water

METHOD

1 Preheat the oven to gas mark 2 (150°C, 300°F).

2 To make the caramel: heat the sugar in a thick-bottomed saucepan and add the water and mix together. Leave the syrup to turn into caramel, tipping (not stirring) the pan so that it browns evenly – you want it to be the colour of dark honey: more and it will taste burnt.

3 Carefully (it will be very hot indeed) pour the caramel into an ovenproof dish, rolling it so that the caramel more or less covers the bottom.

4 Take the saucepan used to make the caramel and add the milk and remaining sugar and heat to scalding point (not quite boiling). The caramel left behind will dissolve and add more flavour to the milk.

5 To make the custard: beat the egg yolks and extra whole egg together in a bowl. Add

the coffee. When the milk is hot, pour a little onto the raw eggs (about half a cupful), stirring well as you do this. Then add a little more, stirring all the time. This gradual introduction of hot milk to the raw eggs will prevent them from scrambling. When you have mixed about a third of the milk with the eggs, they should be hot enough to add the remaining milk and coffee. Mix well using an egg whisk for half a minute – this will give it a bit of froth.

6 Using a fine sieve, strain the custard into the dish lined with the caramel. This will remove any stringy bits of egg.

7 Place the dish in an oven tray half filled with some water – you don't want too much or it might overflow into the custard. By putting the dish into a bain marie as it is called, it will prevent the custard from boiling, which would create unattractive air holes. Bake for 1 hour or until the custard has set firm. Test by piercing it with a pointed knife – if it is cooked it will come out clean.

8 Once cool, keep in the fridge overnight or until the caramel has had time to dissolve.

MUM'S TRIFLE *SERVES 6*

1 packet trifle sponges
450 g (1 lb) jar good quality apricot preserve
3 tbsp sherry, e.g. amontillado (any more is too much)
55 g (2 oz) sugar
225 ml ($\frac{1}{2}$ pint) milk
1 heaped tbsp Bird's instant custard powder
150 ml ($\frac{1}{4}$ pint) whipped cream
25 g (1 oz) sliced toasted almonds

METHOD

1 Begin by finding your prettiest glass bowl. Roughly break the trifle sponges into this. Tip the jam into a mixing bowl and add the sherry, mixing well. Drizzle over the sponges.

2 Make your custard: put the sugar and all but a cup of milk into a pan and heat to just below boiling point.

3 Put the custard powder into a bowl and mix thoroughly with the remaining cold milk. Then pour about a cup of the hot milk into the custard mix, stirring all the time, add more hot milk, stir and pour it back into the saucepan. Bring the custard to the boil, stirring all the time to avoid lumps. Cook for 1 minute. You are aiming for a pouring consistency a touch thicker than double cream. It will thicken once cold.

4 Remove from the heat and let the custard cool for 5 minutes before pouring it over the sponges and jam – you don't want the heat to crack your bowl. Cover with cling film – this will stop a skin from forming, and allow to get cold before chilling in the fridge.

5 The next day, whip the cream and spoon onto the trifle. Brown the almonds under the grill. This takes seconds – longer and they burn, or leave them as they are. Scatter them over the whipped cream and serve.

PROPER RICE PUDDING *SERVES 4*

600 ml (1 pint) full cream milk
40-55 g (1½-2 oz) pudding (round grain) rice
1½ tbsp sugar (you don't want it to be too sweet)
15 g (½ oz) butter
¼ teaspoon freshly grated nutmeg

METHOD

1 Preheat the oven to gas mark 2 (150°C, 300°F).

2 Pour the milk into an oven-safe dish and add the rice.

3 Add the sugar, stir and dot with butter. Grate the nutmeg over the milk.

4 Bake for about 45 minutes until the top has formed a lovely brown skin and the rice and milk are creamy. If in doubt, take out of the oven and prod around with a fork – if the milk is still watery, put it back in the oven for a further 15 minutes. If by chance it is too solid, add some more milk.

5 If you have an Aga, put the dish in the top oven until golden brown and then put in the bottom oven for at least another hour more to cook slowly.

BAKED LEMON SPONGE PUDDING *SERVES 4*

There are dozens of variations of this, but this is my mother's version, therefore obviously the best.

1 tbsp flour
115 g (4 oz) sugar
Pinch of salt
2 egg yolks
200 ml (7 fl oz) milk
Zest and juice 1 lemon
2 tbsp melted butter
2 egg whites
Double cream, to serve

METHOD

1 Preheat the oven to gas mark 4 (180°C, 350°F).

2 Sift the flour, sugar, salt and blend with the beaten egg yolks.

3 Add the milk, lemon juice and zest. Beat thoroughly.

4 Melt the butter and add to the mixture.

5 Whisk the egg whites until stiff and fold into the mixture.

6 Pour into a greased oven dish/soufflé dish, and put it into a roasting dish half filled with water.

7 Bake for about 40 minutes – until the sponge is firm and golden.

8 Serve hot, (it is equally good cold) and with double cream.

APPLE PUDDING *SERVES 4*

450 g (1 lb) cooking apples, peeled and sliced
55 g (2 oz) soft brown sugar
1 tbsp water
115 g (4 oz) butter
115 g (4 oz) caster sugar
115 g (4 oz) ground almonds
2 large eggs, beaten

METHOD

1 Preheat the oven to gas mark 4 (180°C, 350°F).

2 Place the apples in a saucepan with the sugar and 1 tablespoon water. Simmer until soft and arrange in the bottom of a 300 ml ($\frac{1}{2}$ pint) buttered pie dish.

3 In a mixing bowl, using an electric hand whisk, cream the butter and caster sugar until pale and fluffy.

4 Beat the eggs separately and add a little at a time to the butter mixture. When fully incorporated, fold in the ground almonds. Spread this mixture over the apples.

5 Bake on high shelf for 1 hour or until golden brown.

BANANA FRITTERS

I have been known to make these in my lunch hour when I was working in London and devour the lot in one go.

2 ripe bananas, sliced (for two people)

BATTER
115 g (4 oz) flour
Pinch of salt
1 egg
300 ml ($\frac{1}{2}$ pint) milk
Oil for frying
Sugar for dredging

METHOD

1 To make the batter: sift the flour and salt into a bowl. Make a well and drop in the egg, incorporating the flour and adding the milk by degrees. Mix thoroughly using a whisk. It should have the consistency of single cream.

2 Peel and slice the bananas and add to the batter.

3 Heat about $\frac{1}{2}$ inch of oil in a frying pan. To test whether or not it is ready to receive the fritters, place the tip of a handle of a wooden

spoon into the fat. If it sizzles and bubbles on contact, the temperature is right. If not, continue heating a few moments longer.

4 When the fat is hot enough, drop in tablespoonfuls of the banana batter. They will rise to the surface and begin to turn golden. After a couple of minutes, turn the fritters over to cook on the other side. After a further 2–3 minutes remove with a slotted spoon and drain on kitchen paper. Dredge with sugar and eat immediately.

TIP •

Apples can be used instead of bananas (see recipe below).

If you are preparing bananas some time before they are cooked or to be used as a side dish to a curry, cover them in lemon juice – this will prevent them from going black.

APPLE FRITTERS

I love these 'moreish' mouthfuls. When I lived in central France, the winter months could be bitterly cold. It would be dark by half-past-three in the afternoon and to see the bright, inviting lights glowing in a patisserie shop was an irresistible lure. The windows would be partially obscured with condensation and once inside I would be in a magical world, enveloped in the indulgent scent of chocolate and vanilla. On the counter, in front of the racks of baguettes, rustic loaves and croissants, would be a wooden tray lined with greaseproof paper and filled with neat rows of golden apple fritters, dredged with caster sugar. Wrapped in a paper napkin these tangy, sweet, crispy *friandises* never lasted the journey home.

Use Granny Smith or Golden Delicious apples – these will hold their shape when cooked.

**140 g (5 oz) plain flour (for the batter), plus an
extra saucer of flour to dust the apple rings
Pinch of salt
335 g (8 oz) medium sweet cider
2–3 apples, peeled and cored
Corn oil or sunflower oil for frying
Caster sugar for dredging**

METHOD

1 Sift the flour and salt (this will enhance the flavour of the apples) into a bowl and make a well in the centre. Puddle in the cider, incorporating the flour bit by bit, whisking as you go until you have a smooth, lump-free and cream-like batter.

2 Cut the apples into rings about 5 mm (¼ inch) thick.

3 Heat some oil in a frying pan - enough to cover the base generously. To test that it is hot enough, don't allow it to smoke but dip the end of a wooden spoon into the hot fat. If it is the right temperature, the fat will bubble around the end of the spoon. If not, continue heating for a further minute or two and test again.

3 Dip the apple rings into the saucer of flour, shaking off any excess and then into the batter – the coating of flour will make the batter stick to the apple ring. Carefully drop them individually into the hot fat and cook on each side for about 3 minutes, or until golden brown.

4 Remove with a slotted spoon and drain on some kitchen paper. Dredge with sugar and eat straight away.

5 These can be eaten on their own in your fingers, or accompanied with some good quality vanilla ice cream.

BAKED BANANAS

Prepare this before you put it in the oven or the bananas will go black.

1 banana per person

Juice 2 oranges

Juice 1/2 lemon

1 wine glass liqueur – dark rum is nice or Cointreau or Grand Marnier

2 dessertspoons demerara sugar

Sprinkle of cinnamon

Freshly grated nutmeg

25 g (1 oz) butter

Double cream for serving

METHOD

1 Preheat the oven to gas mark 5 (190°C, 375°F).

2 Place the peeled fruit in a dish and pour on the other ingredients. Sprinkle the cinnamon and grate the nutmeg over the top. Dot with the butter.

3 Bake in the oven for about 10 minutes and serve with thick, double cream.

ELLIE'S AUTUMN PUDDING

This is an excellent way to use up those over-ripe bananas lurking in your fruit basket.

4 bananas

About 2 heaped tbsp blackberries (fresh or frozen)

1–2 tbsp demerara sugar

Juice of 2 oranges (again, use up the older ones first!)

1/2 oz butter

METHOD

1 Preheat the oven to gas mark 5 (190°C, 375°F)

2 Peel the bananas and cut away any bruised bits; lay them in an oven proof dish.

3 Scatter over the blackberries and pour on the orange juice.

4 Sprinkle with the sugar and dot with the butter.

5 Put into the oven for about 15 minutes, or until the fruit is cooked.

6 Serve warm as it is, or with crème fraîche, vanilla ice cream or custard.

BANANA AND APPLE BAKED PUDDING *SERVES 4-6*

6 thin slices buttered bread
450 g (1 lb) apples, peeled, cored and sliced
4 ripe bananas, sliced
Grated zest and juice 1 lemon
115 g (4 oz) demerara sugar
Caster sugar for dusting

METHOD

1 Preheat the oven to gas mark 5 (190°C, 375°F).

2 Prepare the fruit and grate the lemon rind and squeeze out the juice.

3 Line a buttered pie dish with a mixture of apple and banana, sprinkle with lemon juice, zest and sugar, and cover with the thin slices of buttered bread. Continue until the dish is full.

4 Cover the top with the apple peelings and bake in a moderate oven for approximately 45 minutes until golden brown.

5 Remove the apple peelings and throw them away. Dust the pudding with caster sugar and serve.

BANANAS IN PYJAMAS

Now's the time to use up any leftover pastry if you have any.

Ready made all-butter puff pastry
1 tbsp caster sugar per banana
Cinnamon or mixed spice

Grated zest and juice 1 lemon
1 large ripe, but still firm banana per person
1 tbsp milk
225 g (8 oz) strawberries

METHOD

1 Preheat the oven to gas mark 5 (190°C, 375°F).

2 Roll it out the pastry (leftovers will do) as thinly as you wish and cut it into 1–2 cm (½–¾ inch) wide strips.

3 Mix enough sugar to coat the bananas in a dish with a teaspoon of cinnamon or mixed spice. Add the grated zest of the lemon zest and stir in.

4 Peel the bananas. Squeeze the juice from the lemon and pour onto the fruit before rolling them in the flavoured sugar, coating them well.

5 Take a strip of the thinly rolled out pastry and wrap it around each banana in a spiral. There is no need to cover the entire piece of fruit. Lay them side by side on a baking sheet. With a pastry brush, gently paint the pastry with a little milk and then sprinkle the surface with some of the remaining sugar. These can sit for an hour or so in a cool place (not the fridge) before baking since the lemon juice will prevent the bananas from going black.

6 Bake on the middle shelf in the oven for about 15 minutes, or until the pastry is puffed up and golden.

7 Whilst the bananas are in the oven, remove the hulls from the strawberries and put in the blender to make a purée. Sweeten with sugar to taste and pass the fruit through a sieve to remove any pips. Serve this separately in a small jug alongside the hot bananas. A dollop of proper vanilla ice cream completes the trio.

CARAMELISED COMPOTE OF RHUBARB *SERVES 4*

450–650 g (1–1½ lb) rhubarb
175 g (6 oz) sugar
Small glass of water
Juice 1 lemon or orange

METHOD

1 Wash and trim the rhubarb and cut into 2.5 cm (1 inch) pieces – a pair of kitchen scissors is easier to use than a knife and board.

2 Put half the sugar and the water into a heavy-bottomed pan and bring to the boil. You want the sugar to caramelise but not burn – a mid to dark brown is what you are looking for. Do not stir. When the right colour is achieved remove the pan from the heat and swirl the caramel around the inside – this will be very hot indeed. Tip in the raw rhubarb, the rest of the sugar and the orange or lemon juice.

3 Place back on a medium heat and allow to simmer until the fruit is cooked – this shouldn't take long, about 8–10 minutes – and the caramel has dissolved. Taste for sweetness and adjust accordingly.

4 Serve chilled with some cold vanilla custard or crème fraîche.

TIP •

As an alternative serving, make a loosely assembled fool, folding in some whipped cream and a couple of chunks of crystallised ginger cut into small pieces. Pile the mixture into pretty glass dishes.

Substitute the rhubarb with 900 g (2 lb) of apples, peeled and chopped. If there are any white bits of apple left when the rest are cooked, use the hand-held blender and blitz.

FRESH PINEAPPLE AND BLUEBERRY
FRUIT SALAD *SERVES 4-6*

This is a really clean pudding to have after a rich meal and is quick and easy to prepare. Other simple fruit dishes are given in the Tips below.

1 fresh pineapple

About a quarter of blueberries to the weight of prepared pineapple

Caster sugar (optional)

METHOD

1 Prepare the pineapple by cutting off the outside rind, and removing the black bits. Cut into small chunks and place in a glass bowl.

2 Add the washed blueberries and sprinkle with a little sugar to taste if wished. Mix with the pineapple and serve at room temperature.

TIP •••

Orange juice goes particularly well with strawberries and can be added to a bowl of whole, fresh fruit. Allow to macerate for an hour or so before eating.

Marinate fresh strawberries with some lemon juice and a little elderflower cordial.

PEACHES IN ORANGE AND LEMON SYRUP
SERVES 2

2 peaches (choose 'free' rather than 'cling' stone peaches if possible)
115 g (4 oz) sugar
150 ml (5 fl oz) water
Thinly peeled rind of 1 orange and 1 lemon plus juice of another lemon

METHOD

1 Pour a kettle of boiling water over the peaches and leave for a couple of minutes. Drain and run them under the cold tap to cool slightly. Immersing the fruit in hot water will enable you to peel them more easily. Remove the stone and slice the fruit.

2 Combine the sugar, water, lemon and orange peel in a saucepan. Heat and stir until the sugar has melted. Bring to the boil and keep on a high heat for 5 minutes in order to reduce the liquid by about a third. Remove from heat and take out the peel.

3 Slice the peaches and place into a bowl with the lemon juice and pour over the syrup. Leave to cool and chill well before serving.

FRUIT COMPOTE *SERVES 4*

2 peaches, peeled and sliced
225 g (8 oz) black grapes, halved and de-pipped
225 g (8 oz) black cherries, halved and stoned
Juice of 2 oranges
Sugar to taste

METHOD

1 Put everything into a saucepan and bring gently to the boil on low heat, stirring until the sugar has melted. Simmer for a few minutes until the fruit juices run and the peaches are soft but not turned into a pulp.

2 Cool, then chill for a couple of hours at least and serve with crème fraîche.

CHOCOLATE BUNNY RASCAL *SERVES 4-6*

This makes everyone smile: little people love it.

600 ml (1 pint) full cream milk
3 tbsp sugar
1 heaped tbsp cocoa powder
2 tbsp cornflour
1 packet bright green jelly
Canned whipped cream
A few currants

METHOD

1 This *has* to be made in a rabbit-shaped mould. Rinse it with cold water and drain upside down, but don't dry.

2 Set aside a cup of cold milk and heat the rest with the sugar almost to the boil.

3 Sieve the cocoa powder and cornflour into a bowl and gradually stir in the remaining cold milk making a smooth paste. Add the hot milk to the paste and stir well. Return to the saucepan and bring back to the boil stirring constantly. Cook for a further 2 minutes,

stirring all the time, to remove the cornflour taste, then pour into the bunny mould.

4 Cover with cling film to prevent a skin forming and once cold, pop in the fridge and chill overnight during which time the custard will set.

5 Make the jelly according to the instructions on the packet and leave to set in any sort of container – you are going to chop it up later.

6 When you are about to serve, take a serving plate and run it under the cold tap. Take the bunny out of the fridge, shake off the water from the plate and put it over the mould; turn it over and give it a sharp shake and it should come out in one piece. If it doesn't land plumb centre, you can then slide it into position because you have wetted the plate in advance.

7 Next unmould the green jelly and chop it up any old how and scatter it around the chocolate rabbit – this is your grass.

8 Next, squirt a small rosette of whipped cream to create a fluffy tail then scatter the currants on the grass/green jelly. These are your droppings – children think it's very naughty!

TIP •

If you want to make it more grown-up you can use a bar of dark chocolate instead of the powdered cocoa: make the custard with the milk, sugar and cornflour as above and add a drop or two of vanilla extract and while still hot add the chocolate broken into pieces and stir until it is thick and creamy. Pour into the mould and continue as before.

DUTCH BLANCMANGE *SERVES 4-6*

55 g (2 oz) powdered or 4 sheets of leaf gelatine
600 ml (1 pint) water
6 egg yolks
175 g (6 oz) sugar
2 wine glasses sherry
1 wine glass lemon juice

METHOD

1 Swell the powdered gelatine in the water. Heat until dissolved and add the sugar. (If you are using leaf gelatine, follow the manufacturer's instructions.)

2 Beat the egg yolks with the sherry. Add the lemon juice. Add to the water and gelatine mixture and heat together, stirring constantly but do not boil or the egg will curdle. The custard must reach the stage where it coats the back of a wooden spoon (it will continue to thicken as it cools).

3 Pour into a mould and allow to cool. Chill overnight in the fridge.

4 When you are ready to serve, take the blancmange out of the fridge and de-mould as in the Chocolate Bunny Rascal recipe (see page 218).

HOT CROSS BUN AND BUTTER PUDDING
SERVES 4-6

This is a tasty way to use up any leftover hot cross buns after the Easter weekend.

4 hot cross or currant buns
Softened butter
Jar of good quality apricot preserve
425 ml (³/₄ pint) full cream milk (Channel Islands if you want to cast the diet police to the wind)
2–3 tbsp demerara sugar
3 large eggs
Zest of 1 lemon
Zest of an orange
¹/₂ tsp nutmeg

METHOD

1 Cut the buns in half and spread generously with the butter and drizzle with some of the apricot preserve. Cut the buns in half again and place in a baking dish, semi-upright, zig-zag, to look like fish scales.

2 Heat the milk and sugar in a saucepan to scalding point.

3 Beat the eggs in a bowl and gradually add a little of the hot milk, whisking well to prevent the eggs from scrambling. When you have mixed about a cup of hot milk with the eggs, strain this mixture into the remaining hot milk. This will remove any stringy bits from the egg. Whisk well.

4 Grate the zest of the lemon and orange over the buttered buns and pour over the custard. Grate the nutmeg on top and leave the pudding to rest for about 20 minutes so that the buns absorb some of the custard.

5 Heat the oven to gas mark 4 (180°C, 350°F). Place the pudding in a roasting dish and add enough water to come half way up the outside of the dish. Place on the middle shelf in the oven and bake for 30–40 minutes until the top is golden brown and crusty, but fluffy and soft underneath.

FALLEN ANGEL PUDDING

In the middle of the night I had a lightbulb moment and this is the result. Do you remember the crunchy, biscuit-based lemon cream tart that used to crop up regularly in the seventies? It was very Abigail's Party but actually is an extremely pleasant pudding and easy to put together, involving no cooking at all. 'Fallen Angel' is my updated version.

SERVES 6
6 plain chocolate digestive biscuits
25 g (1 oz) unsalted butter
150 ml (5 fl oz) double cream – or light crème fraîche if you prefer
1 small tin condensed milk (you will need approximately 125 ml [4 fl oz])
Zest of 1 and juice of 2 oranges (unwaxed if possible)
Juice 1 lemon
1 small bar of good quality dark chocolate
6 glass or china ramekins, or assorted pretty tea or coffee cups and saucers

METHOD

1 Put the biscuits into a strong plastic bag – a freezer bag for example – and squash them into crumbs either using your hands or the back of a large wooden spoon.

2 Melt the butter, but do not allow to boil. Tip the crumbs into a bowl with the melted butter and mix together.

3 Put a spoonful or two of the biscuit crumb into the bottom of each ramekin and squash down with the back of a spoon, or your fingers, to make a firm, level base about 5–10 mm ($\frac{1}{4}$–$\frac{1}{2}$ inch) deep. Put them in the fridge to set.

4 Tip the double cream/crème fraîche into a clean bowl and add the condensed milk. Whisk lightly merely to blend the two.

5 Wash the fruit and using a fine grater, add the zest of one orange to the cream, then the juice of the two oranges and the lemon. Mix thoroughly and pour into the ramekins on top of the biscuit base. Put into the fridge to set. These can be prepared the day before.

6 When you are ready to serve, remove them from the fridge and grate a small amount of dark chocolate on top of each pot – you could always add a little extra fresh orange zest for flavour and colour.

TIP •

A tablespoon of orange liqueur might be an interesting addition.

Cakes and biscuits

Something happens to me on a bitter winter's afternoon, usually just before the half-time whistle blows when Jimmy is ensconced in front of the television watching a football match. The fire is glowing, it's raining outside and already dark, and lunch is a memory. The kitchen beckons and I have the urge to bake. Scones and Scotch pancakes can be rustled up in no time at all, and a batch of fairy cakes made from our own eggs, rich dried fruit, a sprinkle of spices such as cinnamon and ginger, blended with the juice of and zest of a lemon and orange, appear as if by magic in under 30 minutes.

I love baking, and it is virtually the only time I rely on accurate measurements and use my scales. I relish the sensation of tipping raw cake mixture into paper cases or spreading it carefully into a buttered tin, then waiting ten anxious minutes before peeking into the oven to see if the sponge is rising properly. Delicious smells waft through the house, the kitchen window steams up and I can't wait for the cakes to be cool enough to eat.

If domestic science/home economics – call it what you will – isn't a compulsory part of the school curriculum, then maybe baking should be!

CAMP SITE GINGERBREAD

Here is a recipe for gingerbread without using black treacle – as children it reminded us of a filthy health food called Virol to which we were subjected every day before going to school in the hope of boosting our immune system. This gingerbread uses golden syrup instead.

Ma used to make a large batch of this before we went on our annual camping holiday in Southwold or Walberswick on the Suffolk coast. We always hired a caravan (without fail, with orange curtains) and in those pre-tunnel days we crossed the Thames at Gravesend to Tilbury on the ferry – it felt like going abroad.

The cooked gingerbread was first wrapped in greaseproof paper then stored in the same old square metal biscuit tin used solely for this purpose. The cake just about lasted a week of the fortnight's holiday, and writing about it brings a rush of fond memories of playing hot rice (a game invented by my father) with the children from the neighbouring caravans and tents and shivering on the beach after a swim in the cold North Sea, huddled behind the canvas wind break in our home-made towelling dressing gowns. A slice of this with a mug of warm milk at bedtime guaranteed a peaceful night's sleep.

450 g (1 lb) plain flour
$\frac{1}{2}$ tsp salt
2 tbsp ground ginger
2 tsp baking powder
$\frac{1}{2}$ tsp bicarbonate of soda
225 g (8 oz) brown sugar – I use demerara but
if you want a more treacly taste, use muscovado
175 g (6 oz) butter (the wartime recipe used margarine)
350 g ($\frac{3}{4}$ lb) golden syrup
225 ml ($\frac{1}{2}$ pint) milk
1 egg, beaten

METHOD

1 Preheat the oven to gas mark 4 (180°C, 350°F).

2 Grease a shallow, non stick baking tin – a rectangular or square one makes cutting into fingers or squares easier.

3 Sieve all the dry ingredients bar the sugar into a bowl.

4 In a saucepan warm the sugar, butter and syrup over a low heat (or in a bowl in the microwave). Do not allow the mix to become too hot.

5 Warm the milk in a separate pan then combine all the ingredients, gradually pouring in the egg and mixing well. Pour into the prepared tin and bake in the oven for approximately 30 minutes or until the cake is firm and a skewer comes out 'clean'.

6 Allow to cool and cut up into large sections to fit into an airtight tin to be cut as needed. This heavenly cake grows gooier and stickier the older it is – if it ever hangs around long enough! To add insult to injury, you can always butter the slices before eating them.

TIPS •

I like to keep flour and cornflour in airtight containers but always forget to put in a label telling me which is which. If you are unsure, the following will help: insert your thumb and forefinger into the jar, take a little pinch of flour and rub together. If it is cornflour then it will 'squeak' – if it is ordinary flour, it will remain silent.

Remember (to avoid lumps): hot liquid for flour, cold liquid for cornflour.

AFGHAN BISCUITS

This is a recipe given to my mother before the war. These biscuits can be iced but they are equally good served plain. If you decide to go along the former route, then see below for a choice of toppings.

175 g (6 oz) butter
4 tbsp sugar
2 level tbsp cocoa
140 g (5 oz) flour
55 g (2 oz) crushed cornflakes
1/4 tsp vanilla extract

METHOD

1 Preheat the oven to gas mark 5 (190°C, 375°F).

2 Cream the butter until soft and add the sugar. Beat well and gradually work in the cocoa, flour and cornflakes.

3 Add the vanilla extract, mix well then spoon out walnut-sized pieces of the mix and place on a greased oven tray (not too closely together as they will spread a bit).

4 Bake in the oven for about 15 minutes, checking after 10. It is important that they are cooked through but not burnt. Wait for 5 minutes to allow them to become crisp enough to transfer to a wire cake rack.

TOPPINGS

CHOCOLATE ICING 1
25 g (1 oz) butter
1 tsp cocoa powder, sieved
1 tbsp icing sugar, sieved
1 tbsp hot water

METHOD

1 Beat the butter until soft then add the cocoa, icing sugar and water and work well until smooth and creamy.

2 Spread on the cooled biscuits and top with a walnut or a chocolate-covered coffee bean.

CHOCOLATE ICING 2
6oz plain chocolate
55 g (2 oz) double cream
25 g (1 oz) butter
Walnut halves

METHOD

1 Melt the chocolate with the cream over a low heat, stirring continuously. Add the butter and stir until this has melted as well.

2 Beat for a few minutes until it is less runny and spreadable, put a little icing onto each biscuit. Decorate with a walnut half.

ICING FOR CUP CAKES

Cup cakes have become highly fashionable. They are irresistible to both children and adults alike, and I have seen fully grown men fighting over who has the less girly green or blue ones. If you are decorating a batch with coloured icing, be it glacé or butter, this is an invaluable tip because, if you are anything like me the icing ends up the colour of My Little Pony's shocking pink mane or Shrek's bilious complexion. To avoid such disasters follow the simple procedure below. By the way, if you decide to colour butter icing, remember that it starts off yellow and you can end up with some interesting shades: by adding red it turns orange, by adding green it turns a vivid green and by adding blue another shade of green. On the other hand, it could end up brown or khaki! Great for doing camouflage icing if there is a boy in the family.

1 First find a skewer.

2 Next, prepare your icing, and if you are doing several colours, divide it into little bowls. Work quickly if using glacé icing as it hardens in no time.

3 Dip the end of the skewer into the bottle of cake colouring and hold it over the bowl containing the icing. Tap the skewer and a couple of drops will fall. Stir it into the icing. If at first it is too pale, repeat until you are happy with the colour.

4 Decorate your cakes.

ORANGE FAIRY CAKES

Fairy cakes are delicious reminders of childhood picnics on the beach, or consumed by a camp fire, eaten alongside Marmite sandwiches and sausages cooked on sticks. These are so easy and quick to make that even with only twenty minutes' warning you can have them baked, iced and ready to serve with a pot of proper tea for unexpected guests – or as a totally indulgent moment for yourself.

**Weigh an egg/eggs and then
weigh the equivalent amount of:**

Self-raising flour

Caster sugar

**Butter (if using unsalted butter add
a pinch of salt to the mixture)**

**1 level teaspoon of baking powder per
115 g (4 oz) of any of the above**

**Zest and juice of half an orange per
115 g (4 oz) of the above**

Paper muffin cases and a non-stick moulded muffin tray

NB – 115 g (4 oz) of everything produces 8 cakes

Have everything at room temperature – you
want the butter to be really soft, but not melted.

FOR THE ICING:
115 g (4 oz) icing sugar
Juice of an orange

METHOD

1 Pre-heat the oven to gas mark 4 (180°C, 350°F).

2 Weigh the eggs in their shells and then, into a mixing jug or bowl, weigh the equivalent amounts of butter, flour and sugar. Crack the eggs separately to check there are no bits of shell and add to the other ingredients, along with the baking powder and orange juice and zest.

3 Using a hand blender (or put into a small mixer – a tiny amount will stick to the sides in a large blender through centrifugal force and will not amalgamate properly) and whizz quickly for only a few seconds. If a spoonful won't fall off the end of a spatula after the count of five, add a little more orange juice or water.

4 Pile the mix into the paper cases, filling them just over half full. They will swell up to the top during baking. Put on the middle tray of the oven and cook for 8–10 minutes.

5 When the cakes are risen and golden brown, test to see if they are cooked through by piercing the centre with a skewer or finely pointed knife: if it comes out clean, they are cooked. If not, return to the oven for no more than a minute and test again.

6 Remove the little cakes (still in their wrappers) from the tin and place on a wire wrack. Cover with a clean drying up cloth and allow to cool. A cloth will prevent them from drying out and the sponge will remain moist.

7 Once cold, make your glacé icing: sieve the icing sugar into a bowl and add the juice of an orange. Mix thoroughly and, using a teaspoon and a knife, spread each cake with the icing. While it is still soft, you can decorate them with ready made flowers, silver balls or hundreds and thousands.

8 If I have time, I tint the icing by adding a tiny amount of yellow food colouring: dip the tip of a knife into the bottle and tap the end into the icing, mixing quickly to blend the colours into a light orange colour.

SPONGE CREAM DROPS

3 eggs
Sugar (equalling the eggs in weight)
Flour (equalling 2 eggs' weight less 2 tbsp worth)
2 tsp baking powder
Pinch of salt
Caster sugar for dusting

TOPPING
Jam of your choice
Whipped cream

METHOD

1 Preheat the oven to gas mark 2 (150°C, 300°F).

2 Beat the eggs and sugar and add the other ingredients. Spoon the mixture onto a greased baking sheet (or one lined with baking parchment) and dust with caster sugar.

3 Bake until lightly golden. When cool, sandwich two together with a layer of jam and whipped cream. Prepare these 1½ hours before eating them.

STEP-GREAT-GRANNY ENID'S OAT CAKES

My great-grandmother had an extramarital affair when my great-grandfather was stationed with the British army in India in the 1800s, resulting in their divorce and, because of the scandal, the family was removed from Debrett. This was despite the fact that my great-grandfather had been up to mischief with his servant's wife. Great-granny gave birth to a boy, in Canada, after which she and Ned moved to New Zealand – a prejudice-free zone. Gerald, their son, became a communist and died fighting in Spain in the Civil War. Tragedy was to strike the male line again. My grandmother's younger brother, Douglas, passed out as chief cadet at the Royal Naval College in Dartmouth and sailed on the *Invincible* to the Falklands during the First World War as a mid-shipman, then on to the North Atlantic where, at the age of seventeen, he was killed when the ship was sunk by the Germans in the battle of Jutland.

Some time after Great-granny died, Ned married a sparky New Zealander, Enid. They were blissfully happy and in typical spirit, she held a wake with all her mates before she dropped off this mortal coil, determined not to miss out on the fun. She cooked a batch of these oat cakes every week without fail.

The measurements here are based on a teacup.

½ cup fat (Enid used the dripping in her grill pan which was mostly bacon fat – you could substitute it with ½ cup butter or dripping)
½ cup boiling water in which you melt the fat
2 cups medium oatmeal (or ¾ oatmeal to ¼ plain flour)
1 cup flour
¼ tsp baking soda
¼ tsp salt

METHOD

1 Preheat the oven to gas mark 4 (180°C, 350°F).

2 Pour the melted fat and hot water into the dry ingredients and mix well. Form it into a ball.

3 Sprinkle some extra oatmeal onto a board and roll out the dough as thinly as you dare. Cut out circular shapes and place on a greased baking tray.

4 Cook in the oven for about 5 minutes checking on them to see that they aren't burning. Leave to cool so they can harden before lifting off the tray with a spatula.

5 Store in an airtight tin – recycle that empty tin of Highland shortbread.

CHEESE PUFFS

85 g (3 oz) cup plain flour
1 egg, beaten
115 g (4 oz) grated cheese
2 tsp baking powder
2 tbsp milk
Salt
Butter for serving

METHOD

1 Preheat the oven to gas mark 8 (230°C, 450°F).

2 Mix together all the ingredients and spoon out little heaps onto a baking tray – about a large teaspoonful.

3 Bake for 3 minutes. Split when still hot and pop in a nut of butter. Serve at once. These are great with soup, instead of bread.

CRUMBLY CHEESE BISCUITS

You can either use some fresh, mature Cheddar or bits and pieces of cheese that are hanging around in the fridge, first making sure you remove any trace of mould.

85 g (3 oz) flour
55 g (2 oz) butter
55 g (2 oz) grated strong Cheddar cheese
¼ tsp cayenne pepper

METHOD

1 Preheat the oven to gas mark 5 (190°C, 375°F).

2 Rub the all the ingredients together binding them as you go. Do not add any moisture. The pastry will come together, but try not to be too heavy handed. Rest in the fridge for 30 minutes.

3 When returned to room temperature, roll the pastry out thinly and cut into pretty shapes – at Christmas time use festive cutters. Place the shapes onto a baking tray and bake for about 5 minutes, but keep your eye on them – they will go golden brown very quickly.

4 Allow to cool a few minutes before putting the biscuits onto a wire rack. Once cold these can be frozen or kept in an airtight tin.

TIPS •

Instead of going through the hassle of rolling out the pastry once you have worked the ingredients into a ball, shape it into a sausage about an inch in diameter. Wrap this in cling film and put in the fridge to rest for 30 minutes. When you want to bake the biscuits, remove the pastry from the fridge and slice into thin medallions. Place these on the baking tray and proceed as above.

This avoids possible accidents: for storing a large cake, such as a Christmas cake, place it on the inverted lid of the airtight tin/container it is going to be kept in. Then put the large part of the container over the cake. When you want to serve it at teatime it can easily be lifted off the base/lid onto a pretty plate.

BREAKFAST SCONES

450 g (1 lb) plain flour
Add 1 teaspoon baking powder.
Buttermilk

METHOD

1 Set the oven to gas mark 7, 220°C, 425°F.

2 Mix the flour with the baking powder and enough buttermilk to make into a stiff dough.

3 Roll out to a thickness of about 2 cm ($^3/_4$") and cut out rounds using a 5 cm (2") cutter. Place these onto a non-stick baking sheet, brush with a little milk (or leftover buttermilk) and bake in a hot oven until golden brown and risen – about twelve to fifteen minutes.

4 Serve with lots of butter.

• ANGEL IN AN APRON •

Jams
and jellies

There is something immensely satisfying in making jam and other preserves but I only make it when I have time to cook the fruit within an hour of picking, thus safeguarding the flavours. Here are some useful jam-making tips:

· Make sure your fruit is clean and in good condition. Remove any wobbly ones with mould or bad bits or they will spoil the end product and it won't store well.

· Warm the sugar in the oven before adding it to the hot fruit – it will dissolve more quickly.

· Sterilise your jam jars by running them through the dishwasher. Heat in a low oven before filling.

· Fruit jam can be made with practically anything and I often mix and match. Weigh your fruit and add the same amount of sugar.

· You need to know when setting point is reached – a jam thermometer removes any element of doubt, but the wrinkle test will do: place a small metal dish in the freezer and when you are ready to test, take it out, pour a few drops of the jam onto the dish, wait a few moments and then push it with your finger – it should wrinkle up if setting point has been reached.

· Substitute ordinary sugar with special jam sugar (which contains pectin, the setting agent). This costs a little more but is worth the extra expense. Read and follow the instructions on the packet. The cooking time will be considerably less than with ordinary granulated sugar.

· When making vinegar-based pickles and chutneys, use special lids for the purpose. Save, beg or borrow empty instant coffee jars with plastic lids as these will not corrode from the acid.

· Also, when cooking chutney, use a stainless steel preserving pan, not one made from copper – the vinegar reacts with the metal and taints the flavour.

SOFT FRUIT JAM

Any type of soft fruit: strawberries, raspberries, plums, etc.
Equal amount in weight of sugar
Juice 1 or 2 lemons
A little water to moisten the fruit
1 tsp unsalted butter

METHOD

1 Put the fruit into a basin or bowl and add the same amount of sugar (see Tip below) and the juice of the lemon(s). Stir and allow to macerate over night if possible. In the morning the fruit will be swimming in a gorgeous, perfumed syrup.

2 Put into a preserving pan and bring to the boil. Add the butter, which will help reduce the scum. Skim any off as it rises to the surface and stir to avoid it burning on the bottom of the pan. If you are making strawberry jam, use the potato masher as the fruit cooks and squash it as much as you can to mix it in with the syrup.

3 When setting point has been reached, or you have cooked the jam long enough according to the instructions on the special sugar packet, you can pour it into hot jars using a ladle and wide-mouthed funnel.

4 Seal immediately.

TIP •••
Strawberry jam has a tendency to develop mildew so store it in a very cool place – if there is room, it goes in the fridge.

MARMALADE

Makes about 3.2 kg (7 lb) of marmalade
1.3 kg (3 lb) Seville oranges (available in the New Year)
2.25 kg (5 lb) granulated sugar (warmed in a low oven)
Water

METHOD

1 Wash the oranges thoroughly and place in a pan. Cover them with cold water and bring to the boil. Simmer until you are able to pierce the skin with the head of a pin – this could take about 30–40 minutes.

2 Pour off the orange cooking water and reserve 700 ml (1¼ pints).

3 Orange by orange, cut in half, remove the pips and put to one side in a separate dish. Cut up the remaining skin very finely and put in a separate bowl. Once all the oranges have been de-pipped and chopped, put the pips in a small square of muslin and tie securely. I like to make marmalade on a miserable Sunday afternoon, watching an old weepie film on television as I cut up the cooked fruit.

4 Put the orange water into a saucepan and add the warmed sugar. Bring to the boil and stir for 5–10 minutes. Be careful and do not leave unattended as this can boil over very easily.

6 Add the chopped oranges and the pips in the muslin to the syrup and boil until setting point has reached, stirring every now and then. A good sign is when the orange peel has become transparent – this can take up to an hour.

7 Pour using a ladle and a wide-mouthed funnel into your hot jars and seal immediately.

APRICOT JAM

Once again, I was taught how to make this by my French friend, Sophie, of the *tarte à l'orange* fame.

900 g (2 lb) apricots
Juice 1 lemon
900 g (2 lb) sugar
1 tsp unsalted butter

METHOD

1 Wash and cut the apricots in half, pick out the stones and put the fruit into a large basin. If you have the time (and it is well worth the effort) crack a dozen or more of the stones and remove the little almonds. Add these to the fruit and they will impart a unique flavour to the jam.

2 Add the lemon juice to the fruit followed by the sugar and mix in well. Cover with a cloth and leave over night. By morning, the sugar will mostly have dissolved and the fruit will be swimming in a perfumed syrup.

3 Pour the apricot mixture into a preserving pan and bring to the boil. Add a knob of butter and skim off any scum. Keep it at a good rolling boil until setting point is reached.

4 Pour into hot jars and cover.

FRUIT JELLIES

These are very easy to make but take a little longer as you have to strain the juices.

METHOD

1 Place any amount of clean fruit into a large pan, add enough water to moisten the fruit and bring slowly to the boil. Continue cooking, stirring every now and again, at the same time squashing the fruit until it is thoroughly cooked and soft.

2 Have ready a special jelly bag or a large piece of muslin. If using the former, pour the cooked fruit into the bag and suspend it over a

bowl. If you are using muslin, scald it first in some hot water, wring it out, then drape it over a large bowl. Have ready a length of strong string (about 15" long) and knot it into a circle. Pour the fruit into the muslin, gather up the edges and loop the string around the cloth, pushing one end through the other and tighten. You can now hang the muslin bag over the bowl.

3 Measure the juice and for each 600 ml (1 pint) of liquid add 450 g (1 lb) of preserving (or ordinary) sugar.

4 Bring the jelly up to the boil, add a knob of butter to help prevent scum from forming – if it does, remove it with a jam skimmer or slotted spoon.

5 Test for setting point and pour into the hot jars. Seal at once.

TIP •

Herb jellies can be made with a base of apple jelly. Add a good bunch of mint, rosemary, thyme etc. to the fruit at the beginning for flavour. Make the jelly in the normal way and pour into hot jars. Do not seal at this point. When almost set, add some extra chopped herbs to each jar, stir gently and the herbs will remain suspended. If you do this too soon they float to the top of the jar.

RASPBERRY AND MINT JELLY

This makes a change from redcurrant jelly to serve with lamb and game.

Any amount of raspberries
Water
Bunch of mint
Sugar
1 tsp unsalted butter

METHOD

1 Put the fruit into a preserving pan with a little water – about 600 ml (1 pint) to 1.3 kg (3 lb) raspberries. Add the bunch of mint and bring slowly to the boil then simmer until the fruit is cooked, stirring every now and again. Mash with a potato masher to crush the fruit.

2 Strain the purée through a jelly bag. When it is cool enough to handle, I put on a clean pair of rubber gloves and squeeze any remaining juice into the bowl.

3 Measure the liquid and to every 600 ml (1 pint) of juice, add 450 g (1 lb) of sugar. Put into a clean preserving pan, bring to the boil and add a knob of butter to help prevent too much scum from forming. Remove any that does come to the surface with a slotted spoon.

4 Bring to a good rolling boil and, if you have a jam thermometer, test for setting point when it reaches 105°C (220°F) – this may take about 15 minutes (unless you are using special jam sugar) – or use the wrinkle test. If it remains runny, bring the jelly back to the boil and cook a further 5 minutes.

5 Remove the hot jars from the oven and, using a jam funnel, fill with the hot jelly. Seal immediately.

WILD BRAMBLE JELLY

A bowl of ripe, wild blackberries
A handful of unripe ones (these will help the jelly to set)
Juice 1 lemon
Sugar
Water

METHOD

1 Place the fruit into a preserving pan with a little water to moisten – about 225 ml (½ pint) to 900 g (2 lb) of fruit. Add the lemon juice and bring to the boil. Stir every now and again and once the fruit is soft, remove from the heat.

2 Pour into a jelly bag and allow the juice to drip into a bowl. When cool enough to handle, put on a clean pair of rubber gloves and squeeze to extract as much juice as you can.

3 Measure the juice and weigh the sugar, 450 g (1 lb) to 600 ml (1 pint) juice. Place the sugar in a bowl and put in a low oven to heat gently, along with some jam jars.

4 Put the juice into a clean preserving pan and bring to the boil. Add the warmed sugar and stir until it is dissolved. Bring back to the boil and continue cooking on a good, rolling boil for about 10 minutes.

6 Test for set. If it remains runny, heat again for a further 5 minutes.

7 Using a jam funnel, pour into the hot jam jars and seal immediately.

Chutneys
and pickles

Life would be very boring indeed without chutneys and pickles. I have always enjoyed preserving food, particularly in the form of jams and chutneys, as I feel it is a magical way of introducing summer, sunshine and warmth into the dark days of winter. I used to dream of having a kitchen with a proper, old-fashioned, walk-in larder with a cool, north-facing aspect and slate or marble shelves. These would be stacked and lined with an array of sparkling jars and bottles, with produce saved from a garden glut, neatly labelled and dated.

Sadly my wish for a proper still room never materialised but it did not hinder my creative urges, and in our cupboards there is always an enticing selection waiting to be opened and tasted, to maximise the flavour of cold roast beef, a doorstep cheese sandwich, or simply to use as a dip for crisps. From late August until the end of October, the house is perfumed with the heady scents of cinnamon, vinegar, garlic, allspice and bubbling fruit and vegetables. Some of these concoctions are labour intensive, others easy to produce, to be enjoyed immediately, while others need a few weeks or months to reach full maturity of flavour. Whatever the demands, it is time well spent.

SWEET CUCUMBER PICKLE

900 g (2 lb) cucumbers
2 large onions
1 large green (bell) pepper
25 g (1 oz) salt
600 ml (1 pint) cider vinegar
$\frac{1}{2}$ level tsp ground turmeric
$\frac{1}{4}$ level tsp ground cloves
1 level tsp mustard seeds
$\frac{1}{2}$ level tsp celery seed (not celery salt)
Fresh chillies or dried chilli flakes to taste (optional)
450 g (1 lb) soft brown sugar (warmed)

METHOD

1 Put half a dozen clean jam jars into a warm oven to heat and sterilise.

2 Wash and dice the cucumbers but do not peel unless they are outdoor ridge cucumbers whose skin could be tough and bitter.

3 Peel the onions and slice finely. Tear the peppers in half and remove the pith and seeds, then chop finely.

4 Place the vegetables into a non-metallic bowl and add the salt. Mix well with your hands. Cover with a cloth and leave in a cool place for a couple of hours. Rinse thoroughly in a colander under running water, then squeeze out as much liquid as you can.

5 Put into a large stainless steel pan and add the vinegar. Do not use a copper preserving pan as the vinegar will react, tainting the flavour. Stir and bring to the boil, then simmer for approximately 20 minutes until the vegetables are soft.

6 Add the spices and warmed sugar in one go and stir until the latter is dissolved. Bring back to the boil and cook on a high heat, stirring frequently to prevent the bottom from burning. Remove from the heat when you can divide the chutney with a wooden spoon and it is slow to fill in the gap. If it is still too runny, continue boiling and stirring to allow more liquid to evaporate.

7 Pour the chutney into the hot jam jars and seal with vinegar-proof lids. This is ready to eat straight away.

SWEET PICKLED SHALLOTS

2 pints water
115 g (4 oz) cooking salt
1.8 kg (4 lb) shallots
1.3 kg (3 lb) moist brown sugar
1.2 litres (2 pints) malt vinegar
2 tbsp mustard seeds
1 tbsp whole cloves
1 stick cinnamon

METHOD

1 Make the brine by heating the water with the salt until it dissolves. Allow to cool.

2 Boil a kettle of water. Put the shallots into a bowl or basin and pour over the boiling water. Leave for a couple of minutes, then rinse under the cold tap. This will enable you to peel the skins off the shallots with ease. Put the shallots into a clean bowl and cover with the cold brine. Cover with a cloth and leave for 4 days.

3 On the fourth day, put the brown sugar, vinegar, mustard seeds, cloves, and cinnamon into a pan and bring to the boil. Cook for 1 minute, then strain through a piece of muslin placed in a colander. Discard the spices.

4 Put the liquid back into a large saucepan. Strain the shallots and add to the spicy liquid. Bring to the boil and remove from the heat.

5 Allow to cool before spooning into clean, sterilised jars and seal immediately.

TOMATO CHUTNEY

There must be as many recipes for tomato chutney as days in the year, but this does what it says on the tin.

MAKES ABOUT 2.7 KG (6 LB) CHUTNEY
2.7 kg (6 lb) ripe tomatoes
1.15 kg (1½ lb) onions, peeled and sliced thinly
225 g (8 oz) green peppers
450 g (1 lb) cooking apples, peeled, cored and sliced or chopped
850 ml (1½ pints) wine vinegar (red or white)
350 g (12 oz) demerara sugar
115 g (4 oz) salt
½ tsp ground ginger
½ tsp ground black pepper
2 cloves garlic (optional)
½ tsp cayenne (optional)
1 cup sultanas (optional)

METHOD

1 Pierce each tomato with a pointed knife and pile into a bowl. Pour some boiling water over them and leave for a minute or two. Drain and the skin will come away easily. Cut the tomatoes into quarters, remove the seeds and strain the juice into a preserving pan.

2 Cut the pepper in half and remove the seeds and slice thinly.

3 Add these and the apples to the tomatoes plus the other (and optional) ingredients and bring to the boil. Continue boiling gently for 1–2 hours until thick enough to run a wooden spoon down the middle and the chutney separates.

4 Bottle into hot jars and seal.

MAKE-DO-AND-MEND MANGO CHUTNEY

I have lost count of the times I have been tempted to buy mangoes when they are on offer, only to find them a week later at the bottom of the fridge over-ripe and wrinkly. Don't throw them into the compost bucket – turn them into a sweet, spicy chutney. If you only have one mango, halve the following quantities.

2 very ripe mangoes
2.5-cm (1-inch) piece fresh root ginger
225 g (8 oz) onions, peeled and thinly sliced
350 ml (³/₄ pint) vinegar (not malt)
175 g (6 oz) demerara sugar
¹/₂ tsp salt

SPICES
¹/₂ tsp ground coriander
1 tsp cardamom pods
1 tsp whole allspice
6 whole cloves
¹/₂ stick cinnamon

METHOD

1 Sterilise your jam jars in a warm oven.

2 Put the spices into a square of muslin and close it with a piece of string.

3 Peel the mangoes and roughly cut the flesh from the stone and put into a saucepan.

4 Peel and grate the ginger and add to the pan along with the onions, vinegar, sugar and salt. Add the bag of spices. Bring to the boil, reduce the heat to a slow boil and stir until the chutney thickens – this shouldn't take more than 15 minutes or so.

5 Remove the bag of spices and ladle the chutney into the hot jars using a jam funnel and seal immediately. This can be eaten straight away, but once opened, keep in the fridge.

RHUBARB CHUTNEY

This recipe was given to my mother by her gardener's wife, Mrs Hyde. In her youth, she had been the poultry cook in a large household and whenever we were lucky enough to be given a brace of pheasant, she very kindly plucked and trussed them for us.

TO MAKE ABOUT 2.25 KG (5 LB) CHUTNEY
1.8 kg (4 lb) rhubarb, washed, trimmed and cut into 2.5 cm (1 inch) pieces
350 g (12 oz) raisins
450 g (1 lb) apples, peeled, cored and sliced
450 g (1 lb) onions, peeled and sliced
900 g (2 lb) light brown sugar
25 g (1 oz) salt
1 tsp ground allspice
1 tsp ground ginger
25 g (1 oz) mustard seed
850 ml (1¹/₂ pints) vinegar of your choice – I use wine or cider not malt vinegar

METHOD
1 Place all the ingredients into a pan. Stir over a medium heat until the sugar is dissolved. Bring to the boil, then simmer, stirring frequently to prevent burning on the bottom of the pan, until thick. You want a really jammy consistency.
2 Pour into hot, sterilised jars and seal.
3 Wait patiently a good six weeks before tasting. Store in a dry, cool cupboard.

BLACKBERRY AND BEETROOT CHUTNEY

One evening I happened to tune in to BBC2 to catch the end of the Hairy Bikers' programme. They were filming in a top chef's restaurant and watched him conjure up a magical but most unusual dish with venison, blackberries and beetroot. He reassured the two cooks that the marriage of blackberry and beetroot was one made in heaven. It made me think. The next morning I filled a colander with huge, juicy, very ripe blackberries from our cultivated plants, pulled a few beetroot roughly the size between a golf and tennis ball, gathered up a couple of windfall apples and some onions left to dry out in the greenhouse. This is the resulting recipe. As I was impatient to see how it tasted once cold, we ate some the next day with French bread and a good, meaty cheddar. I can guarantee that it can be enjoyed immediately but will probably increase in flavour if left to mature for a few weeks.

225 ml (8 fl oz) vinegar of your choice: red, white or cider
175 g (6 oz) light, soft brown sugar
450 g (1 lb) blackberries
450 g (1 lb) beetroot, peeled and grated
2 large cooking apples, peeled and chopped
2 large onions, peeled and chopped
3 garlic cloves, peeled and chopped
1 scant tsp ground allspice
$1/2$ tsp ground cloves
1 red chilli or $1/2$ tsp dried chilli flakes
$1/4$ tsp coriander seeds, roughly crushed
$1/2$ tsp salt

METHOD

1 Put the vinegar and sugar into a preserving pan (not one made from copper or this will react with the vinegar) and gently heat through until the sugar has dissolved.

2 Add all the ingredients to the vinegar/sugar mixture and gently bring to the boil, stirring every now and again. Allow to boil on a gentle roll for about 30–40 minutes until most of the liquid has evaporated and the consistency is sufficiently thick and jammy, allowing a wooden spoon dragged across the bottom of the pan to leave a gap.

3 Tasted the hot mixture to see if you need to add any further vinegar, salt, etc., then fill and seal the chutney into hot, sterilised jars.

HOT PEPPER JELLY

4 large coloured peppers – green, yellow, red and orange
8–12 chillies
1¹/₂ cups (350 ml) cider vinegar
1 kg (2 lb 4 oz) bag preserving (jam) sugar suitable for strawberry jam plus 2 tbsp ordinary granulated sugar

METHOD

1 Place a small metal dish into the freezer.

2 Break the peppers in half and remove the seeds and pith. Put into a food processor and, using the pulse setting, chop them very finely, but don't overdo things – you want very fine spangles and not a purée. Put into a large saucepan.

3 Remove the seeds and pithy rib from the chillies and zap them in the blender.

4 Add to the peppers and then pour in the vinegar. Stir and bring to the boil over a high temperature – the fumes from the chillies will be very powerful, so open a window! Turn down the heat slightly and cook for a further 5 minutes.

5 Read the instructions on the packet for the preserving sugar as timing is all important. Pour in the sugar and stir until it has dissolved. Increase the heat to high to achieve a good, rolling boil. After the time stated on the sugar packet (most likely 4 minutes), remove from the heat and test for setting: take the metal dish from the freezer and drop on a teaspoon of the jelly. It will cool quickly and if it wrinkles when you run a finger across it, the setting point has been reached. If not, put back on the heat for a further minute and test again. It is vital not to overcook the jelly at this point or it will turn into a thick, sticky jam.

6 Pour into hot, sterilised jars and seal with vinegar-proof lids.

SWEDISH PICKLE

This is a marvellous stand-by for emergency catering as it can sit quietly in a cool larder (or fridge) for 6 weeks without going off – if it isn't eaten beforehand! This is very good with any sort of cold meat or in a cheese sandwich.

1 small white cabbage
3 large carrots
4 green (bell) peppers
450 g (1 lb) white onions
225 g (8 oz) sugar
1.2 litres (2 pints) water
1.2 litres (2 pints) white vinegar
4 tbsp salt

METHOD

1 Finely shred the white cabbage. Peel and grate the carrots. Cut the peppers in half and remove the pith and seeds, then slice finely. Peel and slice the onions equally finely.

2 Put all the ingredients into a non-metallic bowl or basin and add the salt. Mix thoroughly, cover with a cloth and leave overnight in a cool place.

3 The next day, rinse the vegetables thoroughly and squeeze out as much of the water as you can. Then scoop into a wide-mouthed glass jar (an old fashioned sweet jar is perfect for this) or a large plastic container with a lid.

4 Heat the sugar, water and vinegar together in a saucepan until the sugar has dissolved. When cold, pour over the vegetables, shake the jar and it is ready to eat straight away. Store in a cool, dark place – there's no need to refrigerate.

PICKLED CLEMENTINES

These would make a lovely present as they conjure up the smell of Christmas. Make a month in advance in November so it can mature to be enjoyed over the festive season with cold roast meat and gammon. You will need a Đ litre (18 fl oz) glass jar with a lid.

650 g (1¹/₂ lb) tangerines or clementines
600 ml (1 pint) water
225 g (8 oz) white wine vinegar
225 g (8 oz) soft brown sugar
5-cm (2-inch) stick cinnamon
1 tsp cloves
2 blades mace
³/₄ tsp mixed peppercorns

METHOD

1   Warm the jar in the oven to sterilise.

2   Wash and dry the fruit. Slice thinly and discard the end slices. Put into a pan with the water and bring to simmering point. Simmer very gently for about 45 minutes – until tender. Drain in a sieve over a bowl, saving the liquid.

3   Return the liquid to the pan and add vinegar, sugar and spices. Boil for 10 minutes and return oranges to this liquid and simmer for a further 20 minutes. The fruit should have become transparent.

4   Transfer the slices to the warmed jar. Pour some liquid over the fruit, let it settle by prodding with a knife, pour in some more, prod and so on until the liquid is up to the top and there are no air bubbles. Cover and keep for a month before eating. Once opened consume within 3 months.

TIP •

Keep a look out for attractive jars and bottles when visiting charity shops as they make great containers for preserves or flavoured vinegars and alcohols such as sloe gin.

Drinks

I believe there remains a place for bowls of punch or exotic cocktails, both alcoholic or otherwise, and with a little care these special welcoming drinks can be whipped up in next to no time. They are eminently suitable for large gatherings. By having only one alcoholic option (remember to have plenty of soft drinks as well), those giving the party enjoy themselves without having to deal with multiple requests for this drink or that, red wine or white, and so on. These are old family recipes and can still hold their own today.

INNOCENT SPICY FRUIT PUNCH

ENOUGH FOR APPROXIMATELY 20 GLASSES
115–175 g (4–6 oz) caster sugar
600 ml (1 pint) water
600 ml (1 pint) freshly squeezed orange juice
225 ml ($\frac{1}{2}$ pint) pineapple juice
1 lemon and 1 orange, sliced
Juice and thinly pared rind of 1 lemon
$\frac{1}{2}$ level tsp ground nutmeg
$\frac{1}{2}$ level tsp ground mixed spice
6 cloves
3 large bottles Canada Dry ginger ale
Crushed ice

METHOD

1 Dissolve the sugar in the water over a low heat. Put to one side to cool.

2 Blend together the fruit juices, lemon and orange slices, lemon juice and zest, and spices. Add the sugar syrup. Chill.

3 Strain into a large bowl or jug and just before serving, add the ginger ale and crushed ice.

SLOE BOOZE

These little darlings appear in the hedgerows from late summer on but really need a good couple of frosts before you venture out with your basket (see Tip below). Some years there is hardly a sloe to be seen, yet others there are loads on offer.

Ideally you need a wide-mouthed jar which can hold a litre (1$\frac{1}{2}$ pints) of gin/vodka or brandy plus the fruit and sugar. I use a jar I was given by the local chippy which once had pickled eggs in it.

Alcohol of your choice: gin, vodka or brandy
Sloes
Sugar

METHOD

1 Once you are home with your harvest, give them a good rinse in a bowl to remove any dust or bits of twig. Then prick them before you immerse them in the alcohol.

2 Tip the pricked fruit into the glass jar – filling it about half way. Pour in about half as much sugar as fruit and then fill to the top with the gin, vodka or brandy – there is no need to go overboard with the quality. Put the lid on and secure and give it a good shake to mix everything together.

3 Leave in a dark cupboard and shake daily until the sugar has dissolved.

4 Before you share it with friends, you need to strain it. Get a jug, insert a funnel and line this with a piece of muslin or kitchen paper then pour the liquid so that it leaves the fruit and any debris behind. Pour into a bottle and seal.

TIPS •

If you gather sloes before the frosts, throw them into a bag and into the freezer for a couple of weeks.

When you gather your sloes take care as the branches are prickly – gloves don't help as the berries grow in tight little groups and you need your fingers free to pick them. A walking cane is a good prop since nine times out of ten (as with blackberries) the best are high up and out of reach.

Pricking the fruit is a pain to do, but I find one of those pincushion affairs with sharp little nails made to support flowers in a vase speeds things up. Charity shops often have them but make sure that they are neither rusty nor dirty before you start. Put the fruit in a bowl, hold the spike in the palm of your hand and stab away. You don't need to perforate everything – enough to release the juices will be adequate.

The longer you leave the sloes in the alcohol the better the end product, but if you want to enjoy it at Christmas and the frosts are late that year, it may not have had quite enough time to mature. In this case, miss out a year and drink it the following one when you will have made, hopefully, another batch to wait its turn.

ELDERFLOWER CORDIAL

This makes a great alcoholic drink if mixed with gin and fizzy water. Before you use the elderflower heads, make sure they smell of muscat grapes and not tom cat.

2 pints water
1.3 kg (3 lb) sugar
1 sliced lemon
20 heads sweet-smelling elderflowers
85 g (3 oz) citric acid or tartaric acid
(bought from the chemist)

METHOD

1 Bring the water to the boil in a large pan and add the sugar and lemon. Remove from the heat and stir until the sugar is dissolved.

2 Bring back to the boil and add the flower heads and citric acid. Bring back to the boil once more, then remove from the heat and allow to stand until cool. Once cold, strain and bottle. It will keep for up to 3 months after which it may become cloudy.

3 Serve it diluted with fizzy or plain chilled water.

ELDERFLOWER CHAMPAGNE

4.8 litres (8 pints) water
650 g (1¹/₂ lb) sugar
7 elderflower heads
2 lemons, sliced
2 tbsp white wine vinegar

METHOD

1 Bring the water to the boil. Put the sugar into a large bowl and pour on the water. Stir until it has dissolved. Allow to cool.

2 Don't wash the elderflower heads or you will remove the natural yeast needed for fermentation; just make sure there are no stray insects! Put the heads into a clean plastic bucket – I buy a new one each year from the pound shop. Pour over the cold syrup then add the sliced lemons and vinegar. Stir.

3 Cover with a cloth and leave for 24 hours (48 hours if you prefer) in a cool place, stirring when you think about it.

4 Next day, strain the liquid through a fine muslin and pour into clean bottles with screw-tops if possible – save your Australian wine bottles for the purpose. Leave in a dry place, neither too hot nor too cold, like a garage or tool shed for 2 weeks whilst the fizz develops. Chill thoroughly before drinking. This bubbly drink has a strong Muscat taste and can keep for quite a while – some say it improves with age, provided the bottles haven't exploded first! In case you are concerned about the alcohol content, this is either non-existent or minimal – not enough to worry about.

SAKE

The following recipe for this Japanese rice wine was given to us by a friend who met her husband in Changi jail in Singapore during the Second World War. They lived in the Far East for many years in peace time and this is something they brought back with them. The measurements are translated from the Japanese. You will need two 9.6-litre (2-gallon) plastic buckets. Traditionally saké is served warm in small porcelain beakers. Be warned – this is strong stuff so don't drive afterwards.

1.050 kg (4 lb 9 oz) round grain pudding rice
375 g (13 oz) sultanas
375 g (13 oz) raisins
2. 175 kg (4 lb 13 oz) sugar
55 g (2 oz) fresh yeast
½ cup warm water
1 tsp sugar

METHOD

1 Wash the rice well to remove as much starch as you can – about three rinses, squishing the grains with your hands.

2 Put the rice, sultanas, raisins and sugar into the bucket and fill with cold water to within 2.5 cm (1 inch) of the top.

3 Cream the yeast with the warm water and sugar until smooth and stir this into the bucket, mixing well with the fruit and rice using a **wooden** spoon not a metal one.

4 Stir the concoction four times a day. Do this for 4 days. Put on a lid to keep insects out but not air – place a piece of muslin over the bucket and rest the lid on top, slightly off kilter. Leave for a further 10 days.

5 Strain through a large piece of muslin into the second bucket and then syphon off into a 5-litre (1-gallon) jar. (These are easily found in charity shops for next to nothing.) If at this stage you squeeze the fruit and rice to extract all the liquid, it will give the saké a fruitier flavour.

6 Leave a further 24 hours and syphon off back into another container. Rinse the jar and return the saké using a funnel.

7 Cork the jar leave to mature for 3 months.

ANDREW FUSE

Heaven only knows where the name for this lethal concoction originated. I found it in one of Ma's recipe books dated 1948 and since it wasn't her handwriting, I can only presume that the perpetrator named it after himself...I wonder what happened to him? The instructions are written verbatim.

Glass: champaigne [*sic*] glass smeared with lemon juice and dusted with sugar.

Base: equal parts of Benedictine, rye whisky, brandy and square [*sic*] gin.

This should be mixed in an iced shaker.

Topping: suggest chilled dry ginger ale with coiled lemon and orange peel.

Note. This drink sounds vicious (and is) but it tastes very (harmful) harmless [*sic*]. I once gave a teetotal aunt four in quick succession telling her they were soft drinks. NB. She cut me out of her will.

JUNE CUP

1 bottle Beaujolais, chilled
4 tbsp brandy
Sliced strawberries
2 bottles (600 ml [1 pint]) chilled fizzy lemonade

METHOD

1 Pour the wine and brandy over the fruit and leave in a cool place (fridge) for at least 30 minutes.

2 Just before serving, add the lemonade. This makes approximately 12 glasses.

QUICK QUENCHER

Perfect for after a tennis party.

1.2 litres (2 pints) chilled dry ginger beer
425 ml (^{3}/$_4$ pint) lime juice, preferably
freshly squeezed and sweetened
Ice cubes
Fresh mint
Large glass jug

METHOD
1 Put all the ingredients into the jug, stir and serve.

TIPS •

Over the years we have collected several small, individual sized teapots along with a selection of pretty bone china teacups and saucers. Mixing and matching, we use them for herbal teas as the delicate porcelain seems to enhance the fine flavours of the infusions. It makes the occasion more special and I am absolutely convinced that they taste completely different in a chunky mug!

If the weather is very hot, one of the best thirst-quenching drinks is the following: boil some freshly drawn water and make a pot of weak Earl Grey tea and allow it to infuse for 2–3 minutes. Then put a sprig of mint into your chosen teacup and pour the tea on top. Add sugar to taste if required.

APERITIFO

MAKES 10 GLASSES
1 bottle chilled, dry Italian vermouth
2 large bottles tonic water
6 tbsp Grand Marnier
Ice cubes

METHOD
1 Pour the first three ingredients over the ice cubes, stir and serve.

PRIDE OF OPORTO

MAKES 12 GLASSES
1 bottle chilled tawny port
4 tbsp orange curaçao
Juice 1 lemon
1 large bottle soda water, chilled

METHOD

1 Mix the port, curaçao and lemon juice together and chill well.

2 Just before serving, pour in the soda water.

EVERYMAN'S BUBBLY
(A SORT OF SPRITZER)

MAKES 8–10 GLASSES
1.2 litres (2 pints) chilled soda water
1 bottle white pudding wine – Graves (if you are feeling flush) or Sauternes (if you are not!)

METHOD

1 Mix together in a large jug only at the moment of serving.

CHURCHWARDEN'S PUNCH

A different Christmas warmer, ideal for after Midnight Mass.

MAKES APPROXIMATELY 1.2–1.4 LITRES (2–2$^1/_2$ PINTS)
1 large lemon
6 whole cloves
600 ml (1 pint) unsweetened weak tea
350 g ($^3/_4$ lb) sugar
1 bottle red wine

METHOD

1 Stud the lemon with the cloves and roast in a hot oven to a rich dark brown. Place it whole in a saucepan with the tea and sugar, stir well. Add the wine, cover and bring slowly to simmering point.

2 When white foam appears on the surface, remove from the heat and press the lemon gently to extract the juices.

HOT RUMOUR

Lovely for open house on Christmas morning.

MAKES APPROXIMATELY 800 ML (1½ PINTS)
1 orange
12 whole cloves
1 bottle red wine
3 tbsp rum
2–3 tbsp demerara sugar

METHOD

1 Preheat the oven to gas mark 2 (150°C, 300°F).

2 Stud the orange with the cloves and bake in the oven for 30 minutes.

3 Heat the wine in a saucepan until near boiling point, then add the rum and sugar to taste.

4 Float the orange on top and simmer for a few minutes. Serve piping hot.

WYNDHAM'S PARACHUTE

MAKES APPROXIMATELY 30 CUPS OF PUNCH
2 bottles full-bodied red wine
2 bottles dry white wine
600 ml (1 pint) orange or lemon juice
Fresh orange and grapes, de-pipped and diced

1 small can pineapple pieces, drained
1 can peach slices
¼ bottle of brandy

METHOD

1 Mix wine, fruit juice and fruit in a serving bowl and leave to rest for 2 hours in a cool place.

2 Just before serving, pour the brandy over the top. Do not stir. Ladle into punch cups.

TRADITIONAL WASSAIL

An eighteenth-century recipe.

Makes approximately 25 servings
450 g (1 lb) brown sugar
600 ml (1 pint) brown ale
1 large piece fresh ginger root, peeled and cut into slices
Freshly grated nutmeg
4 good-sized glasses sherry
2.8 litres (5 pints) light ale
½ oz yeast
Fresh fruit to decorate

METHOD

1 Heat the brown ale, and dissolve the sugar in it, together with the ginger and a little grated nutmeg.

2 Add the sherry and light ale and the yeast. Stir and leave to stand for a few hours. Then pour the mixture into a clean, 4.8-litre (1-gallon) glass jar fitted with a fermentation lock and leave to ferment for 2–3 days.

3 Serve hot (but not boiling) decorated with fresh fruit.

MADISON MULL

MAKES APPROXIMATELY 1.4 LITRES (2¹/₂ PINTS)
1 apple
600 ml (1 pint) vintage cider
1 bottle red wine
2 tbsp sugar (optional)
6 whole cloves

METHOD

1 Stud the apple with the cloves and bake in moderate oven for 30 minutes.

2 Heat the cider to near boiling point, add the wine and the apple. Continue heating but do not boil.

3 Strain into a serving bowl and serve hot.

Miscellaneous bits and pieces

The last three recipes in this book are given their own chapter, because they don't really fit in anywhere else but deserve to be included. I hope they give you as much pleasure as they have to us.

THE BEST CARAMEL FUDGE IN THE WORLD

For this recipe, a sugar/jam thermometer is very handy if you have one. A teacup is used here as a measure.

2 cups sugar

2 tsp glucose (if available – normally available at the chemist)

³/₄ cup milk (full cream)

55 g (2 oz) butter

METHOD

1 Boil 1½ cups of the sugar (and glucose) with the milk. You want to get this really hot without it boiling over.

2 In a strong-bottomed pan, place the remaining sugar and put on the heat for it to caramelise. Do not stir but shake the pan now and then shifting the sugar so that all of it caramelises. You want it to reach a dark honey colour, no more or it will taste burnt. This is very hot indeed.

3 Very carefully and quickly, pour as much of it as you can into the boiling milk. Stir and continue boiling until it reaches what is known as the 'soft ball stage'. You want to make a granular fudge not a smooth toffee and this is where the thermometer is useful as it has this temperature marked on the side.

4 The water content of the milk is evaporating as the milk gets hotter and hotter. If you don't have a jam thermometer, prepare a cup of iced water and drop a little of the fudge mixture into it. If it solidifies and you can roll it up into a firm (not hard) ball, then remove the caramel milk from the heat.

5 Add the butter and beat thoroughly. You want to incorporate the butter and cool the fudge before you pour it into a buttered dish. Carry on beating and the time to stop is when the fudge begins to thicken and stick to the sides of the pan. Hurry and empty it into the dish – one with straight sides is best because you can cut it into pieces easily.

6 Before it is completely hard, cut the fudge into squares and leave to continue cooling.

7 If it doesn't set properly, scrape the fudge back into a saucepan and reheat. It might work or it might turn into toffee. I succeed every other time, but it's worth having a go!

MY LOOSE TEA BLEND

It may seem odd to include tea in a cookery book but here it is nevertheless. I haven't used tea bags for years (except for reducing puffy eyes...) but in the past when I did, I added a teaspoon of loose Earl Grey to the pot. I soon started to experiment with different flavours and heaven knows how, came up with the following mixture, which is about the nicest cup of tea you could wish to drink. Everyone comments on it favourably, but when I told the chap behind the counter in Fortnum and Mason's about my special brew, he looked horrified!

2 packets loose Assam
1 packet loose Earl Grey
1 packet loose China tea (Keemun)

METHOD

1 Mix all the teas together in a bowl and decant into in an airtight tin.

2 For a normal pot of tea for three to four people, I use about 2 heaped teaspoons of loose tea, but you will need to experiment because it depends a lot on the water in your area.

3 Serve with milk and sugar to taste.

PRETEND SNOW FOR THE CHRISTMAS TREE

I'm including this 'recipe' because, if ever there was a smell which conjures up the whole essence of my childhood, it is this one: fresh pine needles and soap. The end result is an amazingly realistic 'snow' which brings a tree to life. Long before electric all-singing, all-dancing food processors, we only had an old-fashioned whisk with a handle you had to turn very fast and, out of pure nostalgia, this is what I use now. By the way, it is definitely **not to be eaten!**

1–2 cups Lux soap flakes or equivalent
Blue food colouring
Boiling water

METHOD

1 Put the soap flakes into a basin and pour on enough boiling water to moisten – half a cup to start with.

2 Whatever implement you use, whisk the soap and water until if forms firm peaks like a meringue.

3 Dip the tip of a skewer into the blue cake colouring and add a tiny amount to the soap mix – the hint of blue will make it whiter.

4 Whisk again to incorporate the colouring and you are ready to decorate your tree. Do this before you add the lights and baubles. Using your hands, scoop out dollops of the 'snow' and spread it onto the branches trying to look as natural as possible – you may need to make a second batch of soap mix (any leftover can be used to wash a pullover). This will dry after a short space of time like cake icing. It has no harmful effect on the tree. If your tree has roots, before replanting it in the garden after Christmas, wash as much of the 'snow' off as possible.

5 Sometimes we sprinkled silver glitter onto the soap while it was still soft. This was magical when the fairy lights were lit.

INDEX

Note to reader
Page numbers <u>underlined</u> indicate entries in the introduction that are of descriptions of life or a story rather than a recipe. Page numbers in italics indicate a cook's Tip. Page numbers in **bold** indicate a main section. The entry for 'vegetables (*general*)' indicates recipes where a selection of vegetables are used or used mainly for flavouring as opposed to the main ingredient.